Disappointment

Disappointment

Toward a Critical Hermeneutics of Worldbuilding

Jarrett Zigon

FORDHAM UNIVERSITY PRESS

New York 2018

Fordham University Press also publishes its books in a variety of electronic formats. Some content that appears in print may not be available in electronic books.
Visit us online at www.fordhampress.com.

Library of Congress Cataloging-in-Publication Data
available online at https://catalog.loc.gov.

Printed in the United States of America

20 19 18 5 4 3 2 1

First edition

for Sylvia

CONTENTS

Disappointment

Introduction

If it is the case that philosophy begins with disappointment,[1] then politics must be the most philosophical of all human endeavors. Politics, which in this book I define as agonistic and creative experimentation with an otherwise,[2] begins not merely with the disappointment of our inability to know, understand, or grasp the world, but with the overwhelming disappointment that a world has become unbearable. When one can no longer dwell in the world in which one is, then two choices remain: either wait and hope against hope that something, somehow, might get a little better; or act. To act in an unbearable world is to act agonistically, since it is likely the case that some*thing* (*thing* here is meant in the broadest possible manner) must be acted against and changed in order to allow one to dwell again. To act in this manner is also creative and experimental, since prior to such political action there is no way of knowing or conceiving how one can act and what kind of action will be successful. Such political action is, as Giorgio Agamben might put it, a politics of a "means without an end."[3] The creative and experimental nature of political action is doubly so in that if acting is successful, then the result is not having been folded into, or included in, or accepted as belonging to the already existing world—the world that was unbearable—but rather the creation of an entirely new world.[4]

It seems that in our times it is not possible to create new worlds. Here we have perhaps the most disappointing fact of contemporary politics: there are no political alternatives other than being folded into the status quo. For many today it truly feels as though history has come to an end. This feeling of being trapped, this feeling of no alternative, this feeling that this, just this, is all there is and can be, is what has rendered contemporary politics so disappointing. There have been plenty of studies, analyses, and theories that tell us why this is so, and capitalism and late liberalism[5] tend to be the two biggest boogeymen. I wouldn't necessarily disagree with this, but I would like to go further. I would like to suggest that it is not capitalism and late liberalism *as such* that have led us to this point, but rather that we find ourselves at this point of exhaustion because of the ontological grounding of our age, which capitalism and late liberalism, along with science and technology, simply enact more exemplarily than any other ontic practices.[6]

This book is meant to address this disappointment by offering a framework for a politics that rises to the demand of our radical finitude. By *radical* I mean the groundlessness not only of politics and morals but also of existence in general.[7] By finitude I mean the fact that not only do our political problems and demands arise from the worlds in which we find ourselves, but so, too, do the possible responses to these, and this is so because there is no other place, sphere, domain, field, or what have you from which we can pluck meaning, value, guidance, or grounding. A politics that rises to the demand of radical finitude is a politics that finds its problems, antagonists, motivations, strategies, tactics—in a word, its call to action—in a world grounded in nothing other than the situations and existents that constitute it. Such a politics cannot hold onto metaphysical bannisters—such as rights, responsibility, dignity—that no longer, if they ever did, hold any meaning or have any effect in our time. As I hope to make clear throughout this book, and particularly so in the first two chapters, such bannisters do little more than close off worlds and their existents to the opening of possibilities while shrouding them in the fantasy of possible completion, totality, and wholeness.

This book takes up the challenge of offering such a framework by showing how ontological starting points have real political implications. In fact, a central argument of this book is that what normally gets called ontology, politics, and ethics are actually three aspects or modalities of the same tradition, and therefore a critical engagement with one necessitates a critical engagement with the other two—that is, with the ontological tradition as a whole. This realization allows us to see how an alternative ontological starting point may lead to alternative political and ethical possibilities.[8] In this sense, this book offers a critical hermeneutics of the dominant ontological tradition of our time and does so by means of both deconstruction and conceptual creativity. What I hope becomes clear is that if we hold out any hope of no longer being disappointed by political (non)possibilities, then we must begin by leaving behind the worn-out and no longer useful metaphysical bannisters we have become so accustomed to in our political-moral discursive practices and, as the phenomenologists might say, return to the world. For as I hope to convince the reader, politics as agonistic and creative experimentation with an otherwise—that is, politics as worldbuilding—only becomes possible when we leave behind the exhausted ontology of a priories that have left us disappointed, and we begin to enact an ontology of worlds.

A significant aspect of this is the process of imagining and creating new concepts. For I take it as a starting assumption that political activity needs a conceptual apparatus. The question then is: what kind of conceptual apparatus is available and what kind of politics does it allow? Throughout this book I argue—and in Chapter 1 I will show how this came about—that the dominant contemporary ontological tradition provides us with a conceptual apparatus for political activity based solely on a very limited and predefined essence of things and thus narrowly limits possibilities for being and becoming. This is what I call the politics of the a priori. Because of this limitation, perhaps the preeminent intellectual and political demand of our time is the creation and development of a new conceptual apparatus that could become the basis for an alternative ontological tradition. These new concepts, however, cannot simply be a refurbishing, if you will, of familiar concepts such as dignity or responsibility because, as the philosopher Lee Braver puts it, "no matter [how we might do so] the very word smuggles in the older meanings [we want] to dispense with. If grammar and vocabulary can contain philosophical assumptions . . . then we need to be innovative with our words if we are to be innovative with our thoughts."[9] This smuggling in is akin to what in Chapter 1 I call conceptual proclivity, the avoidance of which necessitates conceptual creativity.

It is my contention that these new concepts would need to be fidelious to the radical finitude of existence, and as such remain open and not predefine and limit the possibilities for the being and becoming of worlds and their existents. However, and as I hope becomes clear in Chapters 3–5, just because these new concepts would remain fidelious to the openness of radical finitude does not entail that they can be created willy-nilly. Rather, the very fact of remaining fidelious to the openness of radical finitude entails that the concepts created must articulate precisely what this openness is and how it is to exist in it. In other words, these new concepts would articulate what might cautiously be called the "essence" of openness. Such a conceptual articulation would differ from the a priori of metaphysical humanism in that while the latter very narrowly predefines and limits possibilities to what I call in Chapter 2 differential sameness, a conceptual apparatus of openness would articulate the processes by which a minimal ontological sharedness gives way to actual differences in worlds. It is the hope of this book that such a conceptual apparatus would one day allow not only for the emergence of an alternative and open form of political activity, but also for the emergence of an ontological tradition characterized by finitude and openness rather than closed totalities predefined by the a priori. It is this kind of concept creation that I attempt in this book, and *situation*, *world*, *dwelling*, *worldbuilding*, and *attunement* are just such open concepts.

Ontologies

Ontology has become trendy. Across the social sciences and humanities it is not difficult to find any number of ontological arguments, claims, and hopes. But as Laidlaw and Heywood have pointed out in the case of the so-called ontological turn in anthropology, the use of this term *ontology* often involves a slippage between the analysis of ontologies and the proclamation of an ontology.[10] In other words, it is not uncommon to find a conflation between ontology as the study or science of being, and ontology as the being that the study attempts to explain, describe, interpret, or what have you.[11] When it comes to ontology, however, this conflation may in fact be unavoidable. For as I will try to argue throughout this book, what I call an ontological tradition consists of not only the study of being but also that which comes to be as such, as the very theories, concepts, and practices of this study—and the ways they are taken up in everyday life in ordinary practices—over time come to play a significant (but not determining) role in what actually exists and how. Increasingly this fact is becoming well accepted and is often articulated with the notion of the anthropocene, but this is something that has already been critically understood for nearly a century by some, most notably Martin Heidegger and Hannah Arendt.

An ontological tradition grounds a multiplicity of worlds over a *longue durée* of historical time.[12] Talal Asad has written of Islam as a discursive tradition that is, as Charles Hirschkind characterizes it, a "historically evolving set of discourses embodied in [practices and institutions] and hence deeply imbricated in the material life of those inhabiting them."[13] As Saba Mahmood points out, Asad's notion of discursive tradition draws heavily from both Foucault's analysis of discursive formations and MacIntyre's notion of tradition, and "draws attention to both mircropractices of interpersonal pedagogy, through which the truth of a particular discursive practice is established, and to the macrolevel of historically sedimented discourses, which determine the possibility of what is debatable, enunciable, and doable in the present."[14] I would like to take this a step further and make the case that a discursive tradition is best understood as an articulation of the ontological tradition that grounds it. This I hope to make clear in Chapter 1, where I hermeneutically disclose what Gadamer called the effective history of the discursive tradition of rights as it has unfolded within its ontological tradition.

If discursive traditions establish a range of possibilities for speaking and acting, then ontological traditions establish a range of possibilities for being, including the range of possibly existing discursive traditions. In this sense, an ontological tradition will consist of multiple discursive traditions, and it ultimately accounts for how these discursive traditions can have similar and shared notions of such things as space, time, causality, humanness, and non-humanness, to name only a few. Thus, part of how an ontological tradition grounds a multiplicity of worlds over a *longue durée* of historical time is by grounding the diverse discursive traditions that allow for meaningful and imaginable practice in these worlds. It is for this reason, furthermore, that such diverse discursive traditions as, for example, Christianity, natural science, liberalism, socialism, and secularism not only are able to coexist and often "speak" to one another, but also how it is possible that they interact and that aspects of one gets folded into others. Thus, over time and with the repetition and folding together of discursive traditions, the grounding ontological tradition is also repeated, maintained, and more solidly secured. For these reasons, then, we can say that an ontological tradition grounds our worlds, and as will become clear below, the ontological tradition within which most of us have been living can be called metaphysical humanism.

An ontological tradition consists of some key theories or philosophies of being, what I will simply call ontology, and the key concepts of these ontologies, as well as the practices that enact these. Some of the key concepts of the ontological tradition of metaphysical humanism are object, subject, substance, identity, the One or totality, and human, which is ontologically defined in terms of Reason and Morality. Although ontology and ontological traditions might seem to have an aura of intellectual snobbery and ivory tower, head-in-the-sky–ness about them, I hope to make it clear throughout this book that this is not so. For while it is certainly the case that an ontological tradition and its concepts are commonly enacted by intellectuals—even and perhaps especially so when they are unaware of it—an ontological tradition is primarily enacted by means of discursive traditions, institutions, and people in their everyday lives.

It should already be clear that only humans have ontological traditions. For ontological traditions are the primary means by which we humans participate in the being and becoming of what is. In order to head off any knee-jerk reaction by posthumanists, let me make clear that nothing I have said so far excludes nonhumans or reenacts the error of humanism that places "Man" at the center of all things. Unless one's ontology is so flat that no distinction at all can be made between existents—such that, for example, a rock and a human have the exact same capacities—then we must agree that all existents have particular and more or less unique capacities by which they are able to engage and participate in the shaping of their mutually shared worlds. I am simply making the claim that for the purposes of this book ontology, and particularly ontological tradition, will denote the primary capacity humans have for worldbuilding.

Notice that the key distinction that I am trying to make, and what I want to be very clear about here, is that I intend ontology to indicate a speculative theory of being, which through its enactment is able to partially shape existence. To the best of my knowledge only humans have the capacity to creatively speculate in a systematic manner on the nature of existence and then act based on that speculation. Rocks, trees, chimpanzees, climate, alarm clocks, stars, asteroids, photons, amoebas, carrots, tables, light wave-particles, thermostats, or anything else you could name, none of these has the capacity to create a speculative and systematic theory of being and then act accordingly. For better or worse we will just have to accept that only humans can do this. However, just because only humans are capable of doing ontology does not mean that their existence has any more priority, special claim, or hierarchical necessity than that of any other existent. Ontology is just a capacity of being human, like flying is a capacity of some birds. And just as flying plays a significant role in establishing the conditions of being of these birds, so, too, does the capacity to create and enact ontological traditions play a significant role in establishing the conditions of being human. All existents—human and nonhuman alike—have their unique and particular capacities for establishing the conditions of their being, and this is done through their engagement with and participation in their mutually shared worlds. At times some of those existents may have a more or less significant role in the shaping of worlds, but no existent—human or nonhuman—ever fully determines or even always primarily shapes its worlds. So let me be clear here: by *ontology* I mean a uniquely human capacity to creatively speculate in a systematic manner on being and to act accordingly. As such, ontology is one of the uniquely human ways of engaging and participating in worlds. Therefore, it plays a significant role in establishing the conditions for being human and, as a consequence, a more or less significant role in the becoming of the worlds humans share with nonhumans.

Conditions

When I write about ontological conditions I do not intend conditions in the logical sense of sufficient or necessary conditions. Existence is not logical, and nor can it be represented through logic or mathematics. Both logic and mathematics, despite their claims to the contrary, are merely human instruments for grasping what is. Here I use the term *grasping* to indicate two consequences of the use of logic and mathematics. First, logic and mathematics are human instruments for becoming aware of and comfortable with what is, a consequence indicated by the Greek root of *mathēsis*, which can be rendered something like "getting used to" or "growing accustomed to."[15] Second, logic and mathematics have become instruments of control and security, such that it can be said that logic and mathematics today are our preeminent tools for enacting a sense of security and control by means of "grasping" existence and existents, and becoming comfortable with it and them. In this sense, the mathematization of existence is just another form of the metaphysical humanism I will address in the next section.

When I write of ontological conditions I mean it in a sense similar to how Hannah Arendt wrote of the human condition. For Arendt "human existence is conditioned existence," and this conditioned existence is nothing like an a priori human nature that precedes any actual being in any actual world.[16] Rather, the human conditions that Arendt wrote of—natality, plurality, worldliness—arise out of human intertwining with nonhuman existents in various worlds. As she put it, "Whatever touches or enters into a sustained relationship with human life immediately assumes the character of a condition of human existence. This is why men, no matter what they do, are always conditioned beings . . . The impact of the world's reality upon human existence is felt and received as a conditioning force. The objectivity of the world—its objects- or thing-character—and the human condition supplement each other."[17] As is clear from this quote, for Arendt, though human conditions are the result of the intertwining of human and nonhuman existents, nevertheless humans have the capacity to intervene and alter the conditions that shape their ways of being-in-a-world. For Arendt this intervention is one of the primary purposes of political activity. This Arendtian insight into the necessity of such political activity is one of the main points of this book.

Similar to Arendt, then, when I write of ontological conditions I mean something like what we mean when we say "weather conditions" or "skiing conditions"—that is, the conditions that enable or hinder or provide limits for possible ways of being, becoming, acting, doing, thinking, saying, and so on, in the worlds where we are. And like weather or skiing conditions, ontological conditions emerge through the confluence of both human and nonhuman intertwining. Furthermore, because conditions emerge at this confluence, they should be understood in terms of having the potential of becoming otherwise. For just as weather and skiing conditions change as the result of both human and nonhuman activity, so, too, can ontological conditions change in similar ways. Some questions arise: If it is possible for ontological conditions to change, is there a possibility that they do not? If so, how does this happen? Furthermore, if ontological conditions can change, what are the processes by which this change occurs and what is its temporality? These are just some of the questions I would like to attend to in this book.

The political theorist William Connolly similarly writes about the significance of conditions for setting the limits, constraints, and possibilities for political, economic, and social life. Although in many ways Connolly's notion of conditions differs significantly from mine, we agree that it is impossible to understand our contemporary political and social worlds, and thus come to act in them in a directed and effective manner, without first disclosing and understanding the conditions of being of these worlds. Furthermore, we agree that although these conditions are always the result of the intertwining of human and nonhuman processes, the import of human institutions such as states, policy, legislation, media, and moral discourses are central and significant. It is for this reason that when Connolly writes of "preadaptations" and "conditions," he regularly does so in terms of the role of the state and institutions or the necessity of "an ideological machine embedded deeply in life in order to produce the submission and self-constraints its putative success demands."[18] It is for this same reason that in this book I focus on political ontologies and how their impact on political discursive practices shape ontological conditions.

Despite this similarity between my concept of conditions and what Connolly intends by it, he stops short of articulating his sense of conditions in ontological terms. Nevertheless, it is clear that Connolly recognizes the importance of ontology in political theory and for political practice, and sees a direct link between the notion of conditions and ontology.[19] This is perhaps clearest with his concept of conditioned creativity. By combining insights from complexity theory with the metaphysics of Alfred North Whitehead, Connolly articulates a notion of becoming that is central to his political theory. Becoming necessitates a process like creativity, which is the spontaneous becoming into actuality of beings-in-the-world. But this spontaneous becoming should not be thought of as an unconditioned process. For as Connolly writes, "It happens within preconditions and constraints, so there is never creation ex nihilo. The constraints are explained in large part by the fact that at any moment in chronotime the universe is composed of 'actual entities' of innumerable types which help to set preconditions for new events."[20] As will be clear throughout this book, I have much affinity for this ontological articulation. Nevertheless, while Connolly turns to the vitalist and process tradition for inspiration, my inspiration comes from post-Heideggerian philosophy. Ultimately, however, I do not think the differences are as great as they are often made out to be.

Because I agree with both Arendt and Connolly that conditions can always become otherwise, and this becoming is primarily a matter of political activity, I posit that the central political question of our time must be this: how do we think and enact the alteration of contemporary ontological conditions that limit and constrain our possibilities of becoming otherwise? Finding an answer to this question is no easy feat for sure. But attending to this question is the intention of this book. This will be done throughout by means of a critical hermeneutics that moves back and forth between a process of ungrounding the contemporary politics of the a priori and, as a result of this ungrounding, the creative development of an alternative ethical and political conceptual apparatus always open to conditions, beings, and worlds becoming otherwise. First, however, I need to turn to a consideration of what Heidegger called the "modern form of ontology" that is primarily responsible for the limitations and constraints of our contemporary condition for being and becoming.

Metaphysical Humanism

Ontology has become so trendy in the social sciences and humanities because it seems to hold some promise of providing an alternative to the status quo, whether it be intellectual, political, or social. Disappointment seems to be the mood of the day, and many have come to the conclusion that the only remedy is a radical shift not in the way we understand our own being—this, in fact, has been the hope for a long time, from the Enlightenment philosophes to the Marxists to the neo-Kantians to the post-structuralists to the critical theorists—but rather a radical shift in our conceptualization and engagement with existence as such. Perhaps if we creatively rethink the very nature of being—so the thinking goes—and along with it finally realize the promise of the Copernican revolution of decentering the human, then just maybe new possibilities for thinking, acting, and living will emerge.

An ontology, Heidegger tells us, "grounds an age, in that through a specific interpretation of what is and through a specific comprehension of truth it gives to that age the basis upon which it is essentially formed."[21] Metaphysical individualism is what Karen Barad calls the ontology that grounds contemporary science, politics, ethics, and our general way of being-in-the-world today. This is an ontology which posits "that the world is composed of individual entities with individually determinate boundaries and properties."[22] This is the ontology that equally grounds a science still largely based on atomism and objective observation, a politics based on the liberal assumption of independent individuals freely choosing in their best interest, and an ethics that begins from an individual who is endowed with inherent characteristics—such as dignity or autonomy—and who is accountable for her actions and has responsibility toward other individual humans. This is an ontology that may have emerged in a particular corner of the globe, but through the long historical processes of empire, trade, colonialism, capitalism, and media, to name only a few, this metaphysics of individualism has spread throughout the globe and, while certainly not the only ontology, has become dominant.

The fact that much social scientific and anthropological analysis remains grounded in the metaphysics of individualism is just one reason why the critique that ontology is just another name for culture is mistaken.[23] For the concept of culture only makes sense in a world grounded in the metaphysics of individualism.[24] One of the key characteristics of the metaphysics of individualism is that each individual entity is both spatially located and contained. This container notion of space was a hallmark of classical physics and remains so in the political and social sciences. Whether we speak of nation-states and its citizens, or cultures and their peoples, we ground such conceptions in the spatial container characteristic of the metaphysics of individualism.[25]

Indeed, the culture concept acts as both container and individual entity depending on the perspective taken. For culture as traditionally conceived can either be the "container" in which individuals are located or, from another perspective, just one of a multitude of similar individual cultures within the container of the globe. More nuanced conceptions of culture that emphasize process, complexity, fluid and flexible boundaries, and the like, nevertheless, ultimately rest on the ontological assumption of "individual entities with individually determinate boundaries and properties." For on a globe populated with a multitude of different and distinct cultures—even if with fluid and flexible boundaries—if you travel far enough in any direction you will eventually cross a boundary from one culture to the next—that is, from one individual with "determinate boundaries and properties" to another. And even if we conceive of culture as "in the head" or embodied rather than "out there," we remain within this ontological assumption. For while it may seem that such a move addresses the container issue—although we could say that the container has just collapsed to the dimensions of the "determinate boundaries" of the individual human, and that the "properties" of the individual human have, at least to a large degree, become that of the container—we, nevertheless, are left talking about "individual entities with individually determinate boundaries and properties." No matter how you look at the picture of culture, it remains a very good image of the metaphysics of individualism.

This is even more so when the metaphysics of individualism is understood as the ontological ground of representationalism. Whether in scientific, social, or political theories, the "idea that beings exist as individuals with inherent attributes, anterior to their representation, is a metaphysical presupposition that underlies the belief in political, linguistic, and epistemological forms of representationalism."[26] Representationalism, then, relies on the ontological distinction between the individual entities represented, their representation, and the individual entities that actually do the representation.[27] As Karen Barad puts it, "That which is represented is held to be independent of all practices of representing."[28] This ontological distinction is the case whether we speak of a scientist representing a law of nature, a word representing a thing, or an elected official representing her constituency.

While the roots of the metaphysics of individualism far precedes the seventeenth century—for example, in Chapter 1 I will show that one of these roots emerged out of medieval intra-Church debates on poverty—there is much agreement that this ontology found firm ground in the new philosophy of Descartes and the new physics of Newton.[29] Just as Newtonian physics started from the assumption of an observer looking onto, discovering, and representing a reality independent from the observation process, so, too, Descartes grounded the possibility of all knowledge on the self-certainty of one's own clear and distinct existence as consciousness, a consciousness that above all represents. It was this self-representation that provides the foundation from which the objectivity of all other things could emerge.[30] Or as Heidegger put it, "The Being of the one who represents and secures himself in representing is the measure of the Being of what is represented as such."[31] Thus, it is by means of the emergence of representationalism out of the metaphysics of individualism that humans become "the relational center of that which is as such,"[32] a position which was firmly established with Kant's Copernican revolution that "grounded the objectivity of the object in the subjectivity of the subject," and thus cemented what Heidegger called the "modern form of ontology."[33]

This "modern form of ontology"—which projects the subjectivity of the subject onto all that exists, and thus places humans in the godlike position of "the representative of that which is"[34]—can also be called metaphysical humanism. Metaphysical humanism is the contemporary form of the metaphysics of individualism. It is the ontology that places the human as an individualized entity with "determinate boundaries and properties" at the center of all existence, from which it projects these properties onto all other existents and worlds in the attempt both to understand and know them by means of representation, and in the process to control them. But even more important, metaphysical humanism enacts this project not merely for the sake of knowledge and control, but primarily as a means to secure and fix those "determinate boundaries and properties" that supposedly constitute its humanness. This ontological circle of metaphysical humanism, then, in the words of Dana Villa, "reifies the 'open possibility' of human existence into a 'what,' the better to provide an answer to the question 'Why is it necessary for man to exist at all?'"[35] In other words, in the attempt to understand its own existence, humans have created an ontology—metaphysical humanism—that secures and fixes this existence by foreclosing all other possibilities for its own becoming.

For Heidegger this foreclosure is enacted by means of the project of "gaining mastery over that which is as a whole."[36] This project results in what he calls Enframing, by which "the impression comes to prevail that everything man encounters exists only insofar as it is his construct. This illusion gives rise in turn to one final delusion: It seems as though man everywhere and always only encounters himself."[37] Hannah Arendt echoes this sentiment in her characterization of modernity when she writes, "Instead of objective qualities . . . we find instruments, and instead of nature or the universe . . . man encounters only himself."[38] For Heidegger, Enframing enacts this final delusion of finding humanity in all of existence not because the science was wrong or the technology not yet powerful enough, but because of the very starting point of metaphysical humanism: that is, the assumption that existents are individually distinct entities and that one of them, namely humans, enjoys a particularly privileged position—an Archimedean point—from which they can come to know and control all that is. As Heidegger continues, this delusion that has arisen through the project to secure and fix a posited essence for humans "[in] truth [results in the fact that] precisely nowhere does man today any longer encounter himself."[39] Thus, the very ontology that begins from the assumption of the self-certain knowledge of oneself actually manifests as an assemblage of worlds in which humans have lost themselves.

This is so because in carrying out the ontological project of metaphysical humanism, humans have covered over and forgotten the open possibilities of existence. By means of the subjectivization of all existence, humans have covered over the very worldliness of not only their own existence but also that of all other existents as well. In doing so they have managed to turn away from the open possibilities available to these worlds and their existents, humans being just one. As Dana Villa puts it in describing Hannah Arendt's critique of modernity, "Science, philosophy, economic and political theory [and I would add social theory as well]: all conspire to cover over both the phenomenon of world and the worldliness of phenomena."[40]

Within the ontological conditions set by this metaphysics, worlds and their existents become fixed. Worlds and the existents that populate them become quantitated as mathematics is projected onto them and understood as the "language of nature," while humans and their activities, when not themselves quantitated, are secured with transcendental value-properties such as dignity and rights. As a result, Reason and Morality, the twin "properties" of humans posited and enacted through metaphysical humanism, have resulted in what Arendt calls world alienation. That is, this ontology has led to the alienation of humans from the worldly conditions out of which their very being emerge, as well as the open possibilities available to them (as well as all other existents) within those worlds. This ontology results in a leveling or closing off of possibility, and as such a closing off of the possibility of an otherwise that might become available if we lived within other ontological conditions. As it currently stands, worlds conditioned by metaphysical humanism foreclose this possibility of the otherwise while only allowing "normalized" behavior.[41] It is for this reason that Arendt, in a sort of foreshadow of Foucault, could so easily conclude that in the "modern age . . . life, and not the world, is the highest good."[42]

It is important to point out that metaphysical humanism as the culmination of the metaphysics of individualism and representationalism is not simply a matter of philosophical writings and trends. Rather, metaphysical humanism emerged, gained hold, and became the dominant ontology today by means of diverse practices. In this sense, philosophy is itself merely just one of many practices that enact this ontology. Perhaps the most significant of these practices has been scientific and mathematic practice, as their modern forms emerged out of the beginnings of the metaphysics of individualism and have come to stand for many as the sole bases of truth. Capitalist and technological practices are based on the assumption that the earth (and increasingly that which is beyond it) exists simply as standing-reserve—and this includes human labor as well—for the purposes of human use, profit, and progress. But one of the primary practices of metaphysical humanism, and as such one of the primary ways that world alienation has been enacted, has been politics. And it is this political practice of metaphysical humanism that I will focus on in this book.

The Politics of the A Priori and Moralism

I will call the metaphysical humanist practice of politics *the politics of the a priori*. This is a politics that begins with an a priori and fixed conception of human being and then proceeds in the attempt to shape political, social, and nonhuman worlds in the image of this predefined essence. The politics of the a priori has been enacted in the form of, for example, liberalism, socialism, anarchism, Marxism, and human rights politics. Each of these political practices begins from an a priori definition of humanness, a definition that usually and for the most part limits existence to such a degree that the latter is essentially rendered human-centric. Thus, in the attempt to enact political practices that are supposed to address worlds, the politics of the a priori in fact results in the kind of world alienation of which Arendt wrote. This is so because all instantiations of the politics of the a priori cover over the worldliness of the world and our intertwining with it, and in turn level such things as time to linear human history, space to contained geography and borders, and activity to human-centric activity such as knowledge, control, and security.

This covering over of worlds by the politics of the a priori is further accomplished by the centrality of morality in all the respective predefinitions of humanness. For Morality, along with Reason, is one of the twin properties of humanness within metaphysical humanism. The various politics of the a priori all posit political practice based on some predefined moral capacity, and they attempt to realize "a world" in the image of this morality. In this way morality is inextricably linked with ontology, and both become enacted through political practices and programs. Regardless of whether we consider the rational calculative human of utilitarianism that grounds both classical and neo-liberalisms, or the communitarian infused Kantianism that either implicitly or explicitly grounds much socialism and anarchism, or the individualistic Kantianism that grounds contemporary human rights politics, regardless of which politics of the a priori we might turn, we find a predefined moral capacity intimately intertwined with its very ontological being of humanness. Thus, it seems that for the politics of the a priori humans can only be political because of their predefined essence as a fixed and particular kind of moral agent. As a result, political practice is significantly limited in its tactics, strategies, and goals to the limitations imposed by this a priori and fixed essence of moral humanness. This, in turn, leaves us with a politics today that forecloses the possibility of experimentation, creativity, and speculation, because within the politics of the a priori political practice can only be imagined in terms of logical entailments from the starting assumption of its a priori moral humanness. It is no wonder that today politics has taken a so-called ethical turn,[43] and this has resulted in a contemporary political scene characterized by what Wendy Brown calls political moralism.

According to Brown political moralism is the result of the loss of the conceptual, strategic, and tactical possibilities of those on both the left and squarely within liberalism.[44] This inability to articulate the basis for or the aims of politics has led to a contemporary political scene that lacks a clearly defined political "good" for which to strive. The resulting political aimlessness and failure to articulate a clear course of political action, Brown argues, leads to both frustration and political paralysis. Here moralism enters the political scene. For marked by frustration, paralysis, and thus political impotence, left and liberal politics has come to equate moralizing platitudes with political action. Such moralizing tends to begin from the assumption of a moral individual defined a priori by dignity and rights, tends to equate suffering with moral Truth and superiority, and exhibits a fundamentalist attachment to this moral Truth, and thus a disdain for the agonistic nature by which political action is actually performed in worlds. This political moralism that begins from the assumption of an a priori moral individual, furthermore, tends to focus on either identity-based or issue-based activism—and thus, regardless of whether we consider the focus of this political moralism as the individually bounded entities of moral individuals, identities, or issues, it is clear how this politics of the a priori enacts the metaphysical humanism I delineated above.

This ethical turn of politics characterized as political moralism, furthermore, seems to result in a notion of politics that is particularly shortsighted. For when a politics of the a priori focuses exclusively on individually bounded entities—moral individuals, identities, issues—this politics must end when the particular project concerning the individually bounded entity is realized. Thus, for example, when an issue is resolved or addressed, or an identity group has its interests met, the politics, so it seems, must end. This shortsightedness of the politics of the a priori is what normally is called reform, which we can characterize as the folding of the excluded into the already existing order of things, an order that fundamentally relies on this very exclusion. This attempt to be included in that which simply cannot be inclusive is part of what in Chapter 2 I will call the fantasy of progress.

Recognizing the essential connection between metaphysical humanism, the politics of the a priori, and the ethical turn in politics allows a significant entrée for a critical hermeneutics. It is precisely such a critical hermeneutics that I will undertake in this book. The result, I hope, will make clear that this link between ontologies, politics, and moralities is essential for any study that intends not only to understand contemporary worlds, but more important, to contribute to the opening of possibilities within them. I would argue that within the anthropology of moralities and political anthropology—that is, within the academic realm that I know best—this essential link has been missed. Just as most anthropologists who have taken up an explicit study of moralities and ethics have done so with little or no concern for politics,[45] political anthropologists have not engaged in a serious study of the significance of moralities and ethics to political discursive practice, other than in a fairly straightforward Foucauldian manner. And none of them has taken seriously the centrality of ontology to both. It is just this lacuna that the critical hermeneutics of this book attempts to address. In doing so the hope is not merely a further contribution to academic literature, but a contribution to the opening of possibilities for an otherwise.

Critical Hermeneutics and an Anthropology of Potentiality

Critical hermeneutics is a theoretical-analytic for the disclosure of the limiting conditions of worlds and ways of being-in-them.[46] Indeed, despite the unwarranted (and seemingly uninformed) reputation that phenomenology and hermeneutics now has in many academic circles for being both conservative and subject-focused, critique as ungrounding, or what is also called deconstruction, has always been central to this tradition.[47] Phenomenological hermeneutics is more than the critical disclosure of limits, however, for in this disclosure there is always an opening to something otherwise.[48] That is, critical hermeneutic disclosure of limits always opens new possibilities for thinking, saying, doing, or being. Hermeneutics, then, is essentially a theoretical-analytic for becoming otherwise.[49] In this sense, to do hermeneutics—whether of a text, a concept, a history, a political practice, or what have you—is to open possibilities.

Opening possibilities is exactly what is needed today to counteract the disappointment of which I have been writing. This is understood and felt not only by many of the political agonists I have come to know over the years, who despite regularly telling me of their frustration with their currently available political strategies, tactics, and concepts go on repeating these same old, exhausted options because they feel as though they have no alternative. It is also increasingly articulated, for example, by anthropologists[50] and political theorists[51] who have tired of mere criticism without offering alternatives for being and acting in our worlds—alternatives, that is, they would like to create in collaboration with those with whom they do research. Such alternative possibilities are precisely what critical hermeneutics offers through its analysis.

However, unlike many other approaches that claim to offer an alternative future by means of so-called ontological anthropology, critical hermeneutics begins with critique.[52] For as already mentioned, to do hermeneutics is to open new possibilities in the very process of ungrounding the already is and the taken for granted. In this sense, critical hermeneutics can be understood as the interplay between deconstruction and experimental creativity. Such creativity, however, should not be thought of as creation ex nihilo, but rather as the creative disclosure, or the creative release of potentialities that already exist right here and now but are covered over, or trapped within, or held back by that which currently is.[53] To be clear: a critical hermeneutic approach, unlike other anthropological approaches of the so-called ontological turn, does not assume that such creative disclosure is only possible through ontologies of the "non-modern"[54] or that it is necessary to return to or be inspired by something called a "primitivist anthropology,"[55] to the extent that either of these necessitate an exposure to a radical alterity that seemingly can be only found far off somewhere and preferably in the Amazon. And neither does a critical hermeneutics

enact a neo-structuralism[56] of cosmogonies and myths[57] while eschewing the centrality of history, politics, and power in the assemblages of that which is.[58] A critical hermeneutics is skeptical, to say the least, of such latter-day Rousseauian fantasies.[59] Rather, a critical hermeneutic perspective begins with the assumption that sites of potentiality abound, and that it is not necessary to return to or become inspired by the "primitive" to find them, but rather that sites of potentiality can be found anywhere if one begins not with myth but with deconstructive critique. Thus, critical hermeneutics opens these already existing potentialities by destructing that which currently makes them seem impossible, wherever these sites of potentiality may be found.

This process of creation through destruction is precisely the task of this book. Therefore, my approach in writing and organizing the book oscillates between deconstructive ungrounding and disclosive opening. Primarily this hermeneutic oscillation will work across the various discursive practices of the global anti–drug war movement, with which I have been doing research for eight years. Although this political movement primarily articulates and understands its activity, strategies, and tactics in the language and terms of late-liberal rights politics, I contend that critical hermeneutic analysis discloses the potentialities this movement has for showing us an alternative form of political language and activity, an alternative that has become necessary as a response to the disappointment about which I wrote above.

This is so because critical hermeneutics is a theoretical-analytic for disclosing, tracing, and describing the contours of the not-yet. For a fundamental assumption of hermeneutic analysis is that existence—human and otherwise—is always other to itself, and as such, constantly engaged in an existentially responsive process[60] in the attempt to become that which it never is, a process that creates gaps of being that can never be filled.[61] Put another way, existence is a hermeneutic process. Because of this, a critical hermeneutics cannot take existents to be what they "claim" to be or concepts to mean what they are "supposed" to mean, but rather asks what they point us toward. By interrogating this gap between the "supposed to" and that to which we are pointed, critical hermeneutic analysis discloses the potentialities that are already there partly shaping what is, but as of yet, are not fully possible. Thus, in this book I will work this critical hermeneutic oscillation across the late-liberal political-moral triad of rights-dignity-responsibility as it is utilized by the anti–drug war movement in order to deconstruct the limitations this triad establishes and to open potential possibilities this utilization points toward.

Furthermore, in this book another critical hermeneutic oscillation will run between some contemporary academic engagements with the themes of this book—that is, ethics, politics, and ontologies—and the analysis being offered here. Thus, I also interrogate some of the more significant anthropological, philosophical, and political theoretical engagements with ethics, politics, and ontologies in order to reveal and deconstruct their metaphysical humanist foundations so as to show the way to potential new modalities of analysis. The hope of this hermeneutic strategy, then, is not only to reveal the continuing dominance of metaphysical humanism in academic work—perhaps most perniciously so in that work that claims to go beyond it—but also to disclose potential avenues out of the academic repetition of this ontological tradition.

This book is not—and should not be read as—a traditional ethnography. For although this critical hermeneutics begins from an ethnographic archive accrued over the course of eight years of research I have done on anti–drug war political activity, I approach this archive as a hermeneutic opportunity to explore the possibility of studying potentialities. In a future book, I intend to offer a more ethnographically focused analysis of potentiality. Here I offer the theoretical notes or framework, as it were, from which that analysis will begin. Therefore, in this book I will take up such questions as: If we were to begin to articulate a study of potentiality, how might we do so? To what extent could we begin with already established anthropological methods and conceptual apparatuses, and to what extent would we need to look elsewhere for inspiration or create new ones? Indeed, to what extent would an anthropology of potentiality necessitate—perhaps above all else—imagination and creativity, not in our writing per se, but in our thinking? In this book I try to address these and similar questions as I begin to trace the contours of the possibility of studying potentiality. As such, this book is itself an experiment in what anthropology could be; perhaps we could tentatively call this an anthropology of potentiality.

Outline of the Book

If one of the tasks of this book is to provide an alternative approach to the analysis of the intertwining of humans and worlds in terms of the politics that enacts this intertwining, the moralities that motivate and shape this politics, and the ontological tradition that frames both of these, while at the same time providing a possible alternative for being and acting in our worlds today, then we must begin with the ungrounding of the dominant onto-political-moral assemblage within which we are entwined. To this end, a main thread that runs throughout the chapters, and which is the focus of the first two, is the deconstructive ungrounding of the dominant political-moral discursive articulation of metaphysical humanism—that is, contemporary late-liberal rights-based politics. This ungrounding draws on much critical analysis already done of such politics, and particularly that of human rights politics.[62] But the fact of the continued dominance of human rights discursive practice in global politics today, as well as the current state of anthropology's supportive relationship with human rights politics,[63] necessitates a revisiting of this critical analysis—a revisiting, that is, in ontological terms.

Thus, in this book, and especially in Chapters 1 and 2, I hermeneutically disclose the ontological conditions for being-in-the-world that this dominant form of politics enacts. As the reader moves through the book, it should become increasingly clear that rights-based politics, as the epitome of the politics of the a priori and the metaphysical humanism that grounds this politics, enacts the ontological conditions of totality and repetition. Similar to how Lee Edelman describes reproductive futurism,[64] I will show that the enactment of totality and repetition in political-moral terms is a politics that aims at little more than the folding of the excluded into a fantasized totality, a morality narrowly conceived in terms of a priori and transcendental properties of an individually bounded subject, and an ontology that closes any possibility of worlds or its existents becoming anything other than another version of what they already are. Ironically, as I will show in Chapter 2, these ontological conditions of totality and repetition, which enframe limits and closure, are articulated as progress.

To help the reader understand how this has become so, in Chapter 1 I trace the historical emergence of the supposedly transcendental and a priori concept of rights in order to disclose its link to the metaphysics of individualism, and metaphysical humanism in particular, and in so doing come to understand the limitations on political and moral possibilities this concept enframes today. This is a process of tracing what Gadamer called the effective history of tradition, or the way "we are always already affected by history."[65] Critically tracing the contours of this effective history is crucial for a critical hermeneutics of contemporary politics, for the deconstructive analysis of the ontological grounding of our currently available political possibilities reveals much about the way such politics are practiced and the kinds of consequences—intended and otherwise—we can expect from these practices. Thus, beginning with the intra-Church poverty debates of the late medieval period, this chapter traces the emergence of the concept of rights and its solidification in terms of what I call its conceptual proclivity over the course of some of the key political moments of the coming to dominance of the ontological tradition of metaphysical humanism. As I will try to make clear, ultimately the concept of rights as it is utilized today emerged from, is grounded in, and repeats a particular ontological tradition that by means of its concepts, posits and enacts ontological conditions of totality and repetition through processes aimed at sovereignty, security, and control. Thus, not only does this chapter serve as a necessary background for the following chapters and for understanding the ontological grounds of late-liberal rights-based politics, but more important, it does the critical deconstructive work necessary to begin to find the interstitial gaps in this discursive tradition from which sites of potentiality may be disclosed.

Chapter 2 will consider the centrality of the concept of progress in the enactment of these ontological conditions of totality and repetition. In this chapter I move between an ontic and ontological analysis of progress to disclose the limits of the political possibilities of the ontological tradition of metaphysical humanism. After hermeneutically considering the temporality of progress as utilized in liberal discourse, I then consider it in terms of the moral progress articulated in human rights discourse. In particular, I analyze the way rights arguments are made by anti–drug war agonists working in Russia in order to disclose the repetition of differential sameness enacted through their discursive practice. What becomes clear is that ontically the enactment of progress ultimately works to limit political and moral activity within a narrowly defined range of possibilities, and thus reveals the essential conservatism of human rights discursive practice. Ontologically, I will argue, progress is best understood as the temporal projection of the subjectivity of the subject onto existence as a whole. In this sense, we can understand progress as the central temporal concept of metaphysical humanism and its totalizing enframing. This chapter concludes with the suggestion that when this complete projection of metaphysical humanism occurs—or perhaps better put, when the fantasy of this complete projection becomes our reality—we find ourselves living in the ontological conditions of totality and repetition.

In the first two chapters, then, I show how this phantasmatic projection occurs by means of political-moral practice, and why as a result of these ontological conditions of totality and repetition we find ourselves today living ontically not with hope but with disappointment. Ultimately these chapters lead us to the realization that the politics of the a priori is the political "fulfillment" of metaphysical humanism, and the morality of a predefined and transcendental subject that is one of the central aspects of this ontological tradition. As such, it is hardly surprising that this politics of the a priori enacts the ontological conditions of totality and repetition by means of political moralism, and in so doing enacts the foreclosure of possibilities for becoming otherwise. In the remaining chapters I address this foreclosure through a critical hermeneutics that discloses alternative conceptions for understanding, articulating, and enacting a radical politics (radical, that is, in terms of groundless finitude). Such concepts will be *situation*, *world*, *dwelling*, *attunement*, and *worldbuilding*, and provide a way of conceiving an alternative politics that I suggest we can find the potential for within what is already being done by the anti–drug war movement. Such a politics, unlike the closed totality and repetition enacted by the politics of the a priori, I hope to show enacts ontological conditions of openness and possibilities.

To this end Chapter 3 offers a new way of conceiving the focus of political activity. In contrast to the individualized and bounded issues and identities that much politics of the a priori focuses on today, a politics of worldbuilding begins with situations. Using the drug war as an example of a situation, this chapter delineates the characteristics of a situation and argues that worlds are nothing other than an assemblage of multiple situations and the existents that are intertwined with them. This focus on situations, so I argue, allows politics to remain open-ended rather than closed and shortsighted; demands that strategies, tactics, and aims emerge from a situation rather than an a priori conception of humanity; and as a result is enacted as a politics of becoming rather than being.

Chapter 4 takes up the dilemma posed by what Simon Critchley calls the motivational deficit that accompanies the disappointment in politics today. In contrast to the politics of the a priori that I suggest Critchley perpetuates with his focus on the political subject, I argue for a motivational ethics that begins not with the subject but with a world that has become unbearable. I call this an ethics of dwelling and argue that an anthropological sensitivity to the particularities of situations and worlds is necessary for understanding how such an ethics motivates politics. To make this argument I begin the chapter by considering the metaphysical humanist assumptions built into much of contemporary anthropological analysis of moralities and ethics—with a particular focus on the so-called ordinary ethics approach—and argue that, much like the politics of the a priori, such assumptions do little more than repeat a totalized a priori notion of the human subject detached from its worlds. I then argue that unlike the politics of the a priori that begins with a metaphysical humanist notion of the political subject, a politics of worldbuilding begins with a being-in-a-world with an existential imperative to dwell. Dwelling is here conceived as being-in-a-world in such a way that one is always open to new possibilities that can emerge from one's world. When one's world breaks down and becomes uninhabitable, then one is no longer able to dwell in this world. Some respond to this with what I call an ethics of dwelling, which is the subjective experience of doing a politics of worldbuilding. I will consider such an ethics through the experience of some anti–drug war agonists in New York City and Vancouver.

Chapter 5 attempts to rethink the concept of responsibility in terms of respond-ability. I think of this respond-ability as attunement, and do so in terms of a world becoming attuned with itself. I contrast two approaches to the practice of harm reduction—a key element in the anti–drug war movement—and show that while most harm reduction is still practiced with the assumption of a metaphysical humanist subject, a subject burdened by personal responsibility, a politics of worldbuilding is underway in Vancouver that begins with the demands of an unbearable world and attempts to build one that is attuned with itself. Attunement, then, like an ethics of dwelling, would be a key concept in a politics that begins with a world rather than an a priori subject.

The epilogue attempts to bring together this experiment in analysis and politics by means of delineating the hermeneutic character of existence. Because of this character, so I argue, a critical hermeneutics as an anthropology of potentiality provides the best possibility for coming to understand not only the worlds with which we are intertwined, but also, and ultimately most important, the ways we can best participate in these worlds so as to help make them the best possible worlds for ourselves and our nonhuman cohabitants. Critical hermeneutics, then, provides us with hope that we need not continue to be disappointed.

CHAPTER I

The Effective History of Rights

In this chapter I attempt to trace the historical emergence of the supposedly transcendental and a priori concept of rights, to disclose its grounding in the metaphysics of individualism, and metaphysical humanism in particular, and in so doing come to understand the limitations on political and moral possibilities this concept enframes. In other words, this chapter will trace what Gadamer calls the effective history[1] of the concept of rights. For Gadamer a central component of hermeneutic analysis is the recognition that "we are always already affected by history," and therefore, we must begin with what he called a history of effect.[2] Such recognition entails a realization that we are always an effect of the tradition—I would say the ontological tradition—within which we find ourselves, and despite this recognition we continue to be affected by the tradition. And yet, the way we inhabit this continued affective tradition is a matter of import. From a hermeneutic perspective we must inhabit our tradition, as Gadamer puts it, not as "imprisoned, as if behind insurmountable barriers,"[3] but rather in a modality of openness. This is so because hermeneutics is always a process of disclosing potentialities and opening possibilities. In other words, to do hermeneutics is at one and the same time to recognize the continued effect an ontological tradition has on limiting the contemporary possibilities for being and acting in worlds, and through this recognition to begin to find sites of potentiality from which new possibilities might emerge.

This modality of considering effective history is central to a critical hermeneutics of contemporary politics, for the analysis of the moral and ontological grounding of our currently available political possibilities reveals much about the way such politics are practiced and the kinds of consequences—intended and otherwise—we can expect from these practices. Furthermore, because the moral and ontological grounding of a politics is rarely consciously understood by its practitioners, and thus even more rarely explicitly acknowledged, critical hermeneutic analysis is vital for coming to understand the possibilities and limitations for being-in-the-world made available by a discursive practice. Thus, a guiding question of such analysis would be: what kinds of conditions and possibilities for being are enframed and enacted through a particular kind of discursive practice such as rights-based politics, and how can we understand this as a consequence of the effective history of its grounding ontological tradition?

In attempting to answer this question I begin with the assumption that critical hermeneutic analysis discloses the effective history and thus the limits of a particular politics, and in so doing also discloses that which this politics excludes. This would seem to be an important exercise for any form of politics. But perhaps this is even more urgent and necessary for rights-based politics considering its predominance today among the world's political and social movements, and, perhaps more important, because of the primacy of place of human rights language in much of the public rhetoric of national and international governments. As will become clear, however, the concept of rights in its diverse historical manifestations has always been closely tied to and ultimately utilized to underwrite, stabilize, and support sovereign power, and usually conservative power at that, in the name of security and control. Now that human rights has become both the language of power and of those who seek to resist power, and as such the central political-moral concept of our day, the necessity of critically analyzing its ontological grounding and thus its political and moral assumptions, limitations, and exclusions should be clear.[4]

Human rights have only recently become an object of study by historians, and these studies tend to fall into one of two approaches. The first tends to give a triumphalist account that sees the present dominance of human rights as the result of a long history of progressive evolution into its contemporary manifestation (a history, it should be noted, that seemingly stretches to the very beginnings of human civilization in some accounts).[5]

The second approach tends to see the emergence of human rights as a globally dominant political-moral discourse as a very recent—usually starting in the 1970s—and historically contingent occurrence.[6] As will be clear I am very sympathetic to the latter approach. But while agreeing that human rights as a dominant political-moral discourse is a very recent and historically contingent phenomenon, the critical hermeneutic analysis of this chapter reveals that, in fact, human rights can only be understood as part of a larger conceptual history of rights and, as such, as part of the dominant ontological tradition today.

This is not to say, as do the triumphalist histories, that this larger conceptual history necessarily led to the contemporary concept of human rights as if a kernel of an idea snowballed through history and emerged in 1948 in the form of an unavoidable avalanche. Far from it. But it is also not correct, I will show, that human rights be viewed as initiating a completely new discourse—or at least one significantly distinct from the natural rights tradition—as the contingent histories seem to argue at times. Rather, I argue that the very notion of human rights and the ways it is manifest today can only be understood against a larger effective and conceptual history[7] of rights. This history reveals what I will call a conceptual proclivity that, despite changes and shifts in the meaning and social uses of the concept, tends to lead to conceptual manifestations that support certain kinds of social and power relationships, institutions, and practices over time. It is a view of conceptual history that acknowledges change and shifts, as well as similarities and tendencies. It is a view of the concept that at one and the same time recognizes its singular historical manifestation at any particular space-time as well as the fact that this particular singularity always exceeds itself in its reference to, and thus its inescapability from, its unique effective history. It is, finally, a view of the concept that emphasizes that because a concept always exceeds its singular historical manifestation, it also exceeds the intentions of those who use it at any particular historical moment.[8]

This is so because, as Gadamer puts it, our contemporary understanding and use of concepts are but "the furthering of an event that goes far back. Hence [we are not able to use our] concepts unquestioningly, but will have to take over whatever features of the original meaning of [our] concepts have come down to [us]."[9] The critical hermeneutic analysis of this chapter reveals that this conceptual proclivity of rights is best understood in terms of how this concept emerged as a key concept of the incipient metaphysics of individualism taking shape in the high and late medieval periods. While it may be the case that this metaphysics did not become manifest until the mathematical and natural scientific grounding of Descartes and Newton,[10] in this chapter we will see that the moral and political aspect of this metaphysics began much earlier than its mathematico-scientific ones.[11] Indeed, this order of conceptualization is not surprising since before the mathematicians and natural philosophers could ground the objectivity of "the world" on the subjectivity of the subject, an individualized subject needed to come into being. As will become clear, the concept of rights, and most specifically the idea of an individual with a priori inherent rights inextricably linked to an institution of power, was a necessary political-moral conceptual move for the emergence of and eventual establishment of the ontological tradition of metaphysical humanism. It is no surprise, then, that this key political-moral conceptual foundation—rights—has today become the dominant conceptual expression for legitimate political-moral ways of being and acting in our worlds, and as such, doesn't so much express a political or moral aim as much as repeats and reaffirms the dominant ontological tradition of our age.

What this critical hermeneutics of the effective and conceptual history of rights will disclose, then, is that concepts emerge along with a particular ontological tradition. Furthermore, the ongoing enactment of these concepts—by means of such things as everyday practices, governmental policies, laws, narratives, architecture, design, and technology, to name only a few—is also the ongoing enactment, repetition, maintenance, and perpetuation of the ontological tradition of which the concepts are a part. What becomes particularly clear in this chapter, then, is that the concept of rights has accumulated a conceptual proclivity to become manifest as a political-moral foundation of a metaphysical humanist ontological tradition that today has its most significant consequence as the foundation for state sovereignty primarily concerned with security, control, and the disciplining of life. In what follows, I hope to make clear how this has unfolded historically, and why political agonists such as those in the anti–drug war movement, about whom I write in the rest of this book, can only conceive and articulate their political activity in terms of the rights-dignity-responsibility triad.

A Critical Hermeneutics of Rights

In the beginning there was already property and ownership. Or at least that is how John XXII saw it in his papal bull *Quia vir reprobus*, in which he effectively put an end to the long-standing debate over poverty and property within the thirteenth- and fourteenth-century Church.[12] This consequential debate centered on the Franciscan doctrine of apostolic poverty, which made the claim that members of the order could use the commodities necessary for daily life without having property rights in them. From the Franciscan point of view this doctrine was necessary to maintain fidelity to the ideals of the order's founder, as well as to remain an organized order within the institutional setting of the Church.[13] The position of the Franciscans can be articulated as follows: because property only comes about through civil law—that is, it is socially and humanly created—it is not characteristic of humans as such and their natural relationship with one another and the world. Therefore, because *usus simplex facti* (simple use) or mere consumption[14] does not entail ownership, the ability to consume some thing or place does not entail that one must own it and therefore exercise property rights. This argument, then, was essentially opposed to rights in that it took the position that property rights, which in the late medieval period were quickly coming to be considered the quintessential right,[15] only existed within the temporal order of civil law.[16] The 1279 papal bull *Exiit qui seminat* by Nicholas III supported and protected this Franciscan claim.[17]

Just two generations later the radical implications of this doctrine became clear to the Church hierarchy and the new pope, John XXII; as Richard Tuck expresses the concern, "If it was possible for some men to live in an innocent way, then it should be possible for all men to do so."[18] The Church as the most powerful and richest institution in medieval Europe simply could not accept this potentially revolutionary doctrine from one of its own orders. The response, therefore, necessitated the articulation of an alternative view of human life under God's law or the law of nature; it necessitated a view that individuals could have property naturally, outside of any social order.[19] The answer finally came in John XXII's *Quia vir reprobus*. Claiming that a human's *dominium* over his possessions is conceptually the same as God's *dominium* over the earth, John XXII went on to argue that Adam, before Eve, had "by himself *dominium* over temporal things."[20] The "by himself" is essential to John XXII's argument, for even in this state of innocence when Adam had no one with whom to exchange commodities he still had *dominium* or ownership over these. In other words, John's argument essentially made the claim that Adam—all alone and existing only as a human as such and not in any relation to any society because none existed—had property rights by his very nature as a human.

For the very first time the notion that individual human beings—humans outside of any relationship to institutions, states, or human sociality—had by the very fact of being human certain natural rights, or what we might call today inherent rights.[21] Thus was born the idea that has become the keystone of the modern human rights industry[22]—that all humans are naturally endowed with particular rights—within the context of the medieval Catholic Church defending its institutional position of power against a perceived heretical and potentially revolutionary doctrine which claimed that individuals could consume what they need to live outside relationships of property. As Leff puts it, John's *Quia vir reprobus* had "comprehensively supplanted poverty by dominion [property/ownership/control] not only in the life of Christ but in the designs of God. Lordship not renunciation was the badge of apostolic life." In the defense of property rights and the Church as an institution of power, then, John XXII created a conservative and profoundly individualistic conception of rights founded on property and control that can be understood as an essential conceptual move in the emergence of an incipient metaphysics of individualism. This conception of individual rights founded on property and control was the ground from which, in only a few centuries and with only a few modifications, the classic natural rights theories sprang—for example, Locke's notion of property of the self—and, in turn, gave way to today's conception of human rights.[23]

It is important to note that the Latin terms *dominium* and *ius* are the keywords in this textual debate. *Dominium* is often translated as "property," but it does not quite match with the modern notion of that concept. Rather, in addition to ownership, *dominium* is perhaps best translated as "control" or "sovereignty," as in the English "dominion." Therefore in these medieval Church debates over property or *dominium* the debate is not over simple ownership but about control and sovereignty and whether rights could be exercised without being one who possesses control and sovereignty.[24] It is here that we see the truly significant nature of John XXII's argument, for in defending the institutional power of the Church, John endows individuals with an inherent nature characterized by control and sovereignty. This is significant because it signals a conceptual shift from the notion of passive rights—which since the time of imperial Rome had been the most dominant institutional articulation of rights—to that of active rights.[25] In other words, John's argument entailed that rights could only be exercised by morally sovereign individuals. This is language that already gets us quite close to many of the assumptions of the modern human rights industry.

Indeed, the centrality of *dominium* in this conceptual shift also mirrors a broader conceptual shift in the midst of what could be described as the incipient moment of the ontological tradition of metaphysical humanism. This is so because John XXII's argument for the *dominium* of Adam in the defense of inherent rights can be understood as just one move in what Schürmann describes as a shift in the history of metaphysics. According to Schürmann, in the Middle Ages—and particularly in the thirteenth century despite the rediscovery of Aristotle in Christendom—metaphysics underwent a shift such that the new ontological tradition then coming into being lost "sight of the origin as *incipit*, as the event of nascency, in order to fix its speculative gaze on the origin as pure *regnat*, as rule and dominion."[26] This key shift in the conceptual order of things signified that what mattered ontologically was no longer the potential of things, persons, and worlds to become otherwise—or to realize an immanent *eidos* as it had been for Aristotle—but rather the primacy of an order that had always already been such: an ontological order as *gubernatio mundi* by which God, the prince, and the individual human (in that order) would have, by nature, *dominium* over all existence.[27]

Similarly, *ius* does not simply translate as "right" but also as "law" and "duty." And here perhaps the utilitarian argument that someone's right is nothing other than another's duty toward that person is made a bit clearer. But it is also important to recognize the possible slippage that could occur between *ius* as right and *ius* as law. Thus, to speak of the *ius naturale* could be to speak of either natural law or natural right—and in some sense it is to speak of both. For the *ius naturale* can imply either an objective or a subjective referent. That is, objectively we could speak of a natural law that more or less orders the way the world ought to be, while at the same time we could speak subjectively of natural right as that which individuals are morally capable of or morally owed. It was the merging of or the slippage between these two meanings of *ius* which allowed for the conceptualization of the active notion of rights that became institutionalized in John XXII's *Quia vir reprobus*. For only when *ius* as a right is also seen as a kind of natural law—an a priori moral capability that is also an objective ought—that individuals become morally sovereign. Here, then, we see the political-moral establishment of one of the central characteristics of metaphysical humanism—that is, the grounding of "the objectivity of the object in the subjectivity of the subject."[28] Thus, we see clearly that one of the foundational assumptions of modern human rights can only be understood within a particular conceptual and effective history that is immanent to a particular ontological tradition, which itself emerged through a particular rhetorical use of language within institutionally based debates.

John's papal bull set the scene for a fundamental shift in the way rights would be considered inherent to humans as individuals, and this was possible because of the very fact of the inherent *dominium* of humans over the world. When John took up the concept of rights its history was still relatively short and limited—it was a concept still open to interpretation and change—but it was, nevertheless, a history that had been essentially connected to institutions of power. So when John sought to mobilize the concept to defend and support his institution of power—the Catholic Church—this move was perfectly understandable within its conceptual history. The radical shift he initiated toward active rights, however, constituted a seminal historical moment in that it fundamentally transformed the way the relation between the concept of rights, institutions of power, and individuals would be conceived from that moment on. It was the shift, then, that initiated what in time would become the conceptual proclivity of the concept of rights—that is, the proclivity always to ultimately connect individuals to institutions of power by means of a notion of active rights that emphasize individual sovereignty and ownership/control.

Indeed, William of Ockham's response to John on the latter's terms exemplifies the fact that John established the grounds of this new proclivity almost immediately; as Richard Tuck puts it, the arguments that would develop in response to and in support of John's bull would quickly lead to the conclusion that there "had to be *some* owner of everything."[29] To this day this notion has hardly changed, and the idea of the property of the self that in the seventeenth and eighteenth centuries built off this notion remains central to human rights. It is, in a sense, that aspect of the conceptual proclivity of rights that cannot be shaken. In order to account for how this came about, I will continue with this critical hermeneutics and move forward from John a few centuries. For nearly three hundred years after John's bull, at the advent of the European colonial adventure, many of John's arguments would be taken as starting assumptions in the great natural rights-based debates and defenses of sovereignty, slavery, and colonialism in the context of mercantile capitalism. It is little surprise, then, that rejuvenation of rights-based argumentation would begin and flourish in the centers of the slave trade—Portugal and the Netherlands. What is perhaps surprising, however, is that this rejuvenation began once again amid intra-Church debates—this time between the Jesuits and Dominicans—a central piece of which was the question of free will.

The Rights of War and Peace

The details of this debate are not important for our purposes. What is important, however, is that the Spanish Jesuit Luis de Molina would make a key move by combining a psychologically based argument of free will with a notion of active rights in order to make a claim about human liberty. In doing so, Molina set the stage for a view that individuals have the capacity to either forego or trade away their rights or to demand or regain them.[30] While clearly the latter capacity has become central to the modern human rights industry, in Molina's time and for the next two hundred years the former capacity would be central to natural rights theories, debates, and politics. Simply put the argument goes like this: because by nature rights are the property of individuals, and because these individuals, by nature, are free to make choices and decisions, these very same individuals are free to forego or trade away their rights (make a property exchange) to another in exchange for something else (e.g., security, a commodity, their life). Here once again we see how this conception of rights articulates and perpetuates the metaphysics of individualism which posits "that the world is composed of individual entities with individually determinate boundaries and properties." From this point forward such an articulation would be the starting point of all major natural rights theories, and for the next two hundred years it would be the basis for arguments both for and against slavery, colonialism, and sovereignty.

Perhaps the most prominent example of this is the political theorist who established many of the grounds of classical natural rights theory, Hugo Grotius. In his *De iure belli ac pacis* (*On the Law of War and Peace*) Grotius takes up the question of sovereignty.[31] While Jean Bodin's response to this question is often considered the strongest defense of absolutism of its time, and Grotius is often held up as a liberal humanist, this distinction is not always so clear, particularly when it comes to the question of slavery.[32] In the early decades of the seventeenth century—as today—the question of sovereignty was at the forefront of political theorizing and practice, and Grotius addressed the issue in a way that in many ways remains familiar. Utilizing the psychologically based notion of free will and human liberty made prominent by Molina, Grotius argued that a particular community or nation of people defined themselves as distinct from others by means of a particular transfer of rights on their part to a ruler.[33] Grotius could make this argument because by extending the assumptions of the metaphysics of individualism out from an individual person to an individually bounded community or nation of people—that is to say, by projecting the subjectivity of the subject onto a world—he could consider this collective as equivalent to and having the same psychologically based powers Molina posited for an individual. From this starting point Grotius argued that the transfer of these rights to a ruler who was from that community would constitute the delimitation of an independent nation-state, and the transfer of these rights to a foreign ruler would constitute the negation of that community as an existing society and the merging of it with the society of the new ruler. The former transfer of rights is thus the original transfer of rights that establish the sovereign order of a nation-state, the latter is the transfer of rights that establish the sovereign order of conquest, colonialism, and slavery. Both are considered free transfers of rights in the Molinian sense because a form of property exchange is understood to have taken place: in the former case the exchange of rights for security, peace, and stability, in the latter the exchange of rights for one's life.

Here it is important to note that regardless of whether this transfer of rights takes place within a society and thus establishes a sovereign nation-state or takes place between societies and establishes a relationship of colonial dominance, the voluntary slave is the (metaphorical?) figure that enacts the particular form of sovereignty by means of a free exchange. In his argument against those who claim sovereignty always lies with "the people," Grotius replies, "I shall refute it with these Arguments. It is lawful for any Man to engage himself as a Slave to whom he pleases; as appears both by the *Hebrew* and *Roman* Laws. Why should it not therefore be as lawful for a People that are at their own Disposal, to deliver up themselves to any one or more Persons, and transfer the Right of governing them upon him or them, without recovering any Share of that Right to themselves?"[34] Once that right of governing has been transferred, "the people" also forego several other rights, such as the right of resistance. Thus, Grotius puts it, "for if that promiscuous Right of Resistance should be allowed, there would be *no longer a State*, but a Multitude without Union."[35] As we will see, a similar position was taken in the 1948 United Nations Universal Declaration on Human Rights against the right of resistance. But for now what needs to be noted is that in one of the foundational texts of rights-based theories of sovereignty, the concept of rights was utilized in defense of an absolutist political theory that envisioned the basis of both national and colonial sovereignty in terms of the free transfer of rights in the establishment of national and global societies of voluntary slaves.[36] In this view, then, rights were the property an individual or a community of individuals freely exchanged in order to voluntarily place themselves in a relationship of subordination to an institution of power that in return provided something like peace, stability, or life itself. Or as Heidegger and Arendt might put it: with each further projection of the subjectivity of the subject onto existence for the sake of control, knowledge, and the preservation of life, there is simultaneously a loss of oneself by means of the forgetting of and alienation from that which the very conditions of being and becoming actually rests.

Nevertheless, Grotius's view of sovereignty would quickly become central to the natural rights debates taking place in England throughout the seventeenth century in relation to the political upheavals of the English Civil War and the Glorious Revolution. If Grotius's arguments spoke well to those on the continent—such as the Spanish, Dutch, Germans, and French—who were enmeshed in colonial and slave trading escapades abroad and social, religious, and political upheaval at home, so, too, they seemed to get to the heart of the matter in England where the political question of the seventeenth century was the relation between the English people and the king: that is, precisely the question of sovereign governance. Grotius's claim of the free transfer of rights to the sovereign became key to both conservative and radical rights theorists in the midst of this nearly century-long domestic crisis. Perhaps the most significant figure of the English scene was John Selden, who with much consequence for future natural rights theories made contracts central to the transfer of rights made between those in a state of nature and the sovereign. In doing so, Selden shifted the debate to the question of obligation, recognition of whether a sovereign has broken the contract, and whether "the people" can break the contract. In many ways these became the main theoretical questions addressed by those on all sides of the English civil wars and revolution of the seventeenth century and those that would follow in other parts of the globe thereafter, such as in the Americas and France.

While Selden's contract-based use of Grotius[37] built off the conservative and absolutist positions of the latter, the English radicals drew from a notion of interpretive charity that can be found in Grotius as well.[38] Although Grotius argued that the right of resistance is foregone when individuals transfer their right of governance to a sovereign, he also held that the right to resistance in extreme cases would not have been relinquished by rational and reasonable beings and therefore was justified and remained a right. It was such interpretive charity that the English radicals such as Overton and other Levellers used to build their arguments for inalienable rights. Thus, for example, Overton, starting from the claim of the inalienable right to self-preservation, quickly deduced a wide range of other so-called inalienable rights, which could be justifiably recovered by means of resistance and rebellion.[39] It is thus through this hermeneutic mechanism of interpretive charity excavated by some English radicals from the deeply conservative theory of Grotius that we arrive at the inalienable rights that would be so central to the revolutionary rights theories of the eighteenth century and would then expand exponentially in the human rights documents of the twentieth century.

What is particularly important to recognize here, however, is that this hermeneutic of interpretive charity relies, ultimately, on the conceptual proclivity established by John XXII in his reconfiguration of the relationship between individuals and institutions of power through the notion of active rights of sovereign individuals. While for a brief historical moment the language of inalienable rights may have provided some limited emancipatory possibilities for the English radicals, through its very proclivity it led to the attempt to enact these possibilities through parliamentary means. Thus, here as in many other instances since, the evocation of rights ultimately entails the necessity of transferring the claimed individual sovereignty to an institutional body of power just as Grotius via Molina had established. To put it plainly, the conceptual proclivity of the concept of rights by this time entailed—and this entailment continues to this day—that to claim a right is always to do so in relation to an institution of power, from which, by means of this very claim, it then becomes nearly impossible to disentangle oneself.

The Rights of Citizens

These debates within the context of the English civil wars and revolution, and particularly the arguments of the radicals, significantly affected the late-eighteenth-century revolutions in the Americas and France.[40] Thus, for the most part, the revolution in France can be understood in quite similar terms to the English civil wars and revolution, and the revolution in the British American colonies can be seen as an extension to the colonial territories of these same arguments over sovereignty and the exchange of rights. Of course the application of natural rights arguments within the American colonies was nothing new. In fact, natural rights were regularly used early in the era of European conquest by the British and other colonial powers as the theoretical, theological, and political foundation for colonial expansion, exploitation, and domination in the Americas and elsewhere.[41] Similarly, the rights of liberty, equality, and fraternity would continue to play a motivating and justifying role throughout nineteenth- and early-twentieth-century British and French colonialism around the globe.[42] But when American colonial revolutionaries and French domestic revolutionaries adopted the natural rights arguments of the British radicals to use against their colonial and monarchical rulers, it initiated a shift of the purview of rights to the realm of nationalism that would have far-reaching consequences for the political and moral uses of the concept of rights well into the late twentieth century.

The Declaration of the Rights of Man and Citizen is perhaps the most aptly named rights-based document in history, for ultimately its claim is that man (and not woman) has his rights only as a citizen of a particular state. Thus this document, often held up as one of the founding declarations in the history of human rights, is in essence a declaration of the rights of citizens and limits itself to the internal relation between citizens and their state.[43] It is, in this sense, the legitimation of Grotius's sovereignty argument and thus the founding political-moral document of the metaphysical humanist projection of a priori subjective properties and values onto the individually bounded collective of people called the nation-state. Indeed, rather than a foundational document of human rights as that which transcends states, the Declaration of the Rights of Man and Citizen is one of the founding documents of the kind of nationalism that would dominate global politics and revolution for the next two hundred years. Thus, sovereignty, as the Declaration states, "resides essentially in the Nation." Similarly, the American Declaration of Independence claimed the sovereign status of the new American states from the British Crown by evoking the authority of "We the People." As would remain the case up to and beyond the 1948 UN Universal Declaration of Human Rights, rights in the context of these two revolutions were utilized and established as the primary political-moral discourse of nationalism.

This remained the case throughout the nineteenth and early twentieth centuries as rights were in essence about rights of citizenship.[44] Even when reformist and revolutionary movements throughout this period evoked rights, they were primarily aimed at expanding the rights of particular kinds of citizens (e.g., the proletariat and women) within particular nation-states.[45] But as the nineteenth century came to an end no longer did such movements reference the abstract foundations of such rights as natural or human; rather, they very clearly saw rights linked to the positive law of each state and mobilized accordingly in terms of changing that law by means of legislation or revolution.[46] For example, despite some desire to inspire revolutions in other countries, most famously embodied by Trotsky, the Bolshevik coup was always aimed at and limited to a revolution within one empire, which by 1926 was articulated as Stalin's Socialism in One Country Policy and legislated in the 1936 Constitution of the Soviet Union, which enumerated any number of citizen rights. Thus, right up to the writing of the UDHR and beyond—for example in the civil rights movement in the United States or the right to self-determination throughout colonial territories—rights were seen as the privilege of citizenship within a particular nation-state and were both politically and morally evoked as such.

Here, as before, rights become manifest in ways that essentially adhere to its conceptual proclivity to link so-called sovereign individuals to institutions of power, even when these various articulations of rights claim to do so for emancipatory ends.

The Twentieth Century

The early twentieth century and the interwar years are often characterized as the period in which liberal democracy rose to prominence through popular social movements, with rights being central to this process. But as Mark Mazower convincingly argues, the widespread support of liberal democracy in Europe, for example, was limited to only a few years before and directly after the First World War, after which it sustained very strong challenges from both the right and left, which in the context of economic depression and political turmoil seemed to offer a more stable, effective, and progressive response to the hardships of modernity.[47] The concept of rights, once again as citizen rights in the form, for example, of welfare, workers', and women's rights, was central to the full range of this political spectrum. This emphasis on rights was increasingly articulated by particular governments that sought to stabilize their nation-state in the face of the interwar crisis,[48] and particularly so by liberal-democratic governments that sought to protect themselves from the political challenge posed by the right and left in the midst of economic depression. Thus, these governments initiated a significant expansion of the social rights linked to a welfare system that had already begun to be put in place prior to the First World War.[49] Similarly, international bodies such as the labor agency of the League of Nations—the International Labor Organization—emphasized social rights and workers' rights.[50] It is important to note that at least in some instances—such as the rise of New Liberalism and state medical services in interwar Britain—rights, as they would be in the post–Cold War period, were already becoming interlinked with notions of personal responsibility.[51]

Inter-war plans to stabilize the liberal-democratic and capitalist system were temporarily derailed by the outbreak of the Second World War.[52] In the immediate postwar period, however, there was a redoubled effort to solidify and expand the political-economic reforms already begun before the war. And it is here, in the midst of the great postwar powers attempting to restabilize a global order on the model of liberal-democratic and capitalist organization, that we find the birth of the modern human rights idea. Although the origin myth of modern human rights is often told as a response to the horrors of the Holocaust, the latter is far from the only motivation for the postwar human rights movement. In fact, human rights was simply one part of a much larger political-economic attempt—which included the establishment of the United Nations, the Bretton Woods system, and the Marshall Plan—to stabilize the nation-state-based liberal-capitalist system in the aftermath of over thirty years of deep crisis. Beginning with the First World War and the Bolshevik Revolution, through to the Great Depression and global social and political unrest, and the resulting political threat from both the extreme right and left in the interwar years, to the unimaginable destruction of the Second World War and the overwhelming call for social reform by the sharp left turn of the electorate of most belligerent and liberated countries—these globally systemic-shaking events led many to the conclusion that unless significant changes were made the socio-political-economic configuration of liberal capitalism would surely come to an end.[53]

In this context the 1948 UN Universal Declaration of Human Rights can be seen as the moral voice of this larger liberal-capitalist project;[54] or as Samuel Moyn puts it, the UDHR was the ornamentalization of a political project of the great powers to restabilize the sovereign nation-state order.[55] Or in ontological terms, the postwar human rights project can be seen as the further metaphysical humanist projection of the a priori properties and values of a particular kind of subject onto yet a larger bounded individual totality—that is, the global order of nation-states. With this move, then, we can read the progression of the political-moral aspect of metaphysical humanism as beginning from the inherent property of rights of the individual posited by John XXII, which becomes projected first onto the bounded individual of the nation-state, and now further projected onto the more encapsulating bounded entity of the globe. Furthermore, with each projection a stronger and more controlling institution of power is required to guarantee the felicity of the projection. Since the eighteenth century this has been the sovereign nation-state.

This becomes particularly clear with a close reading of the Preamble of the UDHR in which each recital addresses the relationship either among states themselves or between states and individuals. The significance within this document of securing the sovereign nation-state system is particularly clear in the third recital and the debate that took place around it: "Whereas it is essential, if man is not to be compelled to have recourse, as a last resort, to rebellion against tyranny and oppression, that human rights should be protected by the rule of law." Johannes Morsink tells us that much debate took place among drafting delegates over the inclusion in the

Universal Declaration of a right to rebellion.[56] Referencing the two great Enlightenment-era rights documents and several national constitutions, some delegates supported the inclusion of such a right. Many others, however, were opposed to an explicit mention of such a right, claiming that it would be, as the head of the UN drafting commission Eleanor Roosevelt said, "tantamount to encouraging sedition"; or as one of the United Kingdom's delegates put it, "Recognition of that right would entail the risk of inciting anarchy." Despite this debate, all delegates agreed in one way or another that rebellion and a right to it are in fact potentially dangerous and therefore should not be encouraged, and it is for this reason that it was eventually included in what Morsink calls a "submerged" right in the third recital, with agreement on some key wording and clausal structure that deemphasizes the right: "if man is not to be compelled to have *recourse*, as a *last resort*, to rebellion against tyranny and oppression."[57]

None of this, of course, should come as any surprise. For despite the rhetoric of an inherence view of individual rights, and no doubt some concern for the protection of these so-called rights for individual persons, the socio-historical fact of the matter is that the Universal Declaration of Human Rights was drafted primarily by elite representatives of state governments with a real interest in securing a new postwar order that, although quite different from the prewar years, would ultimately secure and stabilize the political-economic configuration that had become so fragile in the interwar years, as well as the newly liberal-democratic governments of the early postwar period.[58] In other words, at a historical moment when it seemed possible to conceive of a real shift in the global political order, the attempt to maintain an updated version of the global status quo was the response, and the 1948 UDHR was one part of this larger project of reestablishing the sovereignty of states. As such, the establishment of the modern human rights agenda of the early Cold War years foreshadows the way this agenda would become manifest as an industry in the post–Cold War years.

The "Me" Decade

Just twenty years later events at the end of another decade—often collectively referred to as "1968"—set the stage for a decisive shift in the range of what would become possible not only in the arena of international politics but also for global and everyday discourses of morality, politics, and subjectivity. The Prague Spring; the American civil rights movement; the Tet Offensive; the Paris, Mexico City, Italian, and scores of other protests;

the Polish political crisis; Black Power; the Cultural Revolution; antiwar protests; the Mỹ Lai Massacre; assassinations and bombings; the counter-culture; the Tlatelolco Massacre; the continuation of anticolonial movements; and Third World independence are just a few of the many events of the waning years of the 1960s that radically shifted the ways that politics and economics began to be reconfigured, as well as how persons conceived of themselves and their relations with others both near and afar. This reconception could be understood in terms of a coming into being of the lived experience of being-in-a-global-totality that had emerged along with the political-moral projection of metaphysical humanism.

Of prime importance for our purposes is how these events initiated a shift away from the confines of the Cold War ideological dualism of the postwar years and opened the possibility for human rights to gain prominence as a significant alternative for international, national, and personal relations. For by the end of this decade, and certainly by the mid-1970s, Cold War capitalist democracy and communist rule, along with those elites who depended on the stability of these ideologies, had to a great extent lost their legitimacy for many living within these two great transnational blocs. The détente initiated in the early 1970s is best conceived as a response by the leaders of these two ideological blocs to restabilize their internal affairs by seeking equilibrium in international affairs.[59] By the end of the 1970s, however, détente would prove politically vacuous as human rights redefined in terms of neoconservative and neoliberal political economics would gain prominence and, in so doing, eventually come to supersede the two Cold War ideologies and help usher in a "new world order."

In order for this to eventually happen, however, the third ideological movement of the postwar period—anticolonialism—also needed to lose its appeal. When the Atlantic Charter, which it should be noted did not include the words "human rights," was issued in 1941 one of its most globally celebrated elements was its promise of postwar self-determination. While anticolonial movements and leaders around the globe read this as a promise of decolonization after the war, Churchill was able to convince Roosevelt that self-determination was intended only for those territories that were at the time under Axis control. The postwar global configuration would remain one of empire. Thus, one of the main rights emphasized during the interwar period—minority rights and self-determination—the respect of which gave grounds to Britain and France to appease Hitler's aggression in the Sudetenland, was not included in the immediate postwar human rights agenda due in large part to the potential threat this right posed to the stability and sovereignty of particular nation-states and their colonial possessions.[60] As a result, when the 1948 United Nations Universal Declaration of Human Rights left out any promise of self-determination, it largely became a document void of meaning and utility for the vast numbers of peoples around the globe who sought independence from their colonial rulers.

As Samuel Moyn convincingly argues, for the next thirty years the discourse of human rights took a backseat as the political-moral discourse of anticolonialism was much more central to local aspirations for self-determination and rule.[61] Over the course of the next generation, decolonization gradually occurred by means of diverse levels of violence and resistance to colonial powers, and human rights broadly taken played very little role in the process. When rights were invoked by anticolonial powers it was generally in terms of the older natural rights tradition, which, as I illustrated above, basically stood for the right of national sovereignty—that is, these were rights to sovereign nationalism.[62] In fact, although in the UDHR there is no right to self-determination, the two human rights covenants (the International Covenant on Civil and Political Rights and the International Covenant on Economic, Social and Cultural Rights) adopted by the UN General Assembly in December 1966 each named the right to self-determination (and listed it first, to boot). Thus, for many international observers at the time, not only the United Nations but also the entire human rights project had been hijacked by the politics of decolonization.[63]

Just as the two Cold War ideologies had lost legitimacy by the 1970s, so, too, had recently independent postcolonial nation-states revealed their own set of problems. By the mid-1970s, then, all three postwar utopian political projects had more or less lost their viability as a revolutionary promise. As a result, politics on a grand, revolutionary scale no longer seemed to many a viable option.[64] In the Western capitalist democracies the combination of Vietnam, the counterculture, political scandal, and by the end of the decade new consumer-marketing strategies increasingly led to newly awakened individuals tuning out and dropping out of politics of all kinds. In the communist-ruled countries "normal people" were increasingly fed up with the failure of their governments to deliver what had been promised for over a generation, which led many, for example in the Soviet Union, to performatively enact an accepted Soviet form of political and everyday life while no longer adhering to the truth of the ideology that supposedly founded it.[65] While the roots of this performative shift may have begun with the death of Stalin, it increasingly became a part of everyday life in the 1970s due to such factors as economic stagnation and the increasing use of violent means to suppress any form of dissent; in this context experience belied ideological promise. Furthermore, the newly independent postcolonial countries had problems of their own, which were hardly helped by being used too often as pawns in the international game of Cold War. In this context grand revolutionary politics no longer had appeal, and in its place—particularly in the capitalist West—came the localized politics of what would come to be called new social movements.

By the early 1970s new social movements had already come to replace the kinds of large-scale political movements that had been at the heart of many of the events of 1968. If the latter were largely political movements aimed at significant political and economic change, then the former were primarily social movements aimed at changing the local hearts and minds of people in relation to particular issues such as gay rights, women's rights, and environmentalism. Although rights were often at the heart of these movements—and particularly so for the identity-based movements—the rights sought, like those of the civil rights movement, were primarily nation-based rights of equal citizenship. Similarly, in Eastern Europe and the Soviet Union at this time, dissidents were for the most part not calling for human rights as their supporters in the West on both the left and the right interpreted them to be doing; rather, for the most part they were pointing out that the constitutions of their countries already had written into them particular rights that were not being provided or protected by their governments. In this sense, these dissidents, like the new social movements in the West, are best seen as calling for citizen rights within the context of nation-states.[66] Thus, while new social movements and the Eastern European and Soviet dissident movements are often considered to be based on human rights, most of these began in the 1970s as citizen rights movements.

While there is little doubt that the new social movements in the West were in large part a response to the ideological and political failures associated with 1968, it is important to recognize how an increasing sense of, and emphasis on, individualism helped support the morally focused antipolitics of new social movements that primarily focused on identity- or issue-based concerns that could more easily be understood and experienced by individual persons as affecting their sense of well-being. By the time Tom Wolfe wrote his now-famous article on "The 'Me' Decade" in *New York* magazine in 1976, what he called "the greatest age of individualism in American history" was already well underway.[67] By the mid-1970s diverse social forces had gathered to bring about and support this new age of individualism, or what we might call the height of metaphysical humanism. These included such phenomena as the increased skepticism of politics on a grand scale, as well as politics and politicians in general, the rise of the middle class, the social effects of the counterculture, increased marketing emphasis on individual lifestyles, the rise of psychotherapy and self-help groups as legitimate forms of therapy for the masses, and the increased attraction of religious and spiritual movements, including Christian fundamentalisms, that emphasized individual transformation and development. While this trend was perhaps strongest in the United States, aspects of it could be seen around the globe, including in the communist bloc.[68] By the end of the 1970s, then, the political and cultural context in both Cold War blocs was ripe for a new form of antipolitical-moral politics, which can be seen as the full realization of the political-moral aspect of metaphysical humanism that had been underway since John XXII.

Neoliberal and Human Right Antipolitics Meets Neoconservative Moral Politics

It is only in the late-1970s in this unique global political-moral confluence of the full realization of metaphysical humanism where anticolonialism begins to reveal some of its shortcomings, the two Cold War ideologies no longer deliver what they had once promised, grand politics is replaced by identity and issue politics, and the centrality of individualism begins to dominate everyday life that human rights emerges as a viable last utopian political-moral option.[69] But if 1977–80 were key years for the rise of human rights with, among other events and key players, Amnesty International winning the Nobel Peace Prize and Jimmy Carter standing up as the human rights president, then these very same years were also key for the rise of neoliberal economics and neoconservative politics in the North Atlantic countries. For in this same period Margaret Thatcher would be elected prime minister of Britain and Ronald Reagan would be elected president of the United States, and he would continue the already established neoliberal monetary policies of Paul Volcker, whom Jimmy Carter had put in charge of the U.S. Federal Reserve in July 1979. One result of these neoliberal policies that were widely spread around the globe throughout the 1980s—for example, by means of structural adjustment policies of the IMF and World Bank—was the decentralization of social, welfare, and health programs in various countries. In order to fill the gap in services this decentralization brought about, human rights NGOs stepped in to provide the services no longer available to millions. In effect, by the end of the 1990s rights-based NGOs became the decentralized social, welfare, and health services for the poor and marginalized in the global neoliberal economy.

At the same time proponents of neoconservatism in the United States, which formed in the 1970s as a critique of the perceived soft stance of the Carter administration toward the Soviet Union—as well as its support of international law–based human rights, and particularly social and economic rights—found a home in the Reagan administration. These neoconservatives were the intellectual heirs of early Cold Warriors who largely came from the interwar Old Left anticommunists and were central in shaping early–Cold War U.S. foreign policy in the direction of "democracy promotion" as the best defense against the spread of Soviet-style communism.[70] After falling out of political style in the Vietnam and post-Vietnam eras, however, these Old Left anticommunists increasingly shifted to the right in response to what they perceived as the dangerous totalitarian tendencies of the New Left, finally regaining significant political influence with the election of Reagan.[71]

Neoconservatives had been highly critical of the Carter administration's view of human rights as a possible limit on state power, primarily because they saw it as a potential threat to American interests vis-à-vis the Soviet Union. Recognizing that they could not avoid the growing international influence of human rights discourse, however, neoconservatives merged it with their longtime interest in democracy promotion in order to turn human rights into what Nicolas Guilhot calls "the principled foundation and the moral substance of the state."[72] Thus, throughout the 1980s and into the early post–Cold War years, the link between human rights and democracy promotion was the primary foreign policy objective for the United States. By 1993 human rights may have ostensibly been used as an international legal framework for limiting state power, but it had in fact, by means of late–Cold War policy, shifted to a political-moral discourse for the promotion of a particular kind of state-based political power. This link between human rights and democracy, along with development, eventually became the ideological core of the 1993 Vienna Declaration and Programme of Action, which was the first major international declaration on human rights in the post–Cold War era and set the scene for the explosion of human rights as an increasingly global political-moral discourse ever since.

If the foreign policy goal of the late–Cold War United States and its allies was the promotion of democratic and capitalist political structures as the best assurance against the politicization and turn to the left of Third World persons and their governments, and if neoliberalism can be seen as the depoliticization of social life such that "individual freedoms are guaranteed by freedom of the market,"[73] and if human rights can be seen as the "leaving behind [of] political utopias and turning to smaller and more manageable moral acts,"[74] then it is not difficult to see that each in their own way seem to articulate a particular socio-political moment and resonate quite well with one another. Such resonance left the concept of human rights open as an attractive one for those across the entire range of the political spectrum. This, in turn, led to odd alliances between the right and the left—for example over Latin American policy in the 1980s and human trafficking since the 1980s—as well as a misrecognition by those on the left of just how much human rights had been co-opted by conservative political economics.[75] The result is that today human rights has become a political-moral discourse that, while attractive to many across the full range of the political spectrum, and even more so because it has been nearly equated with democracy, is ultimately a discourse that only finds a political reference in an essentially conservative politics.

The NGO-ization of the Globe and the Etatization of NGOs

Human rights, as Moyn argues, may have emerged in 1948 as the ornamentalization of a great powers project, but at least in Europe it was almost immediately used as a juridical technology for securing a more conservative liberal-capitalist form of governance.[76] Over the next few decades, and through the height of the Cold War and the decolonization era, human rights may have been muted as a viable political-moral discourse; but by the late 1970s, and alongside the anticommunist democracy promotion of neoconservatives and the antipolitics political-economic project of neoliberalism, human rights emerged as a useful moral idiomatic language that would prove ideologically decisive for these newly emerging conservative political strategies. The three would only become more intertwined as the Cold War puttered out and the Soviet Union seemingly disappeared overnight. When in 1993 the Vienna Declaration on Human Rights declared that "democracy, development, and respect for human rights and fundamental freedoms are interdependent and mutually reinforcing," this intertwining was complete such that human rights became embedded as the moral voice and foundation for this conservative politics. Thus, on the one hand, human rights as the political-moral foundation for national democratic nation-states provided a new global post–Cold War foundation for the spread and stability of one particular form of conservative politics; and on the other hand, provided legitimacy for depoliticized and decentralized neoliberal economic policies that emphasized individual freedoms while cutting social services as rights-based NGOs stepped in to fill this gap.[77]

The 1990s, then, was a decade in which the modern human rights industry was founded and exploded onto the international scene. Strongly supported by the neoconservative vision of nationalized human rights articulated in the 1980s, and modeled within the metaphysical humanist constraints expected of the conceptual proclivity of the concept of rights, the very first step in the post–Cold War move to rearticulate human rights was the 1991 Paris International Workshop on National Institutions for the Promotion and Protection of Human Rights, where principles were laid out for the centrality of nationally based institutions within individual states as the primary monitors of human rights abuses. The so-called Paris Principles were adopted by the General Assembly on December 20, 1993, the same day the General Assembly endorsed the Vienna Declaration.[78] In the aftermath of the wave of human rights declarations and documents of the 1990s and the years that followed,[79] human rights have come to work a double movement that while decentralizing up (e.g., through international treaties and institutions) and down (e.g., through local NGOs that provide social services locally) also serves to stabilize and maintain the centrality of the state by making it the ultimate guarantor of human rights. By providing this necessary institutional middle position for states, the political-moral discourse of human rights has further solidified the transition of the contemporary state to that of a managerial institution—which while on the ontic level primarily works to manage the life of populations as a means of maintaining its own existence, ontologically it works to maintain the enframing of existence as a contained totality of "individual entities with individually determinate boundaries and properties."

One way this position of the state is solidified is through the new role of NGOs in the contemporary human rights industry. Whereas in the early 1990s NGOs were held up as key non-state actors meant to provide an independent perspective and voice within the human rights political-moral matrix that could exert significant influence and pressure on state governments,[80] today NGOs are increasingly cultivating close relations with and becoming dependent on states and governments.[81] Since the 1990s NGOs are increasingly dependent on governments for funding and tied to them through contracts for providing services, programs, and projects. Thus, for example, one of the largest international NGOs, CARE International, received nearly 70 percent of its 2001 budget of US$420 million from governments, and the same is true for most other similarly sized international NGOs.[82] The smaller and local NGOs, particularly those in the non-developed world, that are unable to find support from their national governments are increasingly dependent on international funders such as these very same large international NGOs or the World Bank.[83] Thus, in an indirect manner these local NGOs are themselves closely tied to the predominantly Euro-American states that fund these non-state funding agencies, as well as through the funding agencies of the states that directly provide grants to the smaller local NGOs.[84] The result of this increased partnership is that the frontline supporters of human rights now primarily advocate and help enact these rights at the bequest of states by means of providing the local services, programs, and projects that states once did. In this sense, rights-based NGOs have become the organizations through which states outsource services and as such are one of the primary means for the practical realization of neoliberal policies.[85]

By signing on to this global human rights regime, individual states have been able to secure their stability in at least two other ways as well. First, by joining this global order a state claims to belong to a "community of nations," which is the final encapsulating totality that ontologically enframes the multitude of constitutive individualized entities, and which has as its primary political-moral aspect the mutual recognition of human rights. As a member of such a global community, states are relatively secure from outside threats, as such international disciplining tactics as interventions, global policing, and sanctions are increasingly used against states that do not or, perhaps more correctly put, can convincingly be *said* not to respect human rights.

Second, by claiming to uphold and respect human rights as both an international moral and juridical order, states secure themselves against internal threats from below.[86] This, of course, does not simply happen through rhetoric, for actual laws, services, programs, and structural changes must be put in place *in the name of rights* to bear witness to the respect of rights a state claims to uphold. Such rights-referencing changes do not simply provide a moral foundation for the state as many human rights and pro-democracy advocates describe the role of rights to be. More important, these changes, as ethnographic studies are increasingly showing, provide the context for making good citizen-subjects. Thus human rights have become integral and internal to power, in part, through the gradual and eventual disciplining of individuals as good citizen-subjects by means of the discursive practice of rights put in place by these rights-referencing changes.[87]

Here, then, we can see that the ontological tradition has, in a sense, come full circle in that the very political entity—the nation-state—that first appeared as a projection of the subjectivity of the subject onto worlds has become the context in which these very a priori subjects are now made.

Put another way, we have now reached a point where the ontological conditions of totality and repetition have emerged as an effective consequence of this ontological tradition, the result of which is the closure of possibility, the experience of which is disappointment.

The Conceptual Proclivity of Rights

When considered from the perspective of critical hermeneutics, it has become clear that the concept of rights has accumulated a conceptual proclivity to become manifest as the primary political-moral aspect of a metaphysical humanist ontological tradition. The most significant consequence of this is that today the foundation for state sovereignty is primarily enacted by means of security, control, and the disciplining of life. In this chapter I have shown how this ontological tradition has historically unfolded through the concept of rights. With John XXII's move in the poverty debates to tie individuals to the institutional power of the Catholic Church by means of a notion of individual inherent rights and sovereignty, the concept of rights was established as central to the incipient metaphysics of individualism. As this concept increasingly became central to the emerging political-moral order of first Europe and then the rest of the globe as contained individual totalities, a conceptual proclivity was formed with each subsequent iteration such that today the concept of rights is the key political-moral concept of the ontological tradition of metaphysical humanism. As a consequence of this effective history, it has now simply become a fact that to claim a right is always to do so in relation to an institution of power that maintains the bounded totality to which one has been "assigned," and from which, by means of the repetition of this claim, it has now perhaps becomes impossible to disentangle oneself. The critical hermeneutics of the effective history of the concept of rights that I traced in this chapter discloses this conceptual proclivity, and suggests that the historical origins of political and moral concepts—and the accumulated effects of these origins—are vital for understanding the consequences of their current uses and the price we pay for their continued use.[88]

I don't want to be misunderstood; I am not arguing that concepts are predetermined in meaning and the practices they enable. Obviously, as I have shown in this chapter, concepts have a history, and one part of this history is that the social manifestations of these concepts shift and change over time. Rather, I am arguing that concepts are always bound to, because they emerge from, a particular ontological tradition, and as such they come with baggage, or a conceptual proclivity, that despite the changes they undergo over the course of time tend to align conceptual manifestations with a certain kind of ontological enframing of what counts as a "real" person, social and political entity, and world. As a result, and as I tried to show throughout this chapter, these conceptual manifestations also become aligned with particular social and power relationships, institutions, and practices. If nothing else, this is the main point of the argument I am making in this chapter: the articulation and enactment of particular concepts tend to lead to certain kinds of results despite the intentions of those who adopt them. And this is so because concepts over time come to contain within them, as it were, a proclivity that over and over again becomes instrumentalized in similar ways. That is, they contain a proclivity that results in the concept being mobilized for similar ends within similar subjective and power constellations, and thus repeat and perpetuate the ontological tradition that is the ground of such constellations.[89] It is this that I hope to have shown in the critical hermeneutic analysis of this chapter.

In the next chapter I will turn to the anti–drug war movement that will be the focus of much of the rest of this book and provide an example of this proclivity in its political activity. In particular, I will show how their rights-based arguments in support of harm reduction practices, one of the anti–drug war movement's central strategic aims, ultimately leads to a repetition of the very power anti–drug war politics seeks to address. Ironically, this repetition is articulated as progress. In the remaining chapters I will show how despite this tendency to rely on the language of rights and its associated concepts such as dignity and responsibility, the anti–drug war movement offers an opportunity to hermeneutically disclose an alternative conceptual apparatus that emerges from their singular mode of political practice.

CHAPTER 2

Progress; or, The Repetition of Differential Sameness

"We provide a place where [injecting drug users] can have their human rights. It is the most moral thing we can do." This is how a staff worker of a harm reduction center in St. Petersburg, Russia, described to me the services offered at the center one afternoon in the autumn of 2006. By this point Russia had one of the fastest growing HIV rates, a phenomenon overwhelmingly driven by the sharing of contaminated needles by injecting drug users. As a result, since the late 1990s Russia and the former Soviet Union have been a priority area for international harm reduction organizations that initiate on-the-ground harm reduction centers and mobile units. International harm reductionists frame such services as a human right since they provide "a set of evidence-informed strategies and a well-articulated public health alternative to rights-violating drug control measures."[1] As is often pointed out, if a human rights approach to global health arose as a response to the HIV pandemic, then besides access to antiretroviral pharmaceuticals, harm reduction likely has been the most significant project within this new movement. This rights-based approach is considered particularly important in Russia, where police corruption, horrid prison conditions, and a crumbling health care service (which in many cases refuses to treat either drug users or HIV-positive persons) are known to enable the conditions for both human rights abuses and the proliferation of blood-borne viruses related to injecting drug use.

This human rights approach is similarly taken up by Russian-based anti–drug war political agonists and their allies advocating for harm reduction policies in Russia, where these services still have not received complete support or legal sanction by the government. In a document produced by a Moscow-based harm reduction organization for Russian legislators, harm reduction is described as falling under the rubric of the right to health, which is characterized as "the right to the best attainable standard of physical and mental health; the right to access to information and education; the right to privacy; and the right to participate in scientific progress and enjoy its benefits."[2] The services provided at the St. Petersburg center are considered to provide these rights. For example, the center's syringe-exchange service allows access to the latest scientific progress and information for preventing the transmission of HIV and other blood-borne viruses, respects the privacy of those who exchange, and includes informal moments of education on the safest methods of shooting heroin. Nevertheless, because such services have yet to be fully accepted by the government, they also provide injecting drug users with one more venue for a possible run-in with the police, as the latter regularly target and harass those who use such services. Harm reductionists characterize such targeting as yet one more human rights abuse of people who inject drugs.

As in Russia, harm reduction is one of the central pillars of the global anti–drug war movement in general. At the minimum, harm reduction involves the provision of clean syringes and other "works," such as sterile water and cotton balls, for injecting drugs. But ideally it would include a number of initiatives to help "reduce the harms associated with drug use and ineffective drug policies."[3] Such initiatives include, but are not limited to, syringe access, availability of drug treatment, prevention of drug overdose, supervised consumption facilities, and drug replacement and maintenance therapy. Although the implementation of even the most minimal of harm reduction programs anywhere on the globe has provided plenty of evidence of effectively reducing, for example, the spread of HIV and hepatitis C and the number of overdoses, such programs have also been critiqued as places for the disciplining of citizen-subjects.[4] Perhaps the most obvious means of making this citizen-subject is the responsibilization that harm reduction programs have come to be criticized for enacting (which I will address in Chapter 5), but such disciplining can be seen across the full range of the rights-dignity-responsibility triad that I will address throughout this book. Thus, while the "science" of harm reduction is presented in terms of public health, the political-moral aspect of harm reduction is articulated with the language of rights.[5] In this sense, harm reduction is a clear example of how, in the contemporary condition of things, discursive practices of science, politics, and morals intertwine in the reproduction and projection of metaphysical humanism.

Indeed, just like nearly every political movement today, rights language is the primary means by which the global anti–drug war movement in general tends to articulate its political demands and aspirations. Thus, for example, the International Network of People Who Use Drugs puts as first on its list of seven organizational aims advocating "and lobbying at the international level for the rights of people who use drugs." Yet another aim listed is the support of "self-determining networks of drug users that advocate for the health, citizenship and human rights of people who use drugs."[6] Or consider that the Drug Policy Alliance, the world's largest drug policy organization, articulates its vision as "a just society in which the use and regulation of drugs are grounded in science, compassion, health and human rights."[7] Furthermore, similar language is used at the "ground" level of localized drug user political activity. For example, a user agonist in Denpasar, Indonesia, emphasized to me several times in a conversation we had in 2013 that human rights are central to his organization's political activity and aims. Thus, when telling me that in Indonesia drug users are often thought of and treated like "rubbish" and "not human," he told me that much of their political activity "is strategized around human rights for drug users." Even in the United States, where anti–drug war organizations actively avoid the language of human rights since it tends to gain little political traction as American politicians and authorities assume that the United States has no human rights problems, the language of rights is regularly used by local agonists in terms of the right to health, the right to housing, and civil rights. As can be seen, then, no matter the locale or "level" of anti–drug war political activity, the language of rights discursively frames the strategies and aims of this political movement.

It is of course not surprising that the global anti–drug war movement has adopted the political-moral language of rights, since there is hardly a social, cultural, or political movement that exists today that does not take up the banner of rights in one form or another. Whether we turn our gaze toward the so-called Arab Spring, HIV/AIDS prevention and treatment programs, the Occupy movement,[8] indigenous and ethnic politics, or movements to address housing shortages, we find that rights are heralded as both the motivation and aim of these movements. Not only do such movements take up this banner, but so, too, do the state and governing apparatuses these movements so often claim to confront, resist, and oppose. In this sense, rights, and particularly human rights, has become the moral language that grounds both the political status quo and the politics that claims to oppose this status quo. The attempt on the part of both the state-governing apparatuses *and* human rights activists to juridify human rights language at both the international and national levels only serves to codify this increasing conflation of morality and politics. This juridification further serves to legitimize this language as the only viable one for social justice in contemporary global politics. The result is that today nearly every political, social, or public health action taken on the global stage—from military-humanitarian intervention to harm reduction policies—is claimed to be done in the name of human rights. In this sense, human rights has become the dominant political-moral language today.

As a result human rights is also often articulated as the only legitimate means for initiating progress. Consider, for example, the range of articulations[9] linking human rights with a notion of progress as development and improvement: "*Progress* towards achieving all human rights *is* democratic *development*,"[10] or "The principles enshrined in the Declaration are the yardstick by which we measure human *progress*."[11] Indeed, the anti–drug war movement similarly uses this language of progress. Thus, for example, Alex Wodak, a prominent anti–drug war agonist and harm reductionist in Australia, writes that protection "of human rights is an *essential precondition* to *improving* the health of individual drug users and *improving* the public health of the communities where they live."[12]

But perhaps no clearer articulation of this view could be given than that of Michael Ignatieff when he writes, "We make progress to the degree that we act upon the moral intuition that . . . our species is one, and each of the individuals who compose it is entitled to equal moral consideration. Human rights is the language that systematically embodies this intuition, and to the degree that this intuition gains influence over the conduct of individuals and states, we can say that we are making moral progress."[13] The performative capacity of human rights language is here acknowledged by Ignatieff; it is a language that "embodies" a particular and singular "moral intuition," which when articulated has the effect of bringing into being the realization of this intuition and thereby enacting "moral progress." For Ignatieff and the many activists who consider human rights similarly, including the harm reductionist in St. Petersburg with whom I opened this chapter, human rights is a language of moral progress—and it is now considered by many the only option for realizing a future condition that may not be utopian but will surely be better than the current one. In other words, it is a language of progressive hope.

In this chapter I will return to harm reductionists working in Russia and consider their use of this language of hope. In doing so, this analysis will disclose the limitations on political possibilities their rights-based language enacts; furthermore, it will become clear that rather than having a future-oriented temporality that opens new possibilities for political activity and institutions, these harm reductionists' discursive practices of human rights are best understood in terms of repetition. Ontically, this temporality of repetition ultimately works to limit or constrain political activity within a narrowly defined range of possibilities. In this sense, human rights as a political-moral discursive practice is essentially conservative, as are all politics that enact what Lee Edelman calls reproductive futurism.[14]

This is so because ontologically progress is best understood as the temporal projection of the subjectivity of the subject onto all existence. In this sense, we can understand progress as the central temporal concept of metaphysical humanism. Although enacted materially by means of such things as policies, laws, and guns, on such things as human beings, infrastructure, and technology, and within spatial "containers" such as cities, nation-states, regions, and the globe, progress is ultimately the temporalization of existence by means of the subjectivization of existence. Through this projection of the subjectivity of the metaphysical humanist subject onto all that is, existence is not only increasingly understood in terms of Reason and Morality but is rendered as "Reasonable" and "Moral." The process of the gradual realization of this projection is what has come to be known as progress. This process has been enacted by such practices as science, which transforms all of existence into "Reasonable" and "law-abiding" entities; colonization and globalization, which transforms the globe into a "Reasonable" and "Moral" planet; and now human rights, which attempts to transform all humans into "Morally" acting beings and all states into "Morally" grounded governing containers—and therefore, by extension, all political and social activity becomes "Reasonable" and "Moral." The history of progress, then, is the history of the projection of this ontological tradition, which can be understood in its full manifestation in the triumvirate of science, globalization, and human rights. The consequence of this total subjectivization of existence—which we might call the aim of progress—is the end of temporalization and the closure of becoming. When the complete projection of this ontological tradition occurs, or perhaps better put, when the fantasy of this complete projection becomes reality, we find ourselves living in the ontological conditions of totality and repetition—or what some have labeled the end of history.

In the rest of this chapter I will try to show how this phantasmatic projection occurs by means of political-moral practice, and why as a result of these ontological conditions of totality and repetition we find ourselves today living ontically not with hope but with disappointment. I will do this by returning to the case of international and local harm reductionists in Russia attempting to implement a rights-based harm reduction policy in that country and considering this attempt in terms of the larger claim that human rights provide a basis for moral and political progress. In particular I focus on harm reductionists' concerns with juridification and the arguments used to persuade lawmakers to enact rights-based legislation. What becomes clear is that not only are such arguments made according to the logic of security, prosperity, and normativity, but also the realization of such legislation would primarily result in the strengthening of already existing state-government apparatuses. Such human rights activism is perhaps better understood, therefore, in terms of post–Cold War democracy building and the good governance agenda disclosed in the last chapter than in terms of a concern for the health of injecting drug users. It is this institution building that the human rights industry calls progress, and it is this notion of progress that will be critically interrogated in this chapter. Such interrogation will reveal that human rights in practice ultimately results in both the reproduction and strengthening of the very state-governing apparatuses it confronts, and as a consequence ultimately undermines its own aims. This repetition, then, marks a limit for possible political and moral activity since it merely repeats in a different form the very socio-economic-political conditions it attempts to overcome. It is this repetition of differential sameness that I will call the fantasy of progress. Before turning to the harm reductionist case in Russia, however, I will briefly consider the idea of progress within the human rights industry in order to provide a better discursive context for its attempted enactment.

Progress

The idea of progress has been essential to post-Enlightenment modernity and perhaps found its clearest expression in liberalism's conception of politics as the progressive betterment of life. To this end liberalism tends to expand the domain of the political to encompass more and more aspects of life in order to realize the latter's improvement.[15] This link between progress, betterment of life, and politics has been enacted by liberal practices in terms of a politics of reform. While such reform has most certainly taken place domestically in order to secure—in the view of J. S. Mill—self-protection or—in the view of American liberalism—life, liberty, and happiness, it has also been carried out internationally by means of empire, intervention, structural adjustment conditionality, and other such means. Whether domestically or internationally—but most certainly and obviously in the latter case—such liberal reform is directed at the "modification of the various histories it encountered, so as to make them conform to that universalistic vision" posited by liberalism.[16] It is in this sense that liberal reform conceived as progress was central to European colonial rule, as, for example, such colonial reform in the context of the nineteenth century British Empire was conceived as a process of dragging stalled societies through history so that they could reach a stage of civilization commensurate with self-rule; thus the "white man's burden" of bringing progress to the rest of the world provided the rationale for liberalism's imperial exploits.[17]

According to Reinhart Koselleck this concept of progress emerged at the end of the eighteenth century as diverse historical experiences—the Copernican revolution, advances in technology, and the "discovery" of the "global" and the vast array of peoples living within it—came together and provoked categorizations of difference and thus comparison. In Koselleck's phrasing, progress emerged as a concept due to "the knowledge of noncontemporaneities which exist at a chronologically uniform time."[18] The concept of progress emerged, then, because of the possibility of making hierarchical comparisons between what was interpreted to be the contemporaneity of the noncontemporaneous—that is, different temporalities existing simultaneously. Progress as a concept, therefore, became possible with the discovery of difference.

It is just this discovery of difference that enabled the temporality of progress as repetition, for as the British example illustrates such difference could not simply be recognized and accepted, but rather had to be leveled through the processes and practices of progress. Ontologically, this leveling is best understood as the projection of the subjectivity of the subject onto all of existence and, most specifically in this case, onto other peoples and societies. The ontic differences between contemporary societies and people could only be accepted by means of the projection of ontological leveling, which ensures not simply knowledge, control, and security but, existentially more important, "self" knowledge, "self" control, and "self" security. Thus, nineteenth-century British imperialism claimed to be enacting a process of progressive reform, for example, by ruling India until it could reach the stage of—or progress to—civilization, at which point India could begin self-rule. In this sense, India's future would be a mere repetition of the present of Great Britain in that the latter already stood as the historical realization of the progressive ideal aimed at for India's future. But the repetitive temporality of progress does not end with this one self-referencing temporal loop. For Britain's nineteenth-century present was also significantly constituted through the future realization of India's maturity—Britain in a very real way could only be the civilization it was through carrying the heavy burden of reforming India. Furthermore, this present and future could continuously constitute each other only by simultaneously reconstituting the past. Thus, both the past of Britain and India had to be remade in the very same vision that constituted the progressive present and future. Such remaking of the past to fit progressive logic was carried out through triumphalist histories such as James Mill's *The History of British India*, which had as its task the establishment of a scale of civilizational hierarchies; it eventually became required reading for all candidates of the elite corps of senior administrators in the Indian Civil Service.[19] Here we see, then, that liberal temporality may be ideologically conceived as a singular coherent time, but this coherence is only achieved through the violence of eliminating the multiplicity of other existing and possible temporalities by continuously realigning the present with a particular and predefined future that reflects the image of what the present ought to be. Ontologically, this violence is the leveling of all existence to the subjectivity of the metaphysical humanist subject.

Far from having a future-oriented temporality, then, liberal progress is best understood as having the temporality of repetition—for as a process driven by the activity of reform at home and often violent leveling abroad, it attempts to enact a particular future by means of referencing its immanence in an already existing present, even if that present is only the form of an idea. This is a notion of progress that, in the words of Hans Blumenberg, "extrapolates from a structure present in every moment to a future that is immanent in history."[20] It is a notion of progress that has the logic of Kantian a priori history in which the future is already known because it is a future to be made by he who knows what is and therefore what ought to be. Within this logic the "future becomes the consequence of actions in the present, and these become the realization of the current understanding of reality."[21] In this sense, then, liberal progress, understood as having the temporality of repetition, posits a future that is conceived as the realization of the *always already there* of the ideal present. The realization of this "always already there" is the result of what is called progressive reform.

Today progress is rendered quite differently—though, it should be emphasized, not absolutely differently. As the temporal metaconcept of modernity—one that liberalism shared with alternative modernities such as socialism and communism because they are each particular political-moral manifestations of a shared ontological tradition—progress has been much critiqued and attacked in the last several decades, and in the post-1989 years the loss of progressive hope seems to have been fully realized. With the arrival of the "end of history" and the absence of any political and economic alternatives to liberal capitalism, progress as an inspiring and believable idea has been all but lost for politicians and intellectuals on both the right and the left, although for very different reasons. For the vast mass of those people around the globe whose everyday lives have become increasingly precarious, these reasons and the ensuing debates matter very little in their everyday struggles. This lost hope of progress appears to be the case up and down the ladder of (global) society, whether expressed by politicians who either adhere to the "end of history" thesis or nostalgically look back to a golden age of better and more moral times; or academics who have leveled attacks against the metaphysical, theological, and imperialist foundations of an assumed homogenous time of history coherently and smoothly marching toward its inherent aim; or an increasingly large mass of people around the globe who are realizing—or who have realized for years—that the promises of progressive modernity were not meant for them. Progress as the defining and guiding temporal metaconcept of modernity in general, and liberalism in particular, thus, no longer carries much weight. Or so it would seem.

Wendy Brown may be right that today "it is a rare thinker, political leader, or ordinary citizen who straightforwardly invokes the premise of progress";[22] however, as indicated above, spokespersons, activists, and leaders of the human rights industry regularly invoke it. In fact, as I described in Chapter 1, although progress may have lost its position as the primary temporal understanding of political economics in the post-1968 years, human rights and the industry that arose around this idea stepped in as the "last utopia"[23] to fill the gap with a notion of moral progress. While the progressive hope of liberal capitalism or communism no longer held much power for anyone but the true believers by the end of the 1970s, and the notion of the developed West/North as the progressive pinnacle of history had all but become a farce by this point, human rights as universally inherent moral rights became a new standard of progress.

Progress, then, is no longer conceived as closing the gap between the histories of different societies and peoples. Rather, now, in its full metaphysical humanist manifestation, progress has become the conceptual articulation for the drive to make up the difference between the full realization of the "Moral" subjectivization of the globe and that which has yet to become so. Unlike the traditional notion of liberal progress, for example—which relied on hierarchical differentiations and the "obligation" of those further up the scale to "help" those further behind—human rights as the new standard of progress is postulated by its advocates as not necessarily more realized in any one particular nation-state than any other. Because of this, no one country or global region today stands as the exemplar of progress. Rather, within the contemporary condition, human rights as the ideal moral aspect of the dominant ontological tradition stands as the mark for which all countries and individuals ought to strive. Thus, for example, while nation-state A may have a clearly more transparent democratic election process than nation-state B, A may not recognize some of the most basic aspects of the right to health within their health care system that B's system does. Setting aside any assumptions of whether so-called civil or social rights should take priority, it is impossible to rank these two nation-states in terms of their respective realization of human rights in toto.[24] In this sense, the globe and its human existents are not yet fully subjectivized as Moral, but the hope of the human rights industry is that progress is being made.

This is indeed a very different notion of progress than that which came to define modernity in the nineteenth and much of the twentieth century. No longer does one country, region, or political-economic system define the standard of progress; rather, a moral ideal that is said to be distinct from any one of them yet possible for all is the mark of this progress.[25] There is no illusion of inevitability about this moral progress; from the perspective of the human rights industry and its advocates, the full realization of human rights is not historically predestined and any progress thus far realized may be lost at some point. Thus, the realization of human rights entails constant moral struggle and vigilance.[26] The triumphalist histories of human rights may track the gradual appearance of human rights by means of this struggle over the *longue durée*, and they may posit this as the gradual manifestation of our full humanity, but they rarely invoke this in terms of necessity. Rather, struggle, defeat, and backsliding are articulated as significant aspects of this history. The victories gained through these struggles, however, can only be read as moral progress—that is, as a step closer to the realization that, in Ignatieff's words, all individuals are "entitled to equal moral consideration." Wendy Brown, then, is correct when she says that the concept of progress has lost legitimacy in the contemporary world, if by progress she means that idea of history that marches, necessarily and linearly, through homogenous time, and is led by a few, as it were, avant-garde countries, regions, systems, or ideas in its gradual but necessary realization of itself. That idea is indeed dead. But within the human rights industry there remains a notion of progress that is very much alive; the human rights notion of moral progress may posit historical development as fragmented, contentious, and driven through human agency rather than the unfolding of history itself, but it is today a notion of progress that stands as the moral and political motivation for activists around the globe.

But if this important difference exists between the human rights industry's notion of moral progress and the traditional liberal/modernist notion of progress, they still share a significant similarity in terms of the temporality each enacts. In the example above of nineteenth-century Britain as the paradigm of liberal progress, it is clear that the temporality of liberal progress is one of continuously looping repetition that constitutes the "lived" present by means of temporal ecstasies emanating from an ideal present into a future and past that serve to mirror, support, and (re)enact the ideal present as the "lived" present. To put it simply, the British Empire maintained its self-image as the pinnacle of progress through a continuous temporal projection of its ideal self into the future as the aim of history and into the past as the Other of that temporality inhabited by its contemporaries who have not yet become Britain. A similar temporality can be seen, for example, in Kant's liberal vision of progress as the repetition of Frederick's Prussia or the progressive vision of postwar American Cold Warriors as the global repetition of the United States. Liberal progress, then, far from having the temporality of futurity, enacts a repetition that aims to ontically colonize and ontologically level political, moral, and social life through the realization of the ideal present.

If in the liberal imaginary Frederick's Prussia, Victorian England, and the postwar United States all stood at one point as the ideal present that marked the aim of history, then what ideal present can mark the human rights notion of moral progress if there is no one country or region that can exemplify this ideal? To ask the same question slightly differently: if Frederick's Prussia, Victorian England, and the postwar United States all stood in their particular historical moment as the constative guarantor (even if a fantasized one) of the performative realization of progressive history, then what can stand as the guarantor of the performative realization of human rights–based moral progress? This guarantor can only be the state as institution—that is, no particular state as such, but the state as an imagined but yet very real contained set of institutional and bureaucratic relations, rules, and legislations through which moral progress can be implemented.[27] Because the human rights industry, for the most part, defines itself as nonideological and does not advocate for any one particular political-economic order,[28] it can only legitimize itself and act through (by attempting to act on) those institutions that take the form of its original guarantor—that is, the state. In other words, because the human rights industry does not, and almost by definition cannot, advocate for a particular political-economic order, it is limited to merely altering the already existing state institutional structures by which moral progress can supposedly be realized. Thus, while the ideal of moral progress is to realize a moral state, instead the result is often the strengthening and legitimation of the institutional structures of a not-quite-yet moral state in the hope that these institutional modifications will eventually, someday, add up to the ideal aim of the moral state. In this sense, then, the kind of moral progress envisioned and attempted by the human rights industry has a very similar repetitive temporality to that of liberal progress, in that the future is always conceived in terms of the as-of-yet unrealized ideal present. In the next section I return to the harm reductionist case in Russia to illustrate this repetition of differential sameness.

Harm Reduction and Human Rights in Russia

By the mid-2000s Russia's HIV epidemic had become one of the fastest growing on the planet. As in most HIV/AIDS "hotspots," local NGOs and international donors and advisers touted a human rights approach as the best possibility for stemming the epidemic. According to one of the leading NGOs in Russia at the time advocating for this rights-based approach, it consists of providing "the right to the best attainable standard of physical and mental health; the right of access to information and education; the right to privacy; and the right to participate in scientific progress and enjoy its benefits," which are all already guaranteed in both international and Russian regulations.[29] The aim of this NGO and others like it, then, is to advocate that such rights-based regulations are actually practiced in Russia, and that new legislation is enacted to help assure this. In this section I will trace how the realization of this aim would result in the differential repetition of the very same state-based conditions that have helped bring about the HIV epidemic in Russia in the first place.

Russia's HIV crisis is unique in that it has been and still is primarily driven by injecting drug use. About 80 percent of the estimated 940,000 people living with HIV in Russia today were infected through injecting drug use, which contrasts with many other parts of the world where sexual contact is the primary means of transmission. This is not unrelated to the fact that Russia today has an estimated four million active drug users, which represents one of the highest user population percentages in the world.[30] This number has exploded in the post-Soviet period, as the Russian Ministry of Health estimates that drug use has risen by 400 percent between 1992 and 2002. Perhaps most worrying is that the Russian Federation AIDS Center says that 56 percent of injecting drug users (IDUs) are HIV-positive, comprising over 80 percent of registered HIV infections. Thus, while the official count of registered people living with HIV/AIDS (PLWHA) in Russia today numbers over five hundred thousand, all agree that the number is much higher. Some observers claim that the number could be as high as 1.6 million, over 1 percent of the population; most, however, tend to cite the UNAIDS estimate of 940,000 as of 2009. Additionally, UNAIDS has reported that as of the end of 2002 the "unfortunate distinction of having the world's fasting-growing HIV/AIDS epidemic still belongs to Eastern Europe and Central Asia."[31] In this region Russia by far has the highest number of PLWHA and the fastest growing number of infections.

Unfortunately, very little is being done about it. Not only does the Russian government continue to underfund programs and facilities related to HIV and drug use, but for the most part it either outright ignores the dual epidemic of HIV and injecting drug use or blames the US-led NATO war in Afghanistan for the increased supply of heroin in the country.[32] In fact, it has been argued that the drug policies of the Russian government are helping to fuel the HIV/AIDS epidemic because they primarily focus on the criminalization of drug use.[33] Thus, for example, the majority of state funding goes toward anti–drug law enforcement rather than treatment and prevention programs. In St. Petersburg, the city with the highest number of injecting drug users in the country, there is only one rehabilitation center, run by the Russian Orthodox Church, that does not charge an exorbitant fee well beyond the price range of most users. Moreover, only two specially designated infectious disease hospitals will treat users for any health problem, and nearly every person I came to know who uses or formerly used drugs had some kind of criminal record.[34]

Additionally, the widespread corruption within the Russian police forces and legal institutions further exacerbates the problem. Thus, for example, while the police often work together with the so-called drug mafia, they also take advantage of drug users by routinely rounding them up to fulfill monthly arrest quotas.[35] Indeed, it is not unheard of that police will sell the drugs they confiscate from those they arrest back to the dealers. Contributing to this nearly ubiquitous corrupt legal environment, several users have told me that in situations of dire medical need they had visited doctors at hospitals and medical institutions that were not designated for drug users and PLWHA and were met by the doctors calling the police. Such experiences help produce the sense that no matter where they turn, drug users in St. Petersburg and Russia in general are always in danger of being caught up in a carceral apparatus fueled by criminalization. In sum, by overly criminalizing and taking advantage of drug users, Russian drug policies and the corruption endemic to the Russian legal system help create a situation in which IDUs do all they can to avoid the world of official institutions, including medical facilities.

As a result, concern with legislation dominates harm reductionist writing and activity. While it is clear that international and national legal prohibitions against using drugs should be a main target for such political activity, it is less clear that attempts to enact new rights-based legislation will deliver its intended results. In the rest of this section I take a closer look at the legislative focus of harm reductionist arguments and projects, and I consider the implications such a focus has on the political possibilities made available. I begin with one of the first international harm reduction organizations active in the former Soviet Union—the Open Society International Harm Reduction Development Program—and trace the argument made by its then director as to why a human rights–based policy is essential for stemming the dual epidemic of drug use and HIV in Russia.

In a contribution to the edited volume *War on Drugs, HIV/AIDS, and Human Rights*, former director Kasia Malinowska-Sempruch and her coauthors argue that these harsh drug policies are in part the unintended consequences of the Russian government following the mandated drug policies of the UN, which emphasize the criminalization of drug use.[36] They claim that because countries like Russia feel international pressure to live up to the UN policies they have signed onto, they are left with little flexibility to adapt their domestic strategies to unique or newly arising drug situations and public health crises. Because two of the three UN treaties on drugs were implemented prior to the identification of HIV/AIDS, Malinowska-Sempruch and her coauthors claim that not only are they outdated, but they continue to force nation-states to treat drug use solely as a legal problem and neglect its public health aspect. Indeed, when it became undeniably clear in 1999 that Russia was experiencing a wave of HIV infections related to injecting drug use, the government's policy hands remained tied by its UN obligations. It is impossible to say whether Russia's drug policies would be any less punitive and harsh were it not for the UN policies, though my suspicion is that they would not be. Nevertheless, it is important to note that nation-states such as Russia do not work in an international vacuum when it comes to how they react to a social and health crisis, particularly when injecting drug use drives that crisis.

But this concern for legislation by harm reductionists goes well beyond international and domestic drug policies, and Russia in particular has been squarely focused on issues that best fall under the rubric of security. For in advocating that the Russian government reject these UN drug policies and other such punitive approaches, and instead adopt a human rights approach to the dual epidemic of HIV and drug use, Malinowska-Sempruch and her coauthors, who are some of the leading figures in the global anti–drug war movement, appeal to the Russian government through the lens of the so-called demographic crisis. The demographic crisis is what many observers call the fact that Russia is the first industrialized country in non-wartime or non-disaster conditions to experience a significantly sharp decline in its population.[37] Since 1992 there have been more annual deaths than births in the country. Perhaps most shocking is the dramatic decrease in average male life expectancy, which in 2004 when Malinowska-Sempruch was making this argument stood at fifty-nine years. Although it has been argued that there were already signs of this population decline as far back as the 1960s,[38] most have associated this demographic crisis with the societal shock of the collapse of the Soviet Union. Whenever it may have begun, it is clear that the post-Soviet years have seen a marked decline of the population and the kinds of socio-economic factors that have contributed to it, such as increased poverty and the erosion of the social safety net, increased alcohol consumption, and a rise in violence and accidents. Utilizing the language of human rights, anti–drug war agonists are attempting to convince Russian legislators and policy makers to see injecting drug use and HIV/AIDS as part of this list.

The Russian government is particularly concerned with this so-called demographic crisis because of the danger it poses to the country's future security, stability, and prosperity. It is precisely this concern that harm reductionists tend to focus on when they address legislators and policy makers on the importance of implementing a rights-based approach to the HIV and drug-using epidemics. For example, Malinowska-Sempruch and her coauthors do this when, just prior to the concluding section of their chapter, in which they offer policy suggestions, they include a section titled "Looming Catastrophe: HIV and the Destruction of a Nation." Under this heading they argue that in the next decade Russia could have as many as eight million HIV infections, which would amount to about 10 percent of the population.[39] They further argue, however, that even if such a high figure is never realized—which it was not—HIV/AIDS will still have a particularly egregious effect on the Russian economy and national security because it is overwhelmingly found in the younger population who are already of or about to become of working age. They point out that projections suggest that even a "mild" HIV epidemic could prevent the Russian economy from growing through 2025, and that an "intermediate" epidemic could lead to a 40 percent decline in economic growth over the same period.[40] Furthermore, the authors note that the Russian military would have difficulty maintaining its current strength, as the number of available young conscripts will also decline since drug use and HIV are overwhelmingly associated with young males.[41] In fact, in my own research I discovered that several of the young men I came to know first started using heroin while serving in the military, and it is well-established that military life provides the opportunity for many to begin using heroin and other drugs. In this sense, it is possible to say that the Russian military has itself become a public health danger. For these authors, then, the argument for a human rights approach to stemming the HIV epidemic associated with injecting drug use is ultimately grounded in how it will help the government maintain the country's political, economic, military, and social stability, and ultimately, though unspoken, contribute to its prosperity. It is, in other words, a rights-based approach that aims at enacting a differential repetition of the same. Notice that the goal is not necessarily to eradicate the drug using and HIV epidemics, but rather to reduce them to a reasonable rate such that they do not threaten the security and stability of the Russian nation. Security, then, and not health, seems to be the primary rhetorical, and perhaps even the practical, aim of this human rights practice.

Transatlantic Partners against AIDS—the Moscow-based NGO that provided the definition of the right to health cited above, and which in the mid-2000s was one of the leading nongovernmentals in terms of their access to and influence on legislators and policy makers—similarly addressed the security concerns of the demographic crisis in its advocacy for the human rights approach of harm reduction. Like Malinowska-Sempruch and her coauthors, it takes a line of argument that links the rights-based approach to fighting the epidemic with the only possibility of the government realizing its plans for maintaining and strengthening Russia's economy, security, and prosperity. For example, in a document written "to assist members of the Federation Council and deputies of the State Duma of the Russian Federation, and other Russian officials on the federal and regional levels," titled "HIV/AIDS, Law and Human Rights: A Handbook for Russian Legislators," the NGO warns Russian legislators and policy makers that "actions taken today will determine the extent to which HIV affects Russia's economy, national security, and social development."[42] The document continues by arguing that if rights-based legislation is not adopted and implemented, then HIV/AIDS will continue to spread in Russia and, for example, hinder "the Russian Government's goal of doubling GDP by the end of the decade," "reduce labor productivity and corporate competitiveness," and intensify "the poverty problem," threaten "Russia's stability and security," all of which "deepens Russia's growing demographic crisis."[43]

The unspoken implication of this argument is that rights-based HIV prevention and treatment may be important for the well-being and health of millions of Russian individuals, but these, shall we say, distal benefits of human rights are only rendered legible, comprehensible, and ultimately practical in terms of the more proximate benefits they bring to the stability, security, and prosperity of the Russian state and economy. Furthermore, because this rights approach is almost entirely advocated for in terms of legislation and the implementation of laws, an additional unspoken benefit of the rights-based approach for the Russian state is the further envelopment of Russians into a juridical and carceral politics of citizenship by which policing surveillance is increasingly emphasized, the citizen-subject is limited to certain forms of recognition, and the reach of the state-government apparatus is further entwined with daily life. The health of the population, then, becomes a proxy for the health of the nation.

In this sense the human rights approach to fighting the HIV and drug using epidemics in Russia can be read as ultimately addressing what is seen by many in the international community as the lack of democratic institutions within the country. Echoing Part I, Paragraph 34 of the Vienna Declaration, which calls for "the establishment and strengthening of national legislation, national institutions and related infrastructures which uphold the rule of law and democracy," the human rights approach to fighting the HIV and drug use epidemics in Russia—as well as other countries—sees those problems not as health issues but as symptoms of the lack of so-called good governance. This reading of rights-based health advocacy reveals the erasure of the suffering experience and potential health of IDUs and PLWHA by the language of legislation, implementation, reformed policing, state security, and economic productivity and prosperity. When the lives and experiences of IDUs and PLWHA come into the rights-based health literature discussed here—and others like it—the stigma they are exposed to, the lack of medical care and treatment they must suffer, the pains they feel, and the deaths that sometimes befall them stand as markers of corrupt police, lack of governmental funding, ignored laws, and the inability of the state to care for its population.[44] In other words, in this literature their lives and experiences can only signify the need for the "establish[ing] and strengthening of national legislation, national institutions and related infrastructures which uphold the rule of law and democracy." These actual lives and experiences, even when presented in narrative form, are all but folded into a statistical register used to indicate the failure of the Russian state and government to live up to its democratic mandate.

In this sense the human rights approach of harm reduction as advocated and practiced in Russia—and a very similar case could be made for rights-based advocacy around the globe—enacts a repetition of differential sameness best conceived as conservative reformism. This repetition can be seen in the policy advice offered by Malinowska-Sempruch and her coauthors as well as by the Moscow-based NGO. In advocating for a human rights approach to fighting Russia's HIV and drug using epidemics, neither offered any possibilities other than legislative-based solutions that would necessitate the further entrenchment of the state-government apparatuses in the lives of drug users, the treatment of those already infected with HIV, as well as in the daily lives of the rest of the population in the name of prevention. In this sense, the rights-based approach advocated by these two parties is little more than advocacy for political reform that would result in the more efficient practice of state-based power, and thus can only envision healthful well-being through the framework of a powerful and well-working state apparatus. Conceptualized as progress, such repetition of differential sameness provides the ontic conditions by which the very same institutions that these advocates blame for the explosion of HIV and drug use in Russia become strengthened and secured. Far from so-called moral progress, then, this appears to be the elision of power by means of the rhetoric of morality.

Repetition of Differential Sameness

This example, and the elision of power it illustrates, suggests that what has come to be called moral progress may in fact be another way of articulating the political moralism that Wendy Brown claims has largely replaced much of politics in the contemporary world.[45] Such moralism can be seen as a symptom of the loss of a coherent political narrative—a narrative that was once held together by the metaconcept of progress, be it liberal, socialist, or otherwise—and the resulting struggle to continue to engage politically despite the loss of any particular good to strive for. Lacking any clear political desire and unable to articulate any clear course of action, moralism as politics is ultimately rendered politically aimless and impotent. This, of course, is not how the human rights industry would see its actions. But through its fetishization of the state as at one and the same time the primary perpetrator of human rights abuses and the primary mechanism for overcoming such abuses and thus actualizing moral progress, the human rights industry finds itself enacting a similar reformist project as that of liberalism, but without the clear political aim of any good other than a vaguely defined world in which all "individuals who compose it [are] entitled to equal moral consideration."[46] This fetishization, combined with the fact that the state as institution stands as the only constative guarantor for the possible realization of human rights as moral ideal, results in the kind of political-moral activity described above by which the only clear outcome is the strengthening of state institutions.

There is no doubt that these rights-based practices by the anti–drug war movement, as well as other human rights projects, can have short-term and localized positive effects, but the larger picture remains that of—or repeats—the essential conditions that gave rise to the problem the reform sought to fix. And is this really any great surprise? For by fetishizing the state as the only recourse for a moralizing politics, and in so doing misreading the state as a potentially benevolent, disinterested, and principle-based sovereign subject, rather than understanding the state as the violently disciplinary and politically, economically, and socially interested institutional assemblage that it is, the human rights industry—as with many of its left and liberal brethren—reveals the limitations of such moral politics and the conservatism it is forced to enact.[47] This misreading of the state and the rights-based practices it engenders does little to change the circumstances that gave rise to that which these practices seek to address. Rather, at best, they provide the conditions for—shall we say—a more humane enactment of those very same so-called human rights abuses they are attempting to eradicate. It is in this sense, and only in this sense, that human rights practices can be understood to enact some form of futurity. Ultimately, however, to call such futurity progress is ontically to define progress as the realization of the capacity to experience such things as exclusion, marginality, poverty, and disease a bit more comfortably.

Such futurity as progress is what I mean by the repetition of differential sameness. Similar to Benjamin's angel of history being blown backward into the future by a storm we call progress, the same storm that must also be that which piles the debris of history at the angel's feet, the moral progress evoked by the human rights industry blows and swirls around the very conditions it hopes to address and in so doing kicks up, redistributes, and creates other piles of the same debris. Notice that this is not a repetition of the same. The human rights industry does make a difference. But the difference it makes is limited within the bounds of repetition and is therefore cut off from any possibility of the new. Thus what is read as moral progress is actually a misreading, for as a repetition of differential sameness human rights do not bring about anything truly otherwise that stands over and against or outside the conditions from which the rights are initially enacted. As a repetition of differential sameness, or what is perhaps more clearly articulated as conservative reformism, the enactment of human rights ultimately only repeats in a differential form the totality of that which it claims to overcome.[48]

What we see here, then, is a notion of moral progress, a sense of futurity, that in fact reproduces in another form the present. Lee Edelman has convincingly argued that this very reproductive futurism lies behind the logic of liberalism—in both its conservative and liberal forms—as it projects on the future the fantasy of overcoming all of the incompletenesses, incoherencies, and inconsistencies that essentially define liberalism and therefore can never be overcome within itself.[49] This is the fantasy of progress—and it is this fantasy of overcoming without going beyond that has come to define the self-delusional moralism that often stands in today for the name of politics and political action. This fantasy is most clearly articulated and put into practice by the human rights industry and its claim to fight for moral progress.

This fantasy of overcoming is only possible because of the ontological grounding of progress as the subjectivization of the globe and ultimately all of existence. For in the attempt to enact progress by means of transforming the globe, its constituent spatial containers, or what we call states, and the bounded individuals said to populate these national "containers" into Moral existents, the human rights industry has run up against the limits of its ontological tradition by attempting to fulfill or close the total projection of this tradition. By attempting to fulfill this ontological tradition by endeavoring to Morally subjectivize all that is, the human rights industry has disclosed for us the limiting ontological conditions of this tradition, and the ways these conditions alienate us from our worlds. This disclosure has, furthermore, revealed an existential demand that we seek, experiment with, and create new and alternative ontological traditions that are better suited for dwelling in our worlds. For by disclosing the fantasy of progress as the fantasy of the subjectivization of all that is, the human rights industry has also disclosed the groundlessness of our ontological grounding.

As a result of this disclosure we can now understand how it is that disappointment—and increasingly anxiety—has become the political mood of our day, and why we find ourselves at an historical moment when we feel the existential demand to create new ways of being and acting in our worlds. In response to this demand, I will attempt in the rest of this book to provide a framework for an experiment in politically and morally becoming otherwise, one that must begin from an alternative ontological starting point—that is, an ontological starting point that begins not with an a priori assumption of a particular kind of sovereign human subject standing over and against a world that it seeks to secure, control, and know, but rather begins with the intertwining of diverse human and nonhuman existents and situations that constitute our shared worlds. With this shift of ontological beginnings I hope to initiate a shift from the politics of the a priori to a politics of worldbuilding.

CHAPTER 3

Worlds and Situations

So far I have been engaged in the first step of a critical hermeneutics of contemporary politics—the ungrounding of what I am calling the politics of the a priori, which has become epitomized in the time of late liberalism as rights-based politics, and most particularly in terms of human rights. By means of this ungrounding, it became clear that the ontological conditions the language and practices of human rights politics enacts and perpetuates significantly limit possible political, moral, and ethical ways of being-in-the-world. These ontological conditions—repetition and totality—are thus the basis for a politics that is essentially conservative, a morality that is totalizing, and an ethics that is restricted. As a result, these ontological conditions and the human rights politics that enacts and maintains these conditions foreclose possibilities for becoming politically, morally, or ethically otherwise. Thus, it would seem that our response to the disappointment of politics today should be the leaving behind of that which has enframed us so. In other words, if we hope to do politics again, then we must stop talking about, seeking, and demanding human rights. For the implications of the ungrounding carried out so far are that any theoretical or practical attempt to revitalize rights-based politics with, for example, a more ethnographically robust notion of rights[1] or rights that emerge from the gap of dissensus,[2] will ultimately result in repetitions of the sort disclosed in the previous chapters. The task ahead of us, then, is to walk away from rights-based discursive practices and seek an opening where we can experimentally forge new ontological starting points and the concomitant concepts that better articulate the activity demanded by contemporary exigencies. The rest of the chapters of this book are a first attempt—the beginnings of notes on—such an experiment.

I have called the politics associated with human rights language and practice a politics of the a priori. This is a politics that depends on, and repeats, a pre-known narrative of political belonging, aim, and practice, and thus attempts to enact an a priori conception of what counts as the privileged political subject, organization, and praxis. Above all this politics of the a priori is grounded in the ontological tradition of metaphysical humanism, and thus on a narrowly defined and totalized conception of the subject and its place in existence, which, itself has come to be understood in terms of this very subjectivity that is projected on it. This totalized subject is what has come to be named "human," which beyond its demarcation as a biological species is also morally marked as imbued with inherent dignity. For the politics of the a priori this generalized total subject is regularly particularized in the form of a totalized identity subject, who as a result of being specified as an identity tends to have all other possibilities of being foreclosed other than its generalized totality of humanness. As a result, within the politics of the a priori all possibilities of being are reduced to a repetition of totality within the limits of humanness and identity. Thus, for example, from the perspective of the politics of the a priori a person living with HIV has his being-in-the-world reduced to a perpetual oscillation between his identification as an HIV-positive person and his humanness. All other possibilities for his being are either elided or considered negligible for the purposes of politics. As a result, the primary theoretical question of the politics of the a priori is that of political subjectivity, and in particular that of the subject capable of demanding rights.

In this chapter and those that follow I will attempt to think a politics that begins not with a subject but with worlds, and in particular a situation of a world. I will think this politics through the political activity of the anti–drug war movement. For although it is the case, as I showed in the last chapter and will revisit in the following two chapters, that this political movement regularly articulates its political aspirations in terms of the a priori triad of rights-dignity-responsibility, I hope to show that some of its *activity* points us toward something the movement has not yet articulated but which it—for the most part—is already doing. Thus, if the first step of critical hermeneutics is the ungrounding of the a priori, the second step is pointing to the openings that emerge through this ungrounding.[3] Here in these openings we can begin to experiment with and articulate other possible ways of becoming and acting. It is precisely this that I hope to do by hermeneutically engaging with the political activity of anti–drug war agonists. In a future book, I intend to offer a more ethnographically focused analysis of this potential not-yet; here I offer the theoretical framework from which that analysis will begin.

A politics that emerges from a world rather than from an a priori subject begins from a demand made by a world. The "site" of this demand is a situation[4] that has rendered the world unbearable. In contrast to the politics of the a priori, which again begins from an ontological tradition that has as its core a narrowly defined and pre-known subject, the politics I will begin to delineate in this chapter emerges in response to a historically specific and undeniable problem. This problem is perhaps best conceived as the "essence" of a situation that renders that situation unbearable or problematic for the vast majority of those who find themselves caught up in it. Because this politics—which I will name a politics of worldbuilding—recognizes that the problematic nature of a situation makes living that situation unbearable, the only appropriate response is a political project of transgression. Thus, in contrast to the repetitive reformism of the politics of the a priori, the politics of worldbuilding recognizes that the problem that arises as a result of a particular situation demands a new situation, and thus a new world. This transgressive politics, therefore, cannot be based on a pre-known and narrowly defined narrative, aim, and subject with its supposed inherent nature. That is, it cannot hold onto what Hannah Arendt called bannisters. Rather, it must begin with the problem posed by a situation and proceed by means of a total transgression of that which brought about the problem. In other words, unlike the politics of the a priori, which is carried out as a repeated projection of a pre-known totality, a projection that ultimately forecloses possibilities for becoming otherwise, a politics of worldbuilding emerges from a world that has become unbearable and creates political language and activity in response to the demand of this unbearability.[5]

The hope that such a politics provides is that by responding to this worldly demand, new possibilities for being and becoming emerge.[6] For rather than enacting a being that is pre-known—for example, a subject of rights or a dignified person—and thus closing off possibilities for the otherwise, a politics of worldbuilding opens a world to the otherwise by allowing possibilities to emerge from the very unbearableness of that world.[7] As I will clarify in the Epilogue, the political hope of critical hermeneutics lies in the hermeneutic nature of existence; that is, the fact that existence, despite its current enframing by metaphysical humanism, always remains open. But I do not want to get ahead of myself. The hermeneutic nature of existence will reveal itself as we work through the coming chapters. For now we should begin with worlds and their situations. In the rest of this chapter I will sketch what I intend by a world as a multiplicity of situations. In particular, I will show how a situation is that from which the demand of politics first arises. So then, what does a critical hermeneutics intend by worlds and situations?

Worlds and Situations

The concept of world has largely and for the most part been a human-centric one. Indeed, the etymology of world indicates this. Derived from the Old English *woruld*, which emerged from the Proto-Germanic **wer* meaning "man" and **ald* meaning "age," *world*'s literal etymological sense is "age of man."[8] Even if world has come to mean something like "everything that there is,"[9] within the ontological conditions of metaphysical humanism this "everything" can only be understood in terms of the subjectivity of the subject projected onto it. In this sense, the world, even when meant as "everything that there is," remains a human-centric world. As I have been trying to argue so far, and as I made particularly clear in the Introduction, this metaphysical humanist projection is precisely the problem we must address in order to work our way toward other modes of being. Indeed, in the late work of Heidegger, the possibility of thinking world beyond human-centricity had already begun, and here I have in mind his notions of the fourfold and thing.[10] However, the existential and political demand to continue thinking such worlds remains.

In fact, perhaps today more than ever the necessity not only of such thinking but also of the political demand to begin building such worlds calls us.[11] And here, with this political demand to build worlds, we see that humans remain vital. For, although the new worlds that have become necessary cannot be human-centric ones, humans must nevertheless build them. Some posthumanists might disagree with such a statement, but frankly it is unclear how it could be otherwise. For although I agree entirely with Anna Tsing that "making worlds is not limited to humans,"[12] existentially (and here I mean the possibility of existence persisting on this earth) and politically the worlds made by such nonhuman beings as beavers or mushrooms can do very little other than offer inspiration for imagining alternative ways for humans to build worlds. For the existential and political fact of the matter is that humans have parasitically colonized the earth to such an extent that barring some apocalyptic catastrophe they will likely remain the primary shapers of worlds on this planet for quite some time. Furthermore, despite the important case made by Latourians, vital materialists, and object-oriented ontologists for the agency of nonhuman things and their inextricable intertwining in worlds, it simply remains unconvincing that, for example, a worm or a thermostat or a rock has the same capacities for creating and shaping worlds as do that range of possible beings we call human.[13]

Humans, like it or not, have become the dominant creators and shapers of worlds. What needs to be recognized is that this in itself is not problematic. The problem, or should I say the danger, arises when these worlds are built in the image of a predefined and narrowly conceived human—as they have under the conditions of metaphysical humanism and, as such, come to dominate, control, and often eliminate other already existing or possible worlds. The existential and political imperative of our time, then, is to stop building worlds in such a manner, and begin building them so that they attune to one another, themselves, and their constituents. So what is this building of worldbuilding?

Perhaps I should begin by considering this in relation to the two ways Anna Tsing has recently written of worlding and world-making. Indeed, Tsing seems to be working here with two altogether different concepts. For on the one hand, what she calls worlding is primarily meant to indicate a methodological process of providing context through which "meaningful interaction" becomes possible.[14] Articulated as such, this sense of worlding and world is in line with the notion of world as the background by which everything that is contained within it is rendered meaningful, a notion I will critically consider below. On the other hand, she articulates a concept of world-making as "projects [which] emerge from practical activities" that assemble as "open-ended gatherings."[15] This conception, as will become clear, gets quite close to how I will articulate worlds and worldbuilding below. Ultimately, however, what I intend by these differs significantly from what Tsing does. This is primarily so because I make an important distinction between *building as an imaginative and creative process*, the outcome of which can only be judged long after the fact of its having been done, and *making as a project*, the judgment of which is often made in terms of instrumentality (consider, for example, the beaver "judging" the instrumental efficacy of its world-making dam project).[16] Thus, the building of worldbuilding must not be thought in terms of development but instead, as I argue in the next chapter, as a poetic and creative opening. Worldbuilding must not be thought in terms of construction, but rather as the creative design of clearings out of which a world worlds in the process of attuning with itself. A politics of worldbuilding, then, does not close off or wall in but rather opens and clears so that worlds may world in a process of gathering.[17]

It is not uncommon that those who draw intellectual inspiration from Heidegger attempt to explicate a worldly politics. Perhaps most famously, Hannah Arendt expounded a political theory that posits the world as both the site of political action and that which is disclosed—or put another way, given significance through such political activity.[18] Inspired by Arendt, Ella Myers[19] has recently written against the individualized and individualizing ethical turn in political theory by arguing for a politics motivated by care for the world. And Leslie Paul Thiele,[20] having offered, in my opinion, the most important political explication of the political possibilities of Heidegger's work, writes, for example, of a politics of dwelling that, among other things, would entail a politics as caretaker and guardian of the world rather than its exploiter and master.

Despite the similarities of these works with what I will write in the rest of this chapter and book, some critical differences remain, the most significant of which is that these theorists all seem to share a single-world ontology, or the view that there is only one world. Each of them conceives of world as that one world where everything is—indeed, we could even say where everything is contained—and where everything interacts. It seems to me that no matter how complexly one attempts to articulate such a notion of one world—for example, Myers describes world as "the meta-assemblage out of which any particular assemblage can emerge"[21]—such a notion cannot help but repeat a container view of world. The one world, then, no matter how complex these theorists try to make it, ends up seeming very much like the totalized container world of metaphysical humanism or the cave wall on which Platonic shadow puppets play. Indeed, as Myers puts it just a few lines before her meta-assemblage description, world "refers to the sum total of conditions of life on earth."[22]

Some anthropologists who have recently taken up the question of world share this single-world ontology. Thus, for example, in a recent two-part article on "world" the anthropologist João de Pina-Cabral argues for a single-world ontology because, as he puts it, without "the triangulation of the world there is no place for communication."[23] In other words, Pina-Cabral is concerned that anything less (or perhaps better put, anything more) than a single-world ontology would make human communication impossible. Thus, if I understand him correctly, Pina-Cabral argues that a single world is the very condition of human intelligibility. Tim Ingold has made similar claims recently in his call for a "one world anthropology."[24] But as I have been arguing, this is a very old story and one that is increasingly unconvincing. For ultimately what Pina-Cabral and Ingold are doing is repeating the assertion that we need some background or horizon or totality or Platonic cave wall that provides the condition of mutual intelligibility, and thus, so it seems, for any being whatsoever. Or again, as Pina-Cabral puts it, the single world provides the "triangulation" for such intelligibility; this single world is the only stage, as it were, on which humans or any other beings could possibly be. In the rest of this chapter and book I would like to provoke the reader to begin to ask the following question: can we conceive of communicative and responsive human and nonhuman beings without this background? Although I do not subscribe to his semiotic approach, Eduardo Kohn has shown that this is indeed possible.[25] He and I might disagree on his choice of the concept "think"—for me, at least, it has the danger of being yet another metaphysical humanist projection despite his claims to the contrary—but it is clear that he has convincingly articulated the fact of the communicability or responsiveness of human and nonhuman beings without the background of a single world. In Chapter 5 I will argue that attunement is another way that we can conceive of such responsiveness across multiple worlds.

For these single-world theorists, then, world remains something like the closed totality of representation and correspondence that has come to us through the metaphysical humanist ontological tradition. Timothy Morton[26] has argued that we now live in a time after the end of the world, by which he means that in the time of what he calls hyperobjects this metaphysical humanist notion of the contained single world no longer pertains. Indeed, it never really did despite its dominance within this ontological tradition. To a great extent I agree with Morton. Nevertheless, our starting assumptions—objected-oriented ontology for Morton and a critical hermeneutics of relational being for me—lead us to very different places. I will address this difference in greater detail. For now, however, I will simply leave it with the observation that while Morton sees our present moment as the time after the end of the world, I see it as a moment of the existential and political demand to build new worlds. This difference, I hope, will become clearer below.

Let me begin by simply saying that if Morton's response to the metaphysical humanist ontology of a contained single world is to posit an ontology of individualized objects—which, in fact, I will argue below does nothing other than repeat metaphysical humanism in another form—I respond to the single-world ontology in an ecstatically relational manner. Therefore, I intend world along the lines of how Andrew J. Mitchell describes the late Heidegger's notion of world in terms of the fourfold. Mitchell tells us that for the late Heidegger "there is no 'world' in the abstract but always only a populated and articulated one of particular situations at particular times, and likewise no encapsulated things, but always these outpouring gestures of relationality."[27] In the following section, then, I will explicate a notion of world as a multiplicity of situations and ecstatic relationality.

Worlds

As a gathering a world is not a container, space, field, or realm in which we find humans and nonhumans standing beside one another individualized and contained. Rather, worlds world. Worlds are a process of gathering, an assemblage that holds together temporarily. Worlds gather proximate existents and assemble for a time until they recede and give way to new emerging worlds.[28] Such worlding is always already underway.[29] Furthermore, it is important to note that new worlds do not emerge within something that might be called *the* world. Such a notion would only be another version of a single-world ontology. Rather, as I hope becomes clear below, new worlds emerge from the sites of potentiality within the interstices of the situations that structure and link already existing multiple worlds. In this sense, we can understand new worlds as emerging across the complex and ecstatic relationality of existence and the interstices that partially constitute this complexity.

Worlds are shared, but never entirely. In a very real way my wife and I share a world, but only partially. To say that we have different perspectives on a world is not quite right, as this suggests that we both stand side by side, over and against a world at which we look and observe slightly differently. Such a perspective is impossible, as we are always already in and of our shared world. This partial sharedness of our world is not a matter of perspective, then, but rather a result of the fact that we are always part and partial of multiple worlds. This essential multiplicity of our particular way of being-in-worlds—or what we could also call a life trajectory—results in the fact that what each of us brings to any particular world can never be fully shared by the others with whom we partially share a world. For this reason, every world is unique and singular each time, and would not exist as it does without us both being intertwined within it right now (but as we will see below, because situations structure worlds these unique and singular worlds also have duration). The singularity of worlds is further ensured by the fact that other specific existents such as our neighbors, housing policy, consumer capitalism, the tree outside the living room window, current drug policy, our friends and family, and the cats are also intertwined in the gathering of this world.[30] All of this and more constitute and share the world I am in right now, partially and temporarily. And this is so because, as Jean-Luc Nancy might put it, "each one of us is . . . the other origin of the same world."[31]

That which is gathered and assembled through worlding becomes limited in its being by the ontological conditions that emerge out of particular processes of worlding. To a great extent—but never entirely—the enactment of ontological traditions limits worlds as they unfold. In the previous two chapters I tried to show how in the realm of political practice this occurs. This "never entirely" is the result of the fact, as will become clear shortly, that every world is ripe with sites of potentiality that emerge out of the multiplicity of interstices that occur as situations assemble to structure a world. Simon Critchley[32] writes that the task of radical politics is the creation of such interstitial potentiality by means of articulation, a notion he borrows from Laclau and Mouffe.[33] But as I will make clear below, such reliance on political articulation ultimately leaves us with the need to assume a political subject who projects potentiality onto the world by means of such articulation. In contrast to this subjectively focused notion of politics and potentiality, I intend potentiality as always already there—in the interstices of situations—regardless of any such articulation, even if, as Schürmann[34] writes of the possibilities of futurity, such potentiality is presently absent.[35] This "always already there" of potentiality, thus, indicates what Agamben in his reading of Aristotle's *De Anima* calls "*the existence of non-Being*,"[36] which is what I am trying to get at by the concept of *sites of potentiality*. These sites of potentiality can be understood as the clearings from which an otherwise potentially emerges;[37] they are the sites from which new possibilities could enter into a world.[38] Because of these sites of potentiality, a world is perhaps best considered as a process of becoming and receding; and the politics of worldbuilding I am writing about in this book, similar to José Esteban Muñoz's notion of queerness, is "the rejection of a here and now" of an unbearable world, and the "insistence on [sites of] potentiality" as the starting point for enacting "new and better pleasures, other ways of being in the world, and ultimately new worlds."[39]

Worlds do not approximate our typical temporal and spatial categories. Worlds are never simply present. Not-yets, could-have-beens, almosts, and hopefullys are just a few of the nonlinear temporalities that gather along with other existents as a world worlds. Such nonlinear temporalities are central to a politics of worldbuilding as it ensures that "pasts" have never been closed off but always remain open as potential "futures," and thus remain potential sites of political hope.[40] Furthermore, as existents gather into a world they do not form a geometric shape or geography. Worlds are not globes. Neither are worlds abstract and mathematicizable such that they may be contained, for example, within sets. Indeed a world can never be contained Newtonian-like. If anything we may be able to speak of a flesh that stretches and splits, flakes and sheds, reconstitutes and heels a world as it affectively binds existents together for a time.[41] As a world gathers it attunes itself so as to become, as it were, comfortable in its own "skin." But even to speak of a flesh that affectively binds a world together suggests a world somehow contained. Globes, sets, fields, flesh—can we ever get away from the container metaphor of world? But if not contained, how do we conceive of this world of gathered existents? If not a container, is there anything that structures, as it were, the worlding of worlds?

Perhaps we could begin to conceive of a world as structured by a multiplicity of *situations* that affectively and materially hold together existents intertwined in that world, as well as constitute a link or a bridge to other worlds. When I write that a world is structured by situations I intend "structure" in the sense that Jeff Malpas writes of an ontological structure "that is constituted through the mutual interplay of multiple elements, a structure that encompasses the entities and elements that appear within it rather than underlying them, a structure to which belongs a unity that is given only in and through the mutual relatedness of the elements that make it up."[42] Indeed, this mutual interplay that structures a world is what Heidegger was getting at when he wrote of the mirroring of the fourfold by which worlds world, and that which gathers in these worlds are bound in their "essential being toward one another"[43]—or as I would put it, become attuned.

By *world*, then, I intend a multiplicity of situations structured by nothing other than this very multiplicity,[44] and because worlds are structured by these situations that are never contained within one world, these situations constitute a link or a bridge between *multiple worlds*. The fact of multiple worlds and their linkage by situations entails not just that worlds can exist separately, as it were—although, to be clear, they are always potentially connected through the "wormhole" of a situation. But also, importantly, some of these worlds can partially overlap such that we have "worlds within worlds,"[45] as Elizabeth Povinelli has put it echoing the words of

Malinowski, which can and do slip into one another, even if temporarily. In this sense, both worlds and the situations that structure and link them can be described as ecstatically relational and emergent multiplicities. Such a notion of world is ripe with sites of potentiality, and thus open for a politics of worldbuilding.

The rest of this chapter will be dedicated to a fuller explication of situations and their centrality to the politics of worldbuilding that I am considering in this book. Recognizing the centrality of situations to such a politics is vital because we live first and foremost in situations. Furthermore, as will become clear below, situations are central to such a politics because, among other reasons, they limit possibilities for being as they account for similarity, diversity, distinction, and differentiation within worlds.[46] In other words, situations account for that which gets misread in terms of identification, recognition, and representation. To put it plainly, situations of a world, and not biology, culture, class, identity, or any such marker of closure—only situations—are the settings for being and becoming, and thus for politics. For this reason I hope to make clear in the rest of this book that in order to change a world one must begin by changing a situation.[47]

This is so because situations, as the "wormholes" that link multiple worlds, are that which allow the possibility of either "jumping" to other worlds or, more to the point of politics, transgressing a world so as to alter that world. Situations, then, not only get us beyond a concern about potentially incommensurable worlds,[48] but as such are the scenes of political activity. By *politics* I mean the agonistic and creative experimentation with an otherwise. This is always a collective activity, although the collective need not be very large.[49] Furthermore, situations are the scenes of politics because to be in a world is always to be in at least one situation in that world, and as such it is in situations that we discover sites of potentiality. In this sense, the politics of worldbuilding I will consider in the following chapters is perhaps best understood as the activity of disclosing and acting at sites of potentiality within particular situations so as to open clearings in the hope of altering the range of possibilities that limit a world.

If situations are the scene of politics, then it is imperative that we understand what is intended by situation. Thus, in the rest of this chapter I explicate the concept in order to provide a start point for a politics of worldbuilding. I will do this by explicating the drug war situation, and do so in schematic form in order to highlight the key characteristics of a situation. Finally, I will end this chapter with a brief nod to another possible situation so as to be clear that a politics of worldbuilding is not limited to one situation but in fact is a model for acting in response to any number of situations that already exist in our various worlds.

A Situation Named "Drug War"

A situation is a non-totalizable singular multiple, which as such is an assembled intertwining that always has interstices, gaps, incompatibilities, and aspects of other assemblages. The complexity of a situation as a singular multiplicity[50] emerges from its assemblage nature in that multifarious aspects—sometimes contradictory, sometimes complementary—of diverse other assemblages constitute it and render the situation impossible to either totalize or isolate.[51] As an assemblage, external relations with other assemblages constitute a situation rather than the internal relations that are said to constitute totalized individual isolates. For example, what is called the drug war is really an assemblage of diverse aspects of other assemblages such as global militarism, state-based surveillance and control, biopolitical health management, carceral political economics, and national and international inequalities. How does this situation manifest in various worlds?

Take for example the intertwining of global militarism, inequalities, surveillance, and carceral political economics. When U.S. president Richard Nixon declared the war on drugs in June 1971 the battle lines extended well beyond the domestic front. Not only did this declaration result in the increased funding for domestic law enforcement training and cooperation among enforcement agencies, and the creation of new state and federal legislation in support of this law enforcement, it also pressured other countries to fulfill their international obligations of adhering to the 1961 United Nations Single Convention on Narcotic Drugs. In order to do this, Nixon used military and economic aid to force countries "to reduce the manufacture and trafficking of narcotics within their borders."[52] Beginning from this decisive moment the drug war situation increasingly became constituted by an intertwining of national and international legislation, economic aid and development, and military aid and eventually intervention—particularly during the Reagan and Bush years—all of which rested on the international inequalities that characterized Cold War politics.[53] Indeed, as the 1980s came to an end, it became increasingly difficult to discern precisely the distinction between drug war and Cold War military operations.

This was particularly so throughout Latin and South America as the U.S. military became fully entangled with counternarcotics operations. Senator Bob Dole was just one of many at the time to call for a "total war" against drugs; he asserted that it was "time to bring the full force [of] military and intelligence communities into this war."[54] It was only a matter of time, then, before the George H. W. Bush administration fully committed the U.S. military to the drug war, which was clearly demonstrated in the 1989 invasion of Panama. Although many of the top military brass had resisted the military's increased role in counternarcotics operations abroad, with the end of the Cold War many of them now saw the military's participation in such operations as a means to secure the inflated budgets they had enjoyed for the past decade. This concern was echoed by economic analysts who feared the onset of a recession if military expenditures were cut, which adds one more aspectual intertwining to the situation of the drug war—that is, the economic aspect. William Taylor, a military expert at the Center for Strategic and International Studies, offered one solution to this concern that would prove prescient. Arguing that with the "Soviet threat" eliminated the U.S. military would need to "develop some social-utility arguments" in order to defend its standing reserve of personnel, equipment, and funding, Taylor recommended that the so-called Third World might offer a solution in the form of "insurgency, terrorism, and narcotics interdiction."[55]

If one of the initial intertwinings of the drug war situation was that of counternarcotics operations, global militarism, and the Cold War, then by the late 1990s and the 2000s this would morph into counternarcotics operations, global militarism, and counterterrorism.[56] Just as the U.S. government claimed that communist insurgents in Latin America funded their operations with drug trafficking—a claim that at times was tenuous at best—so, too, it currently makes similar claims about terrorist organizations.[57] And just as such claims in the 1980s and 1990s allowed for the increased intertwining of economic and military aid, military and law enforcement operations, and military interventions in the drug war situation, so, too, today have these become tightly knotted and manifest in such locations as Afghanistan, Central Asia, Southeast Europe, and parts of Africa.[58] At both the national and international levels, then, counternarcotics and counterterrorism, which often manifests in the form of military intervention of one form or another, has become a central aspect of the current drug war situation.

This global militarization of the drug war has exceeded itself, as it were, and created an offshoot in the United States with the militarization of domestic police, which has further resulted in the increased surveillance and control aspect of the situation. In the United States this militarization developed throughout the 1980s. From the 1981 Congressional Military

Cooperation with Law Enforcement Act, to the 1988 bill authorizing the National Guard to assist local police in drug interdictions, to the 1989 policy that established regional task forces within the Pentagon to work closely with local police in antidrug efforts, all of this resulted in both the close cooperation between the military and police and the militarization of police equipment, training, and tactics.[59] As was recently revealed by the events in Ferguson, Missouri, American local police are now armed with machine guns, tanks, and military-style surveillance equipment, and trained in military-style siege, combat, and "interrogation" tactics, enabling them to control and occupy entire neighborhoods and regions in military fashion. This capacity, though well underway already with the "law and order" response to urban and revolutionary violence in the 1960s, reached full maturity with the 1980s militarization of the drug war situation.

In day-to-day actuality, though, militarized tactics are hardly necessary for the control and surveillance of neighborhoods and populations. Rather, Stop and Frisk has perhaps been the most "successful" police tactic in the war on drugs. This is particularly so in New York, although similar tactics are used in other cities in North America, Great Britain, and Russia, and likely elsewhere. I will discuss this tactic further in the next chapter, but Stop and Frisk essentially means that police officers with so-called reasonable suspicion can stop any individual on the street, question them, and frisk them. It was initially aimed at getting weapons off the streets but has morphed into a means of controlling and watching populations, and in some cases actually making drug-related arrests. The militarization of the police, the increased number of random searches, and the surveillance employed—in 2012 over five hundred thousand individuals were stopped and frisked in New York City alone, 87 percent of whom were either African American or Latino[60]—has significantly contributed to the explosion of carceral political economics. Thus, just in the United States, which has the highest level of incarceration globally, 1.55 million people were arrested in 2012 on nonviolent drug charges, while globally the prison population has skyrocketed in the last three decades to over ten million, many of whom are imprisoned on low-level drug charges.[61] What is clear, then, is that just as the drug war situational assemblage first became militarized when it became intertwined with Cold War politics and military activity, a surveillance and control aspect has increasingly emerged as part of this situation as it has intertwined with (militarized) domestic policing and transnational anti-terror strategies and tactics. It is no wonder, then, that the anti–drug war agonists I have come to know, and whom we will read more of in the following chapters, refer to the drug war situation as a war on people.

As is clear, then, what we call the drug war is no "thing" in itself, but rather assembled aspects of other assembled "no things" that together create a situation with very real effects in the worlds where they emerge. It is this intertwined character that makes a situation best conceived as a singular multiple. It is important to note, however, that as singular multiples situations resist being categorized or identified. For example, although what we call the drug war can be named such, as an intertwined assemblage its diverse aspects can easily be foregrounded so as to evade such identification; thus as we saw, the global militarism aspect can be foregrounded and reconceived as the war on terrorism or defense against communist insurgents, and carceral political economics can be repositioned as being tough on crime. As a result a situation is quite slippery since it never all at once can be fully grasped in its entirety, for built into its very nature is the capacity for its constitutive aspects to be temporarily refigured. Such refiguration can occur "naturally," as it were, since aspects of situations take on different signification as they are represented, experienced, or considered differently. Or this refiguration can be done intentionally and strategically, as certain persons may wish to emphasize one particular "angle" of the aspect over others—such as mandatory minimum prison sentencing as being tough on crime rather than judicial procedures with clear racial and class prejudices.

This fragmented, intertwined nature of the assembled situation, furthermore, always leaves it with interstices of non-cohesion. These interstitial sites disrupt any possibility for an actually existing totality of a situation and therefore, any possibility for thinking or articulating the totality of a situation. It is at these interstices that problematics of a situation likely occur and sites of potentiality can be found, and therefore, from which a demand for political activity emerges.[62] For example, one possible interstice between the state-based surveillance and control and the biopolitical health management aspects of the drug war assemblage is the problem of harm reduction. The drive to manage the normalized health of a working population by controlling what can and cannot be put into a body has increasingly resulted in the institutionalization of harm reduction programs that were once organized by those people who used the drugs themselves. This has shifted what was once a political project of drug users and their allies to a state-funded therapeutic intervention that is now largely out of the hands of drug users and places the latter in the position of docile beings who must normalize or wait until they are able to do so. Additionally, and as I showed in last chapter is the case in Russia, the attempt by both international and national harm reduction organizations to convince governments to accept harm reduction is regularly posed in terms of supporting security and economic development—and in the Russian case, as a way to address the so-called demographic problem. People who use drugs, however, increasingly recognize this institutionalization, and there has been recent user mobilization around the globe to wrest control of harm reduction practices from state-based and -funded institutions. Thus, the transformative possibilities available at this interstitial site has been recognized by user-organized and -run harm reduction groups, some of which by necessity act outside the law; the consequences have been real, including communally run safe injection sites, housing, and health care. I will consider some of these practices as examples of a politics of worldbuilding in the next two chapters.

A situation is not reducible to an issue. If an issue—that point of focus of the contemporary politics of the a priori—is conceived as specific, isolable, rather easily identified and named, and understandable in terms of causes, perpetrators, effects, and victims, then a situation resists such issuefication. The complexity of a situation is the result of its assemblage nature and, as we just saw, is thus constituted by means of its external relations with other assemblages rather than through the internal relations that are said to constitute individual isolates that come to be known as issues. In this sense if a situation is best conceived as a singular multiple, then an issue is conceived as an individualized singularity.[63]

Those who address the drug war begin with the recognition of the complexity of this situation. As mentioned above, because what is called the drug war is really an assemblage of diverse aspects of other assemblages—for example, global militarism, state-based surveillance and control, biopolitical health management, carceral political economics, and national and international inequalities—it cannot simply be addressed as an isolated issue that can be "ended" by any means "internal" to itself. For as an assemblage of the aspects just named, there is no "internal" to address. Rather, to respond politically to the situation of the drug war entails addressing each one of its external relata, which in turn will alter those relata. As a result, a politics of worldbuilding has consequences well beyond the limits of an issue—in fact, it is potentially transformational and perhaps even transgressive in its outcome. Thus, building on the example above of user-organized and -run harm reduction sites, such facilities might need to be run out of illegally occupied buildings, and if successfully done they could challenge notions of, for example, private property and public space. Indeed, such a result has already been accomplished, for example, by artists in various places in eastern Germany, where once illegally squatted buildings used for artistic performance and production have now become accepted artistic spaces for the benefit and enjoyment of local communities and persons. We could ask, how might well-run and -organized user-led harm reduction sites transform locally provided health care, communal living and working, and abandoned private property? In other words, how might they transform worlds, possibilities for being-in-the-world, and the ontological conditions of dwelling? In Chapter 5 we will see one possible answer to this question as it is currently unfolding in Vancouver.

Furthermore, it should be emphasized that no one person, group, institution, history, or power is responsible for a situation. Unlike the logic of issue-based politics, there are no individuals as perpetrators whose arrest and trial would lead to the end of the situation. Neither would the reform of a certain institution. Thus, for example, demilitarizing the police in the United States will not end the drug war situation, and neither will ending Stop and Frisk tactics or disentangling the drug war from the global war on terror. This is because of the complexity of situations—they have a being and life all their own; and while individual persons may get caught up in the complexity of a situation, agency cannot be said to be solely that of the human variety. Like the Dutch boy who thinks he can stop the flood by sticking his finger in one of the holes in the dam while remaining blind to the fact that what is needed is an entirely new dam, so, too, the issue-based politics of the a priori misses the complexity of situations by focusing on individualized singularities. Because of its recognition of this complexity, a politics of worldbuilding addresses situations and strategizes accordingly.

Clearly this conception of situation as laid out thus far resonates in some significant ways with Alain Badiou's conception of situation. In particular, I find his notion of situation as the presentation of multiplicity structured by the count-as-one extremely compelling.[64] By this, if I understand Badiou correctly, he means that a situation is any closed set of multiples that can be counted-as-one by a process that structures the set as situation. He calls this structure the state of the situation. Furthermore, because each element of a set can be restructured, as it were, as another set, neither a set nor its elements can ever be totalized. It is for this reason that Badiou argues there is only multiplicity, and therefore the One is not. Thus, despite my rejection of Badiou's ontological mathematization—it is, as I argued in the Introduction, a foundational practice of metaphysical humanism—it should be clear that the assemblage nature of situations as I outline it here leads us to similar conclusions as that of Badiou in terms of the singular multiplicity of situations.

Despite this similarity, there are significant differences between what I argue for here and Badiou's approach that, I think, ultimately renders my line of argument more germane for social and political theorization, analysis, and practice. This is most clearly seen in the difference that results from his logico-mathematical ontology and my critical hermeneutic approach. For example, in his most recent explication Badiou has replaced the concept of situation with world, which he defines as "an ontologically-closed set—that is a set measured by an inaccessible cardinal—which contains a transcendental *T* and the transcendental indexings of all the multiples on this transcendental. We can thus say that a world is the place in which objects appear. Or that 'world' designates *one* of the logics of appearing."[65] What is significant here, and especially so as it marks a vital difference between Badiou and myself, is his notion of transcendental. The transcendental, according to Badiou, is the logic that structures or orders a world. As he puts it, "The scale of evaluation of appearing, and thus the logic of a world, depends on the singularity of that world itself. What we can say is that in every world such a scale exists, and it is this scale that we call the transcendental."[66] A world, then, comes into existence, maintains that existence, and is recognizable as such because it has a particular and unique logic—or transcendental—that orders it. If for Badiou "being qua being is thought by mathematics," then "appearing, or being-there-in-a-world, is thought by logic."[67] Indeed, as he goes on to put it, appearing is not simply thought by logic, it *is* logic: "'logic' and 'appearing' are one and the same thing."[68]

For Badiou, then, worlds—and remember, worlds have come to replace situations in Badiou's philosophy—and all that appears in them are nothing other than logic. And this logic is not a procedure that a human subject utilizes to understand a world, so argues Badiou, but rather this logic that orders, and fundamentally *is*, worlds "is altogether anterior to every subjective constitution."[69] That is, the logic of worlds is the case regardless of whether any human exists in that or any other world. A world (or situation) for Badiou, then, is the local emplacement of a logical operation that occurs regardless of human existence.[70] This is what he calls the Greater Logic. This is clearly *not* what I intend by a situation (or worlds for that matter); in fact, it is precisely the kind of metaphysical humanist thinking and politics that I am trying to argue against. Indeed, this logico-mathematical rendering of being and worlds is a clear example of a metaphysical humanist projection of the subjectivity of the subject onto being and existence. Placing himself squarely in the ontological tradition that embraces Galileo's claim that "the world is written in a mathematical language,"[71] Badiou projects an essentially human way of grasping what is onto being and worlds such that these latter are conceived as enacting human ways of "thinking" without the necessity of the human. As Heidegger and Arendt might put it, in Badiou's rendering the human becomes alienated from both its being and its worlds by the projection of its own way of being onto the latter, and in so doing loses itself. It is precisely the politics of the a priori that begins from this double movement of projection-loss—whether initiated through a logico-mathematical projection of Badiou's "materialist dialectic" politics or a Moral projection of a priori rights and dignity of human rights politics—that I seek to offer an alternative to in this book.[72]

A situation is not singularly locatable. Because a situation is never isolable and only ever exists as a singular multiple—that is, as always intertwined with other assemblages—a situation is never located. Therefore, a politics of worldbuilding does not focus its attention on locations other than for temporary tactical purposes, but instead maintains a strategic concern for the dispersed, fragmentary, and emergent nature of a situation. Thus, for example, the situation of the drug war is not located in the veins of heroin users crouched under American highway overpasses, and it is not located in the jungles of South America or the borders between the United States and Mexico or the poppy fields of Afghanistan; nor is the drug war located in the substance called heroin but which is actually a range of potentially infinite kinds of beings as opium derivatives get cut with more contaminants every step it moves through the underground commodity chain; nor is the drug war located in American, Russian, or Thai prisons, or in the infectious disease wards of hospitals around the globe. Rather, the drug war emerges—at times but not always—in all these locales and more. Notice, however, that these locales are not always and only caught up in the drug war situation. For example, there are people in prisons and infectious disease wards for reasons unrelated to the drug war situation. Thus, only by attending to and being attuned to each of these locales and their unique, similar, and shared potentialities and emergent actualities of the drug war situation—or what we can call a situation's widely diffused complexity—can the situation be effectively addressed.

This non-locatability and assemblage nature of situations is similar to how Laclau and Mouffe describe their notion of hegemonic formation. They argue that a hegemonic formation is a constituted chain of equivalence created by means of its articulation.[73] Because a hegemonic formation is articulated through antagonistic delimitations of who and what counts as hegemonic over and against its opposed outside, and because this antagonistic delimitation is done in response to a demand that arises in particular historical and political contexts, a hegemonic formation does not rely on pre-known narratives of political belonging, aim, and practice.[74] Such a hegemonic politics is radical because it is not fixed in any a priori conception of what counts as the privileged political subject, organization, or praxis,[75] and it is this radical groundlessness of hegemonic formations that, in my terms, allows for Laclau and Mouffe's radical politics to emerge from the demands of a world and its situations. In other words, a hegemonic formation eschews what I have been calling the politics of the a priori and enacts a politics similar to that of worldbuilding by means of constituting a chain of equivalence out of those political elements that normally would not be allied but become so in antagonistic contrast to an outside other. To a great extent the anti–drug war movement is a hegemonic formation in that it consists of a diverse assemblage of seemingly antagonistic groups and interests—for example, active drug users, right-wing libertarian politicians, public health workers, anarchists, associations of police chiefs, and mothers of those who died of overdose—but despite this diversity they come together politically because they recognize that their worlds have become unbearable as a result of the drug war situation of which they are, each in their own way, a part.

It would be incorrect to say, however, that a hegemonic formation is a politics of worldbuilding in the sense that I intend here. For if I understand Laclau and Mouffe correctly, a hegemonic formation is articulated by a number of political actors in response to conditions that cut across the chains of difference that might otherwise maintain the logic of difference as separation. The key here is that the hegemonic formation is articulated and thus constructed by political actors. When I write of a politics of worldbuilding, on the other hand, I do not intend something articulated by actors, but rather something articulated, as it were, by a world. In this sense, the politics of worldbuilding as a response to a demand made by a worldly situation is similar to how John Dewey wrote of publics responding to a problem they happen to find themselves thrown into.[76] For if a hegemonic formation only comes into being by means of the analysis and articulation of human actors, a situation, in contrast, *already is* in a world prior to any kind of recognition of it by those humans *already caught up in it*. As a result, a politics of worldbuilding arises out of a situation that already is, rather than as an articulated construction meant to create alliances within a hegemonic formation. Thus, unlike the political actors of Laclau and Mouffe who articulate in order to create a hegemonic formation, political actors in my sense begin by disclosing a certain situation in a world that already is, and through this disclosure discover how to organize, strategize, and act. This difference, then, is one between a human-centered politics that begins with a negotiated articulation, and a world-centered politics that begins with the affective recognition of a demand made by a worldly situation. Thus, while I agree with Laclau and Mouffe in that the resultant political movement assembled in response to the demand of a situation would be very similar to a hegemonic formation, the process by which it is constituted would be quite different. This difference between a human-centered and a world-centered politics is vital for moving beyond the politics of the a priori and its overwhelming concern with political subjectivity.

The political ethics, tactics, and strategy of a situation can never be known prior to the moment of its being done. Because every situation is a unique singular multiple, there cannot be one overall political strategy with its accompanying tactics and ethics that can be applied to all situations globally. For this reason analysis is key to any politics of worldbuilding. In the following chapters, and particularly in the Epilogue, I will show how critical hermeneutics as analysis and practice is key to this politics, but for now we can say that through such analysis questions to be considered might be: What is the specific intertwined nature of *this* situation? Is the situation best addressed as a situation or would a kind of political flanking maneuver against its various aspects be more efficient? How would tactics against one aspect of a situation affect other aspects for better or worse from the perspective of the political project? And so on. Answers to such questions reveal, for example, that the drug war in Russia, which has one of the fastest growing HIV rates on the planet, a rate driven by heroin use, and yet where the government, along with police and medical personnel, persecute, imprison, and leave many drug users to die, is more effectively fought—though dangerously so—using illegal and underground tactics. Whereas in Denmark, for example, where a national union of drug users and allied organizations have been able to convince the government to fund and support a range of initiatives, safe consumption facilities being just one, the tactic tends to be engagement with legislators and government and the strategy is shifting toward decriminalization.

But how precisely do such tactics and strategies come about and how and when do individuals realize they must act? Badiou responds that individuals only become (political) subjects by recognizing an event that erupts within the situation they live and then maintaining fidelity to that event—thereby changing both themselves and the situation. In response,

Levi Bryant asks the fundamental question: how and when is it possible for one to recognize such an event, and even if such recognition were possible, why would one want to become fidelious to it considering this would entail loosing one's place in a situation to which one has likely become attached?[77] In other words, what would motivate a person to give up their attachment and comfort in the already-is for the becoming of the unknown? Note that this question is even more pressing when we recognize that even if one's life is quite precarious it is possible, as history has shown, to become something like attached to and comfortable in this precarity.[78] Furthermore, Bryant raises the political question of the extent to which "preparatory work must be done in order to increase the likelihood of events" occurring within a situation to which one can become fidelious. Clearly, any political ontology must be able to address such questions of motivation, action, and change. In the rest of this section, and in the remaining chapters of this book, I will attempt to address just these questions.

Moods are vital to motivating action.[79] People can live for generations in a situation of precarity and desperation and not act to change the situation. It is possible to say that they have become comfortable in or, in Bryant's words, attached to this situation. But sometimes, and often for reasons that are impossible to pinpoint—that is, no event can be named—a particular mood takes over a situation.[80] This mood transforms a precarious situation into an unbearable situation, and makes clear the necessity of action. Because this mood that a situation evokes is always singular, specific, and temporary, the political urge this evocation brings forth must be acted on in a timely manner.

Unfortunately, although situations are always analytically discoverable, they are rarely affectively knowable, and for this reason they often go unnoticed even by those whose lives are most affected by a situation. This is not to say, for example, that African Americans living in some urban areas of the United States do not notice the constant police surveillance and harassment they experience, the disproportional incarceration that has socially and politically "disappeared" at least a generation of its male population, and the resulting lack of educational, financial, and social growth and stability this "disappearing" has brought to their communities. All of this and more is of course noticed, known, and lived every day. What is not normally recognized, what is not normally affectively known, is the situation according to which this form of life, this way of being, is brought about. Misrecognitions occur regularly in politics; in fact, it is perhaps possible to name the history of the issue-based politics of the a priori a history of political misrecognition. In addition to the reasons I have thus far disclosed in this book for this political misrecognition on the part of the politics of the a priori, it is also true that rarely the moment occurs that a situation evokes a mood that so obviously points to itself. But when a situation does evoke such a mood, when a situation evokes an affective demand that indicates the inability to any longer dwell in this situation, then that clarity and the necessity of action overwhelms one's embodied way of being-in-the-world and compels one to act. It is this moment that a politics of worldbuilding must embrace, and it is this moment, I would argue, that is currently being embraced by the anti–drug war movement all around the globe, and which I hope to show in the following chapters.

William Connolly similarly conceives of political action in response to something like what I call situations. For Connolly the fragility of things is at least partially the consequence of the fact that all things are assembled things constituted by what he calls human and nonhuman force fields that at times may become processes of self-organization.[81] Because what he calls the cosmos comprises multiple force fields that only occasionally interact with one another, it is at the intersection of these force fields—similar to the interstitial sites I wrote of above—that opportunities for political activity are most clearly discerned and possibilities for the new are opened. Some examples Connolly provides to illustrate this fragility of things are terrorism, consumption, investment, and health care. But the one he focuses on the most is climate change, which I return to at the end of this chapter when I briefly consider the situation of the anthropocene.

Connolly argues that in assembled worlds political activity is best done by what he calls a pluralist assemblage of cross-state citizen movements.[82] Such a movement would be non-identitarian in that it would be neither grounded in nor led by any "single class, gender, ethnic group, creed, or generation," but rather would be constituted by an assemblage of those persons around the globe whose lives are affected by—what I am calling—a particular situation. This movement would likely be very similar to Laclau and Mouffe's hegemonic formation, with the proviso of the starting point of a world that I emphasized above. This assembled movement would act at multiple sites around the globe at both the micro and macro political levels, and in response to the unique demands of the manifestation of the situation in those sites, in order to address the political demand made on them by the situation at hand. Again, as I will begin to show in the following chapters, this kind of assembled political movement already has come into being and is acting in response to the situation of the drug war.

Such political action in situations often takes the form of experimentation. Such experimentation is a form of ethics that Connolly calls an ethics of cultivation[83] but I will call an ethics of dwelling, as it is a reflective process of working on both oneself *and* the world in which one finds oneself for the purpose of changing both so as to once again dwell. Indeed, experimentation is vital to doing a critical hermeneutics, for once the kind of ungrounding I did in the previous chapters is accomplished, we must experiment or play with, that is, imagine and create alternative ways of being-together as part of a world and across multiple worlds. For not only is hermeneutics as an analytic an ungrounding that simultaneously opens possibilities, but as a political practice it discloses that we must not wait for an event to usher in the new or for a God who will save us.[84] Critical hermeneutics reveals that such kairological politics are blind not only to the potentialities that are already here among us,[85] but also to the creative and difficult experimentation demanded by political action. In the following chapters I will say more about this ethics of dwelling and the political experimentation it has motivated among anti–drug war agonists. For now, however, it is important to realize that this ethics of dwelling that takes the form of experimentation is aimed at transformation and transgression—that is, the transformation and transgression of aspects of the situational assemblage, those persons caught up in the assemblage, and hopefully and eventually the situation as such so as to allow dwelling to be the mode of being for those caught up in the resulting new situation.

A situation cannot be closed, ended, or eliminated; it can only become another situation. This becoming occurs as either transformation or transgression. Transformation is not reform. Reform is the model for issue-based politics of the a priori by which it is conceived that by "solving" the issue through reforming the current state of affairs things, people, or "the world" will be a little better off. The result, however, is that the current state of affairs essentially stays the same and therefore repeats, although in a slightly different form, that which "caused" the issue in the first place. Transformation, on the other hand, alters the current state of affairs such that the situation that had posed a problem no longer exists but has transformed into a new situation. For example, if in the United States political action led to the decriminalization of all drug use, this would essentially result in the ending of one of the primary means by which the carceral political-economic system is realized, and thus would significantly transform that system—and in turn, significantly transform the situation called the drug war into another situation. This transformation would result in a new situation—an entirely new version of the drug war—that would no longer entail the mass incarceration of the populace of the country. This alteration alone would have consequences that would potentially transform the entire state of affairs of the United States—for example, the elimination of one of the primary means by which African American males become incarcerated and thus lose their rights to such things as student loans, voting, and well-paying, steady jobs.

Notice, however, that decriminalization may have wide-ranging transformative effects, but the new situation that would result would still require the description of "drug war." Decriminalization does not necessarily entail the cessation of global military operations ostensibly aimed solely at drug production and trafficking but yet each year manages to kill thousands of persons in no way connected to drug production, trafficking, or use; it does not necessarily entail access to non-contaminated drugs or clean and safe equipment; and it does not necessarily entail the cessation of state-based surveillance and control that while aimed at people who sell or use drugs extends to the population in general. Only when all aspects of what can be called a drug war situation are addressed by means of all of the relata that constitute the assemblage of the situation can a fully transgressive politics be carried out and accomplished.

Transgressive politics, it should be noted, is not a politics of the immoral in that by transgressing "the norm" one has somehow accomplished a political act. Rather, transgression is meant in the geological sense of the creation of a new shoreline after a flood. Thus, just as during and after a flood, river water transgresses its current shoreline and settles at a new point, so, too, the transgressive possibilities of a politics of worldbuilding is the complete overcoming of the current situation and the settling in of an entirely new situation. And just as the exact location of the new shoreline cannot be known until it has settled as the new shoreline, so, too, a new situation cannot be known beforehand, but only after the political transgression has occurred. All that can be known beforehand is that if a politics of worldbuilding is successful, it will result in an entirely new situation, and thus an entirely new world. In this sense, a politics of worldbuilding is a politics of possibility and becoming; it is a politics for bringing about an otherwise.

We cannot know exactly what our worlds would be like if no situation could any longer be called "drug war," but no one can doubt that the complete elimination of everything related to it—the global militarism done in its name, the carceral political economics based up it, the biopolitical health management that normalizes and marginalizes in its name, the state-based surveillance and control done in the name of protection—the complete elimination of all of this, among other things, would most certainly result in something completely otherwise than we know today. A politics of worldbuilding seeks to enact such a transgressive politics and in so doing bring into being something as of yet unknowable but certainly something otherwise.

Situations Abound

A world is structured by multiple situations. As such, any world can potentially make multiple political demands. In order to see how this is so, and how multiple politics can emerge from a world, a critical hermeneutic disclosure of situations becomes necessary. In the previous section I illustrated just such a disclosure. What becomes immediately clear is that while a critical hermeneutics will likely disclose as of now unimaginable situations, it will also disclose situations that are already quite familiar to us but may be more commonly—if incorrectly—referred to as issues. One such "issue" is often called global warming. I would like to end this chapter, then, with a brief discussion of another situation, one that potentially has truly existential implications, for if left unaddressed it could lead to the end of existence as currently unfolded. This is the situation of the anthropocene.

Anthropocene

The anthropocene is the name given to that situation by which humans play a decisive role in what Timothy Morton calls the "'terraforming' of Earth as such."[86] Morton dates the beginning of the anthropocene to April 1784, the date of the patenting of the steam engine by James Watt, and thus the date from which humans became "a geophysical force on a planetary scale."[87] What has become undeniably clear now that we live in the anthropocene is not that humans affect and alter nonhuman being—this has been clear since at least the dawn of agriculture and the domestication of animals—but that nonhuman being affects human being. It is as if Watt's steam engine drew back the curtain, or drilled a hole in the wall, or pumped away the residue that covered over the fact that human and nonhuman being has always been intertwined in the mutuality of being-together.

But the anthropocene has done more than disclose this mutuality of being-together that has always been the case. It has also disrupted the fragility of this mutuality to such a degree that it is as if nonhuman being were pushing back to reclaim its position within the order of things. It is just this imagery that Morton evokes when he conceives of the anthropocene and its primary consequence of global warming as what he calls a hyperobject. The concept of hyperobject is too complex for me to gloss here, but in short it refers "to things that are massively distributed in time and space relative to humans."[88] Morton characterizes hyperobjects by such qualities as viscosity, nonlocality, phasing, and interobjectivity, among others. Thus, for example, hyperobjects are nonlocal because any local manifestation of a hyperobject is not directly the hyperobject, or at least not the totality of the object. A hurricane or a tsunami, then, may be a local manifestation of the hyperobject of global warming, but it is not global warming as such. Here we see how some of the ways Morton conceives of hyperobjects are similar to how I characterized situations above.

The difference, however, is that Morton conceives of these hyperobjects as real objects, just as he does the glass, the book, oxygen, my ears, viruses, and everything else that is. As an object-oriented ontologist Morton holds that everything that is, is a real object, or a unit unto itself that withdraws from other objects as well as itself, and thus can never be fully known or touched by another object. In this sense, global warming may be a hyperobject that was created by human activity in the anthropocene, but now that it is a real object it is, as it were, untouchable. So the question is this: how does conceiving of global warming as a hyperobject—as a real and massive object—help us to act politically to bring about something otherwise? If objects can't touch or influence one another (by definition according to object-oriented ontology, or OOO),[89] except for perhaps in aesthetic ways, then what are we left to do politically when confronted with the hyperobject of global warming? Ultimately and unfortunately, despite his nod to the role of, for example, social policy or his call to rethink and reenact ontological concepts, Morton provides little to answer this question other than intimating that driving a Prius seems helpful, and that we can draw inspiration from certain kinds of art that seem to "get" the existence of hyperobjects. Not to be too flippant, but the reader of Morton, or at least this reader, is left to believe that driving our Prius to the local hip art gallery is the only political action available with a political ontology of hyperobjects. This is not a compelling political project.

Perhaps turning everything into objects, then, is just as much of a dead end as the metaphysical humanist projection of the subjectivity of the subject onto all that is. And in fact, aren't these actually just two versions of the same metaphysical projection? The hyperobject thesis simply inverts the metaphysical humanist projection, by which all that is becomes anthropomorphized, and posits an OOO projection, by which all that is becomes an object. These are two versions of the same story by which all of existence is leveled to the being of one kind of existent. Politically we also get the inverse outcome, which is the expected result when the same projection simply comes from the other direction, as it were. For just as metaphysical humanism has led to the hubris that humans can and should come to know and dominate all that is, the hyperobject thesis seems to leave us, us objects, incapable of having any political effect in our worlds. When we begin from situations, however, we begin from an entirely other ontological starting point, the characteristics of which I have been trying to delineate in this chapter.

So what is the situation of the anthropocene? William Connolly, I suggest, has gone a long way in disclosing this situation. In describing what he calls the fragility of things, Connolly most often provides examples related to climate change, the ocean conveyor system, and a number of other processes caught up in what we could call the situation of the anthropocene. Although he does not put it in these terms, Connolly's descriptions regularly capture the essence of what I am trying to get at in the above characterization of situations. Thus, for example, Connolly's descriptions depict the assembled nature of the situation of the anthropocene such that it is clear that the anthropocene is an assemblage of diverse aspects of other assemblages such as global capitalism, non-regulative legislation, widespread technological advancement and use, consumer practices driven by what we might call the desire industry, an entertainment-media complex that is the primary driver of the desire industry, transportation infrastructure, and population increases and its concomitant patterns of development, migration, food production, income inequality, and settlement, among others. As a result, any political movement hoping to address the demands imposed by the situation of the anthropocene must adopt a strategy that works at both the micro and macro political levels, across multiple sites around the globe, and learn to communicate its tactics, strategy, and aims in terms of a politics of worldbuilding so as to make more clear the ontological and existential imperative such a situation demands of us all.

As with the situation of the drug war, the situation of the anthropocene is not located but rather exists at multiple, diverse, and often transitory sites around the globe (and perhaps beyond) such that political action aimed at any particular location can only be done as one tactic among many that has the entire situation in view. In other words, to do an effective politics of the situation of the anthropocene, localized tactics such as protesting a fracking site, organizing an urban biking infrastructure, altering consumer practices, or lobbying for legislative changes can only be conceptualized, planned, and carried out as part of a more comprehensive and complex understanding of the situation and with aims derived from that understanding.

As I described above in terms of the drug war situation, because of the non-located, widely diffused, complex nature of situations, political action is usually best done at the interstices of assembled aspects since this is where we can find sites of potentiality. Thus, for example, one obvious interstice of the situation of the anthropocene is that of transportation infrastructure and behavior along with consumer desires and practices. The aim here, for example, in the United States, is not simply to provide an infrastructure suited to biking and public transportation, but to alter consumer desires such that purchasing a bike rather than a car, or traveling by light rail rather than car, become default desires and practices and not simply options. A politics of worldbuilding does not rely on so-called good or rational choices, but rather, like all politics, can only succeed through the transformation of affective ways of being-in-the-world. Put another way, a politics of worldbuilding must seek to change habits.

These political possibilities will only arise by means of the experimentation that is central to the ethics of dwelling that motivates and enacts political activity. As noted above, this form of politics as an experimental ethics of dwelling can lead to transformations and transgressions, and thus bring about some otherwise. Thus, to build on the example from the previous paragraph, the realization of an entirely new transportation infrastructure plus the constitution of new consumer desires that mirror and feed off of this infrastructure would certainly result in the transformation of the urban space as well as the being of those persons who would now desire bikes and light rail instead of cars. What the outcome would be is of course unknowable. And clearly this transformation would not be a transgression of the entire situation of the anthropocene. But the transformation would be significant enough that it could possibly open new and as of now unknowable further possibilities not only for continuing to address the situation politically, but also for simply being and becoming otherwise in our worlds. Ultimately, this is one of the key differences between a politics of worldbuilding and the politics of the a priori: while the latter acts as if it already knows what the end should be, and as such closes off all other possibilities while never actually accomplishing what it hopes to accomplish, a politics of worldbuilding acts so as to open as many possibilities that become available from the situations and worlds with which it is intertwined. In other words, a politics of worldbuilding always has as its primary aim the opening of possibilities.

Finding a Way In

The anthropocene, like the drug war, is another situation that partially structures our worlds. Because the anthropocene is not a hyperobject—a massive object unto itself—but instead a singular multiple constituted by diverse aspects of other singular multiples, we can find a way in, as it were, and attempt to act politically in order to change the situation. What I will try to show in the rest of this book is that critical hermeneutics as an analytic method (intellectually as well as politically) helps "find a way in" so that politics can begin. Part of what a critical hermeneutics can do as a political analytic is to experimentally think alternative concepts. This conceptualization begins in those worlds and their situations that make demands on us, and for this reason I will return to the situation of the drug war and the way anti–drug war agonists are responding to this demand. What becomes clear from their response is that this conceptualization cannot take the form of a reclaiming such that, for example, we find a way to reclaim "dignity" as "our own" and turn it into a usable concept. Rather, this conceptualization takes the form of moving into clearings—the sites of potentialities—that emerge in the interstices of the drug war situation. Once there, in the clearings, we can begin to experiment with new political-moral concepts that may hold up to the burden of a worldly political demand. These new concepts, then, become temporary tools for helping us begin to act, to open further possibilities, and thus to help usher in some as of yet unknowable otherwise.

CHAPTER 4

An Ethics of Dwelling

Simon Critchley writes that our current moment of widespread political disappointment is inextricably linked to the motivational deficit at the heart of liberal democracy.[1] Critchley thinks of this motivational deficit primarily in terms of a lack of what he calls "a motivating, empowering conception of ethics."[2] While I agree entirely with his diagnosis, I have some hesitation regarding his response. My hesitation stems from a concern that a call for "a motivating, empowering conception of ethics" will inevitably repeat the politics of the a priori, and particularly so when articulated, as Critchley does, in terms of ethics as "a self [deciding] to pledge itself to some conception of the good."[3] For such an ethics, as I will demonstrate in the first part of this chapter, has a tendency, despite claims otherwise, to repeat the dominant political-moral discourses of our current ontological tradition, the result of which is a politics that enacts the limiting conditions of repetition and totality.

Therefore, in this chapter I attempt to articulate an ethics that politically motivates without either beginning from the subjectivity of the subject or necessitating anything like a conception of the good. Rather, the ethics of dwelling that I will argue for in this chapter responds to a demand that emerges from a world, and most particularly a situation in that world that has become unbearable. In this sense my formulation has much in common with Critchley's formulation of the link between ethics and politics. The difference, so it seems to me, is Critchley's reliance on the formation of a political subject as the first step of politics, a subject primarily characterized in terms of a Levinasian notion of infinite responsibility. Such a notion of ethics that relies on a particular kind of political subject—and as I will argue further in the next chapter, this is particularly so for one characterized by Levinasian responsibility—leads Critchley back to the individualized, totalized, and conservatively repetitive politics of the a priori. On the other hand, the ethics of dwelling I delineate in this chapter opens possibilities for building new worlds because it is an ethics that begins not with a predefined political subject, but rather with a demand made by a broken-down world that demands change.

This is so because an ethics of dwelling as the motivation for a politics of worldbuilding begins not with a conception of a good, or with a demand for a right, or with the enactment of responsibility for an Other, all of which tend to be conceived in terms of already-known capacities and aims that preexist any particular situation and world. Rather, an ethics of dwelling is the response to an existential imperative emerging from a world that has become unbearable as a result of a very particular situation that has led to the breakdown of this world.[4] In other words, this is an ethics as motivation for political activity that responds to the demand of a world in which it is no longer possible to dwell. This is an ethics that can never be known prior to the breakdown of a world and the demand that emerges from it, and thus an ethics that is only discoverable in the process of being in that particular world. It is for this reason that perhaps anthropology as a critical hermeneutics is perfectly situated to disclose and make understandable such an ethics and its emergence.

Anthropology of Morality and Ethics

In the last decade or so the analysis of morality and ethics has become central to the work of many anthropologists. In particular there have been a growing number of anthropologists who argue that this study needs to be made explicit through a programmatic or theoretically analytic questioning of what counts as morality and ethics. In doing so these anthropologists have initiated a dialogue with philosophers who have been engaged in the question concerning morality and ethics for much longer than have anthropologists. While it remains unclear to what extent philosophers are aware of this anthropological work, it should be noted that these anthropologists have made, so I would argue, at least three significant contributions to the ongoing question concerning morality and ethics: first, the avoidance of simply equating morality or ethics with normative social behavior;[5] second, the avoidance of this consideration solely through the lens of our own moral assumptions, traditions, and concepts;[6] and third, the avoidance of falling into moralizing analysis motivated by the urge, for example, to reveal injustices.[7]

This is an approach to the study of moralities and ethics that takes them seriously as social phenomena, and recognizes them not as distal aspects of primary social practices such as politics or religion but as distinct, yet intertwined, significant factors in shaping these. Perhaps what is most significant about this approach is the possibility it allows for questioning and rethinking some of the most basic assumptions and concepts generally associated with morality. For a critical anthropological study of moralities is perfectly situated not only to disclose the genealogy of moral concepts and reveal their potentially (not so) hidden political-economic implications, but also to offer new concepts that better articulate the moral experiences of actual persons in their worlds.

In the rest of this chapter I will do just this, in terms of rethinking the ethical motivation of political activity. This will be done in two parts. First, I provide a critical reading of one of the most cited contributions to the anthropological study of moralities and ethics—the ordinary ethics approach—and reveal that far from moving this study forward, the ordinary ethics approach actually negates at least two of the three contributions listed above, and in so doing reproduces the kind of a priori and transcendental moral discursive tradition it claims to counter. I have chosen the ordinary ethics approach for this critical reading not because it is unique in the repetition of this moral discourse—indeed such metaphysical humanist renderings of morality and ethics are increasingly common in anthropology—but rather because it is the most clearly articulated metaphysical humanist approach in the contemporary anthropological study of moralities and ethics. Furthermore, because anthropologists increasingly cite the ordinary ethics approach as an authoritative anthropological rendering of moral and ethical being-in-the-world, ordinary ethics and other similarly metaphysical humanist approaches in the discipline threaten anthropology with a deep conservatism that may not be initially obvious. When we consider this reading of ordinary ethics alongside Critchley's call for a new ethics by which a "self" pledges "itself to some conception of the good," we can begin to see the danger of beginning politics with an a priori notion of the ethical subject.

In the second part of the chapter I provide an ethnographic example of anti–drug war political activity that shows how a critical hermeneutics provides a framework that does not simply equate moralities/ethics[8] with everyday social life or with metaphysical humanist assumptions of what defines an a priori "Moral" subject. Rather, a critical hermeneutics allows us to trace the emergence of moralities and ethical demands from a world and its situations. In so doing, a critical hermeneutics recognizes that although many people today may utilize the moral concepts of metaphysical humanism in their ordinary speech and narratives, and this is particularly true for political-moral concepts such as rights and dignity, ethical imperatives often exceed that which is intended or meant by these concepts and thus considers them as the beginning of analysis rather than its end. In this way, a critical hermeneutics seeks to counter the deep and limiting moralism that is the result of the fulfillment of our ontological tradition and has to a great extent saturated much of our social, analytic, and political lives. The result of this critical hermeneutics, I will argue, is the conceptualization of an ethics of dwelling that can reinvigorate the motivational link between ethics and politics.

Ordinary Ethics

The so-called ordinary ethics approach has recently proven appealing to a number of anthropologists addressing moralities/ethics. What is likely most attractive to anthropologists about this approach is the claim that ethics is "intrinsic to action."[9] This is perhaps expressed most elegantly by Veena Das when she writes that the ordinary ethics approach seeks "a shift in perspective from thinking of ethics as made up of judgments we arrive at when we stand away from our ordinary practices to that of thinking of the ethical as a dimension of everyday life in which we are not aspiring to escape the ordinary but rather to descend into it as a way of becoming moral subjects."[10] This argument of the immanence of morality/ethics to everyday life, however, was already one of the key contributions several anthropological studies of moralities and ethics made prior to ordinary ethics arriving on the scene.[11] Therefore, it would simply be incorrect to claim that the ordinary ethics approach has a monopoly on—or was even the first anthropological articulation of—the notion that the ethical is a dimension of everyday life. What is intended by this immanence, however, differs significantly between these other approaches and ordinary ethics, and drawing out this distinction is one of the central concerns of this chapter. In order to do this, we must first be clear about the approach ordinary ethics offers.

Unlike other trends in the social sciences and humanities that emphasize the ordinary—most commonly in terms of affect—the ordinary ethics approach finds its model and influence in ordinary language philosophy. With its roots in the writings of both Wittgenstein and J. L. Austin (despite their clear differences), ordinary language philosophy, broadly characterized, claims that philosophical problems tend to emerge out of "the bewitchment of our intelligence by means of language," and that a turn to ordinary everyday language will clear away the distorted misunderstandings ushered in by abstract concepts.[12] Furthermore, ordinary language should not be thought of in terms of stating truths about the world, but is better thought in terms of how words are used, what they do, and how this is a result of agreement in forms of life rather than structure, knowledge, or belief.

Michael Lambek has described ordinary ethics as assuming that we "find the wellsprings of ethical insight deeply embedded in the categories and functions of language and ways of speaking, in the commonsense ways we distinguish among various kinds of actors or characters, kinds of acts and manners of acting; in specific nouns and adjectives, verbs and adverbs, or adverbial phrases, respectively; thus, in the shared criteria we use to make ourselves intelligible to one another, in 'what we say when.'"[13] As a result, this "implies an ethics that is relatively tacit, grounded in agreement rather than rule, in practice rather than knowledge or belief, and happening without calling undue attention to itself."[14] Only in moments of breach, contestation, social and ethical upheaval, or abstraction, Lambek continues, does this everydayness of ethics become explicit.

So far so good. Other than the differences that emerge due to our different influences—ordinary language philosophy for Lambek and phenomenological hermeneutics for myself—this is more or less how I have described the distinction between what I call embodied morality (Lambek's tacit ethics) and ethics (his explicit ethics).[15] But these differences are essential and my concern is straightforward: it seems to me that a close reading of the two primary advocates of ordinary ethics—Michael Lambek and Veena Das—reveals that the adoption of an ordinary language model relies on the assumptions of the very transcendental moral philosophies—particularly that of Kantianism—ordinary ethicists seek to overcome.

But how is this so? Isn't the ordinary language model meant to help us descend into the ordinary and away from that transcendental realm of morality of which philosophers have supposedly been so concerned? And doesn't Lambek go out of his way to emphasize that ordinary ethics has deep similarities with Aristotelian ethics, in particular with the Aristotelian notions of activity, practice, and judgment,[16] so as to move us away from the transcendental realm of rules and obligation associated with Durkheimianism and Kantianism? Indeed he does, but this alliance with Aristotle is primarily meant to initiate the descent into the ordinary, to get us to move away from thinking of ethics as either a transcendental realm or a separated sphere of everyday life. That is to say, the alliance with Aristotle is meant to help us *locate* ethics, not to help us recognize it. In fact, Lambek opens his chapter in the *Ordinary Ethics* collection by revealing just this when he asks, "Where is the ethical located?"[17] The answer is, "It is intrinsic to action." But what we are never told is how to recognize this intrinsic ethics. It is one thing to claim that ethics is located in the everyday—something that is more or less a truism among those anthropologists who had already been doing explicit studies of moralities/ethics—but it is another thing to provide the analytic toolkit for recognizing those aspects, moments, events, qualities, or what have you that can be recognized as moral or ethical. It is precisely the latter that the ordinary ethics approach does not offer.[18] As a result we are left to draw at least one and possibly two conclusions: first, ethics has been dissolved into the social, that is, all social activity, behavior, thought, speech, et cetera, is ethical through and through; and second, there is no need to tell the reader how to recognize ethics because she already "knows" what it is, that is, ethics is so obvious that it is redundant to have to spell it out.

Now Lambek already tells us he is doing the first, so I will begin there before turning to the second and much more troubling conclusion possibly drawn. Lambek writes, "I hope I have shown that there is no great methodological danger in dissolving the ethical into the social once the social is conceived as (Aristotelian) activity, practice, and judgment rather than (Kantian/Durkheimian) rule or obligation."[19] He writes this in response to those anthropologists who in the last decade have been arguing that in order for there to be an anthropological study of moralities/ethics there must be some way of distinguishing them from social activity in general while at the same time not turning them over to some supposed transcendental realm.[20] But Lambek does not tell us the advantage of "dissolving the ethical into the social." What is gained methodologically or analytically?

It would seem that by "dissolving the ethical into the social" all Lambek is really doing is exchanging one concept for another, replacing "social" with "ethical." In so doing, he performs a metaphysical humanist projection of the subjectivity of the subject onto the worldliness of the social. For not unlike Durkheim's notion of collective consciousness, Lambek's equation of the social with the ethical renders a world understandable only in subjectivist and totalized terms. By "dissolving the ethical into the social," then, Lambek has rendered worlds just another version of the metaphysical humanist a priori assumption of the human subject.

This metaphysical humanist projection, however, is misrecognized and instead labeled Aristotelian. But this so-called Aristotelian move doesn't so much solve the problem of how to study moralities/ethics anthropologically as much as reestablish the problem in other terms. This is not simply the problem of the projection of metaphysical humanist assumptions onto a world, but analytically it poses the problem of how we might ever recognize the emergence of an ethical demand beyond a rather superficial and conservative equivalence of ethics with normative social behavior. For if social equals ethical, we remain at the same impasse of how, if at all, such analysis can be done to identify which aspects or moments of the social might *count* as ethical or moral.

And we can see how "dissolving the ethical into the social" leads to analytic confusion. Consider the various ways Lambek describes ethics in either the introduction or his contributing chapter to the volume *Ordinary Ethics*: ethics is "intrinsic to action"; it is "a property of speech and action"; "we locate the ethical in the conjunction or movement between explicit local pronouncements and implicit local practices and circumstances"; "we use *ethics* as a cover term for recognizing the complexity and perhaps inconsistency of human action and intention"; "it is preferable to see the ethical as a modality of social action or of being in the world than as a modular component of society or mind"; "ethics is a dimension, feature, quality, or entailment of action (acts and utterances)."[21] Although it may be possible to argue that "intrinsic," "property," and "quality" are more or less the same —or at least close enough—these are radically different than, and perhaps even contradictory to, the notion of "entailment," which is a concept of logical consequence as opposed to the immanent nature suggested by "intrinsic" or "property." And each of these is significantly different from ethics, for example, as a "cover term" for complexity and inconsistency.

Ultimately Lambek's analytic inconsistency leads him to provide a list of possible matters to which the study of ordinary ethics might give attention. I will give his list in full:

> The indexical qualities of language; the entailments of speaking, speech acts, and ritual performances; the establishment and recognition of criteria as well as the angst, anomie, vertigo, and, possibly, freedom incurred in their failure or absence; the means of attribution and acknowledgment—public and private, tacit and explicit—of intention, responsibility, and reasons for action; the exercise of practical judgment; the forms of sustained attention and labor subsumed under the concept or practice of "care"; the virtues embedded in or constitutive of any given set of cultural practices and of local depictions of character; the socialization or cultivation of ethical persons; and the confrontation with paradox, chiasm, guilt, rupture, otherness, violence, the intractable, destiny, and evil.[22]

And, as he puts it, "among others." But one wonders, is there anything left to be among these others? My concern here is not to be nitpicky, but to ask very honestly, what is the point of "dissolving the ethical into the social" if all it does is further confuse any possible way of analytically discerning what counts as ethics/moralities while at the same time projecting a limiting and conservative ontological foundation onto our worlds? In terms of the larger concerns of this chapter and book, such analytic ambiguity would make it nearly impossible to understand the motivational link between ethics and politics in any way other than as a repetition of the normative status quo articulated in the limiting metaphysical humanist concepts such as rights, dignity, and responsibility. In fact, as we are about to see, these are precisely the kinds of concepts that are central to ordinary ethics.

My suspicion, therefore, is that the confusion and ambiguity that arises because of this ontological projection of ordinary ethics is elided by this approach's unspoken assumption: ordinary ethics only needs to locate ethics because we *already* know how to recognize it. This is the second conclusion a close reading of ordinary ethics suggests. For by equating ordinary ethics with the social, there is a kind of wink and nod going on, a deferment of the assumed only hinted at through the occasional usage of highly specific concepts that are absolutely central to the political and moral aspects of the metaphysical humanist ontological tradition—whether it's Veena Das[23] relying on concepts like self-respect and dignity, or feeling obliged to address the concept of evil; or Lambek's[24] claim that the people he encountered during research regularly attempt "to do what they think *right or good*," and that "they have acted largely from a sense of their own *dignity*; they have refused positions or attributions of *indignity*, and they have treated, or understood that they *ought to* treat, others as bearing *dignity* of their own." If the embedded categories and tacit agreements of ordinary language all around the globe just happen to be that of Kantian morality, then that is a happy coincidence for Kant. But I suspect what we have here is not Kant proven right by ethnographic research, but rather the descent of Kantianism into the ordinary, or the projection of metaphysical humanism onto our worlds, by means of the built-in moral, political, and ontological assumptions of this form of anthropological analysis. In this sense, it might be possible to call ordinary ethics by the confused neologism of Aristotelian Kantianism.

It is important to recall Talal Asad's critique of Clifford Geertz's definition of religion. According to Asad, Geertz's definition of religion only makes sense within a larger Christian history, and Geertz's claim that religion is a system of symbolic meanings "is a modern, privatized Christian one."[25] In other words, what Geertz did is more or less reproduce in academic form the historically specific Christian self-image. Similarly, ordinary ethicists appear to be reproducing some of the most basic moves of Kantian morality, moves that have today largely become the dominant way of considering and articulating morality and are central to metaphysical humanism. For Kant the categorical imperative provides the procedural formula for determining whether a particular maxim can count as a universal moral law. This procedural formula and the ability to determine the universality of a maxim is available to all humans only because they are a priori rational and legislative beings. Thus, the capacity to be moral beings is transcendental—not in the sense of appealing to a separate realm, but in the sense of being foundational to what it is to be human (this is the Kantian meaning of transcendental). Our capacity to be moral, in other words, is intrinsic to our foundations as particular kinds of subjects. The characteristics and capacities of this subject, including its capacity as a moral/ethical being, are considered to be a priori—that is, existing prior to any engagement with, activity in, or for that matter being in a world at all. Similarly, just as Kant claims that all humans are moral beings because of the legislative capacities made possible because of the categories of Reason that all humans have innately as humans, so, too, the ordinary ethicists claim that "the wellspring of ethical insight [is] deeply embedded in the categories and functions of language and ways of speaking,"[26] or that "grammar" provides the "criteria" for being and acting in the ordinary world.[27]

Ordinary ethics, then, is beginning to look quite similar to Kantian morality. Both claim that ethics/morality are possible because of a transcendental (that is, a pre-worldly defining and foundational) condition of humanness—Reason for Kant, language for the ordinary ethicists; and both claim that this a priori humanness provides the procedural formula or mechanism for enacting this innate capacity to be moral/ethical—the categorical imperative for Kant, criteria or grammar for Lambek and Das; and finally, Kantianism and ordinary ethics share the same moral concepts—right, good, ought, respect, dignity—to describe the motivations for and results of acting morally/ethically. The primary difference, then, seems to lie in that Kant, unlike ordinary ethicists, did not claim that all social life is moral; however, since Durkheim eventually more or less transformed Kantian morality into Durkheimian sociology by projecting the subjectivity of the human onto the totality of society, and in so doing came to equate the social with the moral, this move was already made for the ordinary ethicists.

I have been arguing that ordinary ethicists provide us with an approach for locating ethics but not for recognizing it. This is so, I have tried to show, because there is a built-in assumption to the ordinary ethics approach that "we already know" what ethics/morality is and so there is no need to provide an analytic for recognizing what counts as morality/ethics in any particular situation. But as I have also tried to show, this results in reproducing the dominant moral discourse of our ontological tradition even if the claim is otherwise. However, this seems to me to pass up on the great possibility an anthropological study of moralities and ethics provides—that is, the possibility to reconceive moral concepts by means of anthropological research and analysis; to consider not how the people we study act good or rightly, but rather to ask if good and rightly are the most appropriate concepts for articulating what these people are saying and doing. And if people use the words *good* and *right*, we might be better off asking why these words were used, in what contexts, and to what ends, rather than simply assume that they reflect categories embedded in language or are a result of some tacit agreement. In the rest of this chapter I will offer an alternative anthropological and critical hermeneutic analysis to illustrate how such an analysis need not result in the repetition of the dominant moral discourse of our ontological tradition. In so doing, I hope to show how such an analysis can rejuvenate the motivational link between ethics and politics without falling back on the political-moral bannisters of an ontological tradition that has become exhausted.

Interlude

What might a critical anthropological study of moralities/ethics look like if it did not rely on the moral concepts and assumptions of our ontological tradition? One possible reply to this question would be that we limit our analysis to that which emerges from a world rather than add value to it by means of moral concepts (e.g., right or dignity) that are assumed to preexist that world. This does not mean that concepts in general should be completely eschewed. Rather, I suggest, we find and create concepts that articulate the essential intertwining that constitutes being-in-a-world.

In order to show how this might be done, in the next section I consider the ethical motivations for politically acting of some of the anti–drug war agonists I have come to know. In particular, I hope to show how the analysis of a contemporary activity that is perhaps the example par excellence of moralistic metaphysical humanism—that is, political activism[28]—can be considered in such a way that avoids analysis by means of the very same concepts and assumptions articulated by those about whom we write, as well as avoids the reproduction of our inherited moral discourse and ontological tradition. Such an example works well as a critical response to ordinary ethics because it reveals several weaknesses of the latter's position. First, the example makes clear that even when our informants use moral concepts that are very familiar to us as many anti–drug war agonists certainly do, and Lambek claims his informants regularly do—words such as *rights* and *dignity*—our analysis remains rather superficial if we take these articulations at face value and as simply reflecting embedded categories and tacit agreements for reproducing the social status quo. This is so because, second, although a Wittgensteinian perspective certainly takes account of the historicity of language, the assumption of so-called embedded categories and tacit agreements adopted by ordinary ethicists seems to ignore the fact that much of our everyday articulations are to various degrees influenced by diverse institutions and histories of power that have significantly shaped and limited the available language for articulating what has come to count as morality/ethics in our worlds; in other words, ordinary ethics seems to ignore that the habitus of language has a history that is intimately (but not entirely) intertwined with a history of power, as we saw in Chapter 1. Third, and as a result, it behooves us to consider that when our informants use a familiar moral concept it may be because it is the only concept historically available to try to articulate something about being-in-the-world that exceeds what it is that concept has come to represent, indicate, or mean; and finally, as such, we may recognize this concept as a marker of the problematic of morality/ethics—a place from which our analysis can begin—but not as the end or aim of morality, let alone the aim of politics. It is to such an analysis that I will now turn.

Anti–Drug War Political Activity

The war on drugs was first declared by Richard Nixon, and since the early 1980s it has become a highly militarized, punitive, expensive international "war on people," as many anti–drug war agonists put it, waged to some extent by nearly every country on the globe. It is difficult to conclude that the drug war has been anything but a disastrous failure no matter how one looks at it. From the mass incarceration of a significant proportion of a generation of African American men in the United States, to the street battles, assassinations, and "collateral damage" that has led to over one hundred thousand deaths in Mexico since 2006, to the torturous rehabilitation conditions found throughout Russia, to the extrajudicial killings in 2003 of at least 2,275 suspected drug "offenders" in Thailand by the military and police, to the preventable health risks users and nonusers are exposed to everywhere as the result of stigmatization and lack of harm reduction programs, the drug war seemingly has resulted in little more than the death, suffering, and stigmatization of millions of users and nonusers alike. Meanwhile, drug cartels continue to accumulate wealth and power that in some instances far surpasses that of sovereign nations, and states increasingly tighten security and surveillance that affect the lives of entire populations.[29]

It is precisely this situation against which anti–drug war agonists around the globe are mobilizing. This political movement is carried out at all levels and in all corners of the globe. From international drug policy reform organizations based in such places as New York and London, to regional and national level policy reform organizations based in nearly every North and South American, European, and Asian country, to drug user unions actively mobilizing in countries on every continent and networked through an international users union based in London, the anti–drug war movement is today perhaps the most globally distributed and well-organized political movement. Like nearly every political movement on the contemporary political scene, the anti–drug war movement regularly mixes moral language with its political agenda, and in this sense it could be seen as an example of the political moralism that Wendy Brown[30] argues characterizes contemporary politics. Thus, dignity, rights, respect, and justice are some of the moral key words that members of this movement will regularly invoke.

If we followed the ordinary ethics approach we would be left only to consider how these moral key words are, or reflect, or indicate the embedded categories and/or tacit agreements of ordinary language and, so it would seem, disregard the historical processes and configurations by which possible moral and political utterances have become limited to these and similar key concepts.[31] In Chapter 1 I provided just such an analysis. In this chapter I begin from what we learned in that chapter of the limitations on possible moral and political utterances and carry out a critical hermeneutics by which I seek to disclose an ethical imperative that exceeds the limits of the currently available moral and political language. This disclosure will reveal three significant features of the motivational link between ethics and politics: first, by disclosing this ethical imperative that exceeds possible articulation, I also disclose the transformational possibilities of anti–drug war politics; this is so because, second, this ethical imperative and the transformational politics it engenders can only be considered as emerging from a world that has become unbearable;[32] and third, this emergence is revealed by the very fact of not relying on traditional moral concepts in our analysis. As I hope to make clear, this emergence of ethical imperatives from a world are recognizable because they are first and foremost central to our embodied and affective way of being-in-the-world. That is to say, in what follows I show that ethical imperatives or demands become recognizable not because of their place in language, but because they are responses to singular and particular ways of being, and those situations that either allow or disrupt our ability to dwell in a world.

Dignity

While interviewing a regional director of one of the most influential international drug policy reform organizations, I was told that one of the goals of the organization, as well as her personal view on the matter, is that all drug users should be treated with dignity. Indeed this was not surprising, as dignity is a moral concept regularly used by anti–drug war political agonists in their struggle against prohibition and the negative effects of what they call "a war on people"—drug users and non–drug users alike. I asked her what she meant by "dignity" and she replied:

> Well, I mean our health policies, our criminal justice policies. None of them really treats an individual who is struggling with drugs, whether it's drug possession, drug use, drug selling, with dignity. They don't recognize the fact that an individual's life may have been challenging and that their access to what we would see as normal health care or medication options was limited. Or their job prospects were very lim-

> ited, and so the decisions that they've had to make, that have brought them to this place in their life, may not be decisions that we think are good, but maybe the best decision out of a range of decisions and options that were available at the time those decisions were made. And, I think a lot of the local health-care collaboratives that have sprung up over the last couple of decades like syringe exchange programs and things like that, are some of the only places where there actually is dignity for people who are using drugs and who are struggling in life, whether it's with drug use or life.

It seems, then, that according to this leading advocate of drug policy reform, dignity is not about an inherent essence or capacity of the natural human, as it is so often glossed in human rights discourse.[33] Rather, dignity here is primarily conceived as the outcome of a particular social configuration of non-prohibitionist policies and services that begin not with judgment but with quality care and an understanding of how certain life trajectories may provide limited possibilities for being-in-the-world. In fact, in the director's utterance she locates dignity only once and it is not in or on or as a part of an individual person, but rather in a socio-politically configured space—local health-care collaboratives. It is in particularly assembled and situated worlds of certain practices, policies, ideas, and aims "where there actually is dignity for people." When persons become a part of such assemblages they, too, take on such dignity not because it was a latent aspect of their natural essence, but because this particular assemblage provides certain conditions within which they can dwell. As a result, and as will become clear below, new possibilities arise for them that may allow them to become something that previously would not have been possible. It is this being-at-home in a world and the openness to possibilities that this form of being allows that the director articulates when she uses the word "dignity" but which I will refer to as dwelling.[34]

In the rest of this section I will try to show that what this director refers to as "dignity" may in fact be better conceived as dwelling, and that any analysis of moralities/ethics is most productive when it does not assume that we already know how to recognize these, as I argued above ordinary ethics must assume. Rather, we may be analytically better off accepting that although people often use the moral concepts of dominant moral discourses, they may use them to indicate an ethical imperative that exceeds that which the former can articulate.

Is this, after all, really surprising? Is it unreasonable to consider the possibility that a very particular set of moral concepts that have a very particular history would not entirely or even adequately cover the range of possible moral/ethical concerns, problems, anxieties, or ways of being-in-the-world? The ordinary ethics approach and its reliance on ordinary language philosophy seems ill suited to respond to this all too human likelihood; for although ordinary language philosophy recognizes the sociohistorical situatedness of everyday language use, it does not provide the analytic tools for dealing with the implications of this historicity. This is so because both ordinary language philosophy and ordinary ethics seem to have a kind of literalness built into its perspective such that a word or a criterion or an agreement can only indicate or point to or mean itself. But the director's use of dignity in this utterance clearly seems to be intending some other state of affairs that exceeds what the "ordinary" or dominant use of the word *dignity* would entail. Her use of dignity seems to be pointing to a moral aim that is not covered under the ordinary use of the concept, but she uses it nevertheless.

Perhaps this is so because there is not yet another moral concept available for her to use. It is the gap of this not-yet that a critical hermeneutics attempts to fill. For as I explained in the Introduction, a fundamental assumption of hermeneutic analysis is that existence—human and otherwise—is always other to itself and, as such, constantly engaged in an existentially responsive process in the attempt to become that which it never is, a process that creates gaps of being that can never be filled. Because of this assumption, a critical hermeneutics cannot take concepts to literally mean what they are "supposed" to mean, but rather by doing analysis as a form of the phenomenological method of the epoché a critical hermeneutics asks what the use of the concept points us toward.[35] In so doing, a central task of critical hermeneutics is to offer possibilities for thinking, doing, and being morally and politically otherwise, rather than reproducing the moral vocabulary that no longer clearly resonates with what it is like to be-in-a-world today.

But the director did use the word *dignity*, and when I pushed her a little bit on just this point she responded that she is trying to talk "about the way the social context has impacted this individual's life and how that all goes together to create the current circumstances. Regardless of what those current circumstances are, everyone should be treated with dignity." Here again we see that in response to my slight pushing she more or less repeats—in a much abbreviated form—what she had told me above, but this time seems to put more emphasis on the dignity of individuals rather than how singular assemblages are places of "dignity." It is in the anthropologist's push for clarification, I suggest, in the forced reflection on the use of language, that the director returns to the dominant use of dignity as that which is a characteristic of individuals—that individuals should be treated as dignified beings. In this reflection, return, and reliance on a dominant moral discourse the director shifts her articulation of "dignity" from that of a description of an assembled world, as a part of which one can dwell, to that of the dominant notion of an adjectival being standing over and against "the world" and already pre-known in its moral totality. This shift is not surprising, since our contemporary dominant political-moral discourses—those that utilize the language of rights, dignity, responsibility, good, evil, and so on—begin from the ontological condition of a priori totalized subjects standing over and against "the world" they happen to live in, and stand there as the basis and source of a morality that they, in turn, project onto that world.

Ethics of Dwelling, New York

The police in New York City already "know" the being-in-the-world of a young black man when they (not so) randomly stop and frisk him on the street. Stop and Frisk has been a key police tactic in the war on drugs used in New York. In 2012, for example, 532,911 individuals were stopped and frisked in New York City, 55 percent of whom were African American and 32 percent of whom were Latino. Perhaps most disturbing about this form of surveillance is that 89 percent of all of those stopped and frisked in 2012 were deemed "innocent"—that is, the search turned up nothing. The highest number of those arrested (more than five thousand) were taken in for possessing personal use quantities of marijuana, which under New York City law is not an offence unless it is shown in public, which is exactly what it is when a police officer asks you to empty your pockets. Overwhelmingly those stopped, frisked, and arrested are young African American and Latino men, and this tactic is predominantly carried out in the neighborhoods where these men live.[36] It has created a situation in which one's neighborhood, one's street, one's own front stoop is no longer a place where one can dwell. It is just this inability to dwell in their world that has led many African American and Latin American people in New York City who do and do not use drugs to mobilize politically against this and other tactics of the war on drugs.

Consider, for example, Terrance, who is a fifty-year-old African American man from the Bronx, a former crack user who has been incarcerated twice, and now as a leader of the city's users union—VOCAL—regularly meets with New York State and City politicians and officials in the attempt to end prohibitionist laws and policies. Terrance once told me:

> I kind of think that what really put me, or what really motivated me was, uhm, was seeing the harassment that, you know, people in our community are going through on a daily basis trying to struggle, trying to make ends meet, you know. I mean, it's not fair that you would come to my community, and you don't live there and you can tell me where I can stand, you can tell me that because I live here I can't stand in front of my building, I can't stand on this corner, I can't congregate with individuals in my social setting in front of my building. You know, I'm trespassing in my own neighborhood. Come on! You know, then uhm, and all these unnecessary, all these arrests that were taking place that were just, I can't even find the words to describe it, you know what I'm saying, but it was unorthodox, you know, to a point where if I'm coming out of my building, like I been many times, and stopped and frisked because I'm a person of color and I don't have my sneakers tied or I'm wearing, you know, or I have clothes on that are related to gangsters or whatever, which are the clothings that a lot of people in the neighborhood wear, you know, and I'm going to work and I'm still being stopped. And I got my bag and everything, my ID is out, you know, come on. You're not giving me no freedom to walk in my own neighborhood, but if I was in another neighborhood, another color, you wouldn't be stopping me. So why am I, at this point right here, being profiled? So, profiling was something that really irritated me . . . So that was my motivation for, you know, starting to come to VOCAL and getting involved.

The director of the drug policy organization might characterize the situation Terrance describes as one in which Terrance and his neighbors are treated without dignity. Those who protest against Stop and Frisk policies in front of City Hall often hold signs that call for justice. But Terrance finds no use for what Hannah Arendt called "bannisters" to articulate the breakdown that motivates him to struggle politically against the drug war. Rather for Terrance it all comes down to the fact that the drug war situation has rendered him a stranger in his world, a person who in his total being is assumed from the beginning to be untrustworthy, dangerous, potential evil waiting to manifest. Terrance's motivation for becoming and remaining politically active is not moral outrage erupting from an internal sense of dignity, but is better considered, I suggest, as a moral breakdown[37] that stems from the fact that the drug war situation has resulted in him experiencing himself as if "I'm trespassing in my own neighborhood."

This moral breakdown, however, is not simply about him and his neighbors not being able to live normally and go about their everyday lives, although it is also about that. Rather, this unbearableness points to a deeper and more existential and ontological demand to be in their worlds in a certain way. For not only is Terrance unable to live the everyday in his world, neither can he dwell in his world. This is an important distinction for the purpose of this chapter as it provides a line of flight along which we can reconceive morality/ethics as well as politics. For dwelling is not simply being able to live one's everydayness. Humans have incredible adaptability to all kinds of conditions in which they can live. The innumerable stories of mundane everydayness lived out in extreme contexts of poverty or war attest to this. In contrast, to dwell is to be-in-the-world such that one's being is not reduced to such a degree that being-in-the-world becomes something like being trapped in a world.[38] The everydayness that Terrance and his neighbors are forced to live because of the situation of the drug war is more akin to being trapped in a world than dwelling in one.

This distinction can be seen, for example, in Heidegger's conception of dwelling as both building and care.[39] In considering the phrase "poetically man dwells" found in one of Hölderlin's poems, Heidegger interprets dwelling as ongoing *poiesis*, or as creative building that allows for continued poetic dwelling.[40] Such poetic dwelling ushers forth always already there potential so that it can become possible in the here and now, and is thus a modality of being that maintains openness rather than imposes closure.[41] This would be a modality characterized by *Gelassenheit* or letting-be rather than by ordering or control.[42] It is in this sense that Jonathan Lear has written of the necessity of a poet for radical hope—a poet, that is, in "the broadest sense of a creative maker of meaningful space. The possibility for such a poet is precisely the possibility for the creation of a new field of possibilities."[43] Similarly, Leslie Paul Thiele writes of a politics of dwelling as a letting-be "that allows truth to happen." This "happening of truth" not only opens new possibilities, or what he calls "a founding," but it must also be preserved.[44] This, however, is where the ethics of dwelling as a politics of worldbuilding that I am delineating differs from Thiele. If for Thiele truth as a founding is that which must be preserved, then for me it is the very openness to the happening of new truths and new foundings that must be preserved. Thiele's focus on preserving and guarding truth as a founding concerns me, for, at least to my ears, it has echoes of the security and control the politics of the a priori requires. If the deleterious consequences of the politics of the a priori have come about largely because of the sovereignty of its Truth, the violence of securing that Truth, and the control over possibility this Truth exerts, then an ethics of dwelling responds with the struggle to open possibilities and maintain this openness. This is not to say, of course, that Thiele is espousing another politics of the a priori—I do not claim that he is—it is simply to note that we take care not to repeat some of the same conceptual problems the a priori presents.

Poetic or creative dwelling, then, is being-in-the-world in such a way that as part of that world one is intimately intertwined with and concerned for it and its other existents, and as such participates in maintaining the openness of that world in its ongoing attunement with itself. Here it is important to emphasize that such dwelling is not about being located, emplaced, or even about the space that one occupies. Rather, dwelling is an existential modality for being-in-a-world, a modality that only becomes possible in an attuned world. Thus, to dwell, as Tim Ingold[45] might put it, is to be in a world in such a way that one's being is never pre-limited within a pre-assumed totality, but rather possibilities for becoming otherwise remain open. Becoming otherwise, then, is a process of poetic dwelling, of building and maintaining a world in which such dwelling always remains possible.[46] As such, dwelling is an ongoing process of what Jean-Luc Nancy calls "world-forming." "*To create the world*," Nancy tells us, is "immediately, without delay, reopening each possible struggle for a world . . . against the background of general equivalence,"[47] or what I call the leveling of the a priori. This is an ethics of dwelling as a politics of worldbuilding.

Terrance is struggling to dwell in a world that has made it nearly impossible for him and his neighbors to do so. And yet he keeps going. Despite having a prison record that is a direct result of drug war surveillance—a record that has taken away his ability, for example, to vote, receive student and other kinds of loans, to travel abroad, and to be hired for many jobs—Terrance struggles to find a way to dwell, to be in his world in such a way that not only is existentially comfortable but also provides possibilities for becoming otherwise. A significant part of his ethical struggle to dwell has been his political activity with VOCAL, but perhaps more important for Terrance is his work at the syringe exchange program in his Bronx neighborhood. Similar to how the director of the drug policy reform organization articulated syringe exchanges and other such collaborative health programs as a place where "dignity" is located, Terrance sees his neighborhood program as one of the few places where people who use drugs can dwell. This is so because the program can be understood as a site of potentiality from which new possibilities could emerge. Terrance, of course, does not put it quite like this, but he does describe it as a place where people who use can feel safe, not judged or stigmatized, where they can just "hang out" and socialize with others; he describes it as a place where many of their needs can be met, and where they can learn how to satisfy their own needs. The program is also a place where—through a project run by Terrance—people who use can be trained to become outreach workers, learn skills and become educated in certain ways that translate into other kinds of jobs, and, significantly, become trained to participate in the political activity of VOCAL. All of this—the being and feeling at home, the sociality, and the openness of possibilities to become otherwise—is what I am trying to get at by using the term *dwelling* not only as a moral concept but also as an ethical imperative for human existence.[48]

What is an ethical imperative for human existence and how does it differ from the metaphysical humanism I critique ordinary ethicists of smuggling into their approach (and, it should be mentioned, is characteristic of the discipline of anthropology in general)?[49] Both dwelling as an existential imperative and metaphysical humanist conceptions such as dignity make claims about the essential "nature" of being human. To make a claim that all humans share some essence in and of itself is not a problem. I assume all anthropologists would agree with this despite the discipline's general relativist perspective and concern for difference (if the reader hesitates to grant this, please consider the ontological, social, and political consequences of not agreeing to this; there are plenty of historical examples to draw from). How, after all, could it be said that we study humans and not chimpanzees, dogs, trees, or starfish if we do not acknowledge that there is something essential about what it is to be any one of these particular existents? The problem of metaphysical humanism, I argue, is that it assumes an a priori, predefined human with very specific and limited characteristics and capacities—such as Reason, Morality, dignity, rights, autonomy—that are held to be the case prior to any actual intertwining with any particular world. The only question that remains from a metaphysical humanist perspective is whether these characteristics and capacities will be allowed to manifest and flourish in a particular social and political world. Luckily, built in to this perspective is the answer to the question of what the social and political world ought to be like in order to support this flourishing: it just so happens to be one that resembles very much our own late liberal world.

To claim that dwelling is an ethical imperative for human existence, on the other hand, does *not* assert any predefined characteristics or capacities of humanness. Rather it is simply to claim that to be human is to be intimately intertwined and attuned with a world for which one is concerned, and which becomes attuned, in turn, with itself. It should be noted that this concern makes no normative claim beyond maintaining the ability to dwell in that world.[50] Because of this mutual attunement between oneself and a world, openness always remains such that both oneself and that world can become otherwise so as to maintain this attunement. To speak of dwelling as an ethical imperative, then, does not predefine how or what a human becomes, nor does it predefine what kind of world this human must become a part of. Rather it is simply to acknowledge that to be human is always to be concernedly intertwined in a world with others, and this being-together always manifests differently. Dwelling, then, is that existential imperative of humanness that allows for the very differences of ways of being-in-the-world, ethically acting and valuing, and socially and politically inter- and intra-acting that anthropologists tend to focus on.[51] Thus, while it is certainly the case that I assume an existential essence of the being we call human, this is a minimal essence that provides the open ground for becoming in diverse and differing ways. In contrast, metaphysical humanism assumes a predefined and closed conception of humanness whereby to be human is always and only to be defined by Reason and Morality and their concomitant attributes such as dignity or responsibility. Thus, while the metaphysical humanism built into the ordinary ethics approach is, as mentioned above, analogous to the built-in Christianity of Geertz's theory of religion—and therefore simply repeats and projects a certain predefined conception of humanness—dwelling offers an ontological starting point for understanding how differences manifest *because of* an essential sharedness, as well as offering a link between this ontological starting point, ethical motivation, and political practice.

This is so because when worlds break down, dwelling is no longer possible. When this occurs the demand of an ethics of dwelling is felt, and some respond to the demand. Thus Terrance is not alone in his struggle to enact an ethics of dwelling in New York City. There is also, for example, Martin, who by means of an ethics of dwelling not only opened new possibilities for his own being-in-the-world but, as with Terrance, also politically acts to open possibilities for others. Martin is an African American man in his late forties who formerly used heroin but now only occasionally uses cocaine. Like Terrance, Martin also works at a syringe exchange program in his neighborhood and is one of the leaders of VOCAL and one of its most publicly outspoken members. Once when we were talking about how he got involved with VOCAL, and what his involvement has done for him, he told me that for him it was an "awakening." As he put it, "I guess you could say it was more of an awakening once I saw what VOCAL was actually about. And that's the way I like to look at it now, as basically an awakening." I asked him what he meant by an awakening and he continued:

> When I say an awakening, meaning that for so long being a user, being a user in New York and in Washington Heights, and just not having the understanding that there are opportunities for people like myself to actually meet with our legislators and actually talk to them about things that are needed in our community, when it comes to hepatitis C testing, when it comes to syringe exchange, when it comes to actually being able to have an influence and getting new legislation passed, you know what I'm saying, and moving, and possibly moving policy. To me, that's an awakening as far as being, as far as being, being able to be made aware that, yeah, these things are possible, you know what I'm saying, as your average Joe Simpson. So that's what I mean by saying that's an awakening . . . It was a whole new world that basically opened up and it's a challenge, it's an everyday challenge to try and let others know that they have the same opportunities that I had as far as gaining that awakening.

Martin describes his participation in anti–drug war politics as an awakening, as the opening of "a whole new world" in which he could do, think, and be in ways that he never imagined were possible for him before. VOCAL, which works at multiple interstices of the drug war situation in New York City, disclosed its sites of potentiality to Martin, a disclosure that transformed his very way of being-in-the-world. As he told me later that day, participating in VOCAL and working as an advocacy liaison at the exchange program have provided the possibility for him to become an entirely other person than he was before. Martin's motivations for joining VOCAL, like Terrance's, did not stem from a moral outrage but instead from the experience of having his mother, who was also an injecting drug user, die in his arms from complications related to the HIV/AIDS she contracted as a user who had no access to syringe exchange. The moral breakdown that resulted from this experience brought about for Martin a deep-seated awareness that for drug users it had become impossible to dwell in a world in which the war on drugs is waged on people like his mother, himself, and his friends. Sure, those who did not die could survive within the limiting conditions allowed by this war. But Martin felt that he and his loved ones could not dwell there; that is, they had their open possibilities for being-in-the-world closed simply because they put a substance in their body that the state prohibits.

Martin eventually discovered that the ethics of dwelling as a politics of worldbuilding that he enacts opens new possibilities, new worlds for him and others. He discovered that this ethics of dwelling awakened him. Motivated by this awakening he now seeks to provide this to those users who are still trapped in what he calls the "void" as the result of prohibitionist policies that, among other things, limit users being-in-the-world to a stigmatized identity of an immoral and irresponsible addict who is untrustworthy and potentially dangerous. As of yet Martin and Terrance's activities are limited to building what we might call new "subjective worlds"—that is, worlds that remain rather isolated and subjectively focused. But what is key for the argument I have been making in this chapter is that these political activities have been motivated by an ethics of dwelling—an ethics, that is, motivated to engage in political activity aimed at building a world, even if at this point still a subjective one, in which it is possible once again to dwell. In the next section, however, I will briefly turn to an example of an ethics of dwelling that motivated a politics of worldbuilding that is now currently in the process of building an entirely new and parallel world in the midst of another North American city, Vancouver, Canada. In the next chapter I will then consider how this politics of worldbuilding manifests as a new and attuned world.

Ethics of Dwelling, Vancouver

Terrance's experience in parts of the Bronx shows us that prohibitionist policies render entire neighborhoods zones of uninhabitability. Another such zone of uninhabitability, or what local users referred to as the "Death Zone,"[52] emerged in the Downtown Eastside of Vancouver as a result of the city's drug war situation. A hundred years ago the Downtown Eastside was a center of business, commerce, and government in Vancouver, but by the late twentieth century it had become the front line of the drug war. Businesses and government offices had moved out to be replaced with single room occupancy (SRO) hotels and abandoned spaces. It was not uncommon that commuters who had no other option than to take a bus through this part of town could look out the window and see bodies dead from overdose lying on the sidewalks. The back alleyways that run throughout the neighborhood had become heroin shooting galleries, places of business for sex workers, a place to sleep and congregate and buy and sell drugs, and yet another place to die from overdose. Hundreds of people a year, in fact, would die of overdose in this neighborhood alone. The streets were, as one eventual protest by drug users would call it, "the killing fields."

This neighborhood had become a world in which the people who lived there—an estimated six to ten thousand of whom were drug users[53]—could no longer dwell. This world had become uninhabitable and unbearable. Those who lived there were reduced to objects that metaphorically and quite literally became just another "piece of trash" on the sidewalk or in the alley. Eventually many of these users and their neighbors and some of the organizations already working in the neighborhood mobilized to address the fact of the unbearableness of this world. Here in the Downtown Eastside of Vancouver, then, is an example of how from the breakdown of a world, out of its unbearableness, a demand for another kind of ethics emerges. This is an ethics of dwelling, which we can also call politics—a politics, that is, as a process of worldbuilding.

By the 1990s the Downtown Eastside was ravaged with poverty, homelessness, drug use, and HIV. The potential of a situation-focused politics was already emerging in 1993, when what would eventually become one of the central SRO organizations in the neighborhood was formed and made harm reduction—and particularly the provisioning of clean syringes and works—an inseparable part of their work related to housing. As one of the cofounders of the organization put it, at the time this was quite radical and experimental though now it is common practice. The point, however, is the recognition that for many who found themselves in the world of the Downtown Eastside, the housing problem, drug use, and HIV and other infectious diseases were inextricably linked, and thus addressing only one in isolation would be more or less as if they weren't addressing anything at all. Politically responding to the demands of this situation wouldn't be a matter of building a subjective world, but rather was and is a matter of rebuilding the world where one happens to find oneself.

However, throughout the 1990s the overdoses continued to pile up—two hundred in 1993 alone[54]—despite these efforts and those of others who ran illegal safe injection sites in the neighborhood. Finally, in 1997 an undeniable demand emerged from this world that could not be ignored. The results of a public health survey of drug users in Vancouver revealed that the Downtown Eastside had the highest HIV rate on the planet.[55] This report, which articulated something that many of those living in the neighborhood already felt and experienced, entered the world and motivated some to act (similar to the effect Stop and Frisk had on Terrance). One of these was the poet and incipient neighborhood agonist Bud Osborn,[56] who was also a drug user. Responding to the demand of his world articulated through this report, Bud approached the SRO organization written about above, and together they organized the political event that would become known as 1,000 Crosses. This event for many marks the beginning of the politics of worldbuilding in the Downtown Eastside. It is so named because of the one thousand crosses planted in Oppenheimer Park in the Downtown Eastside, which stood in place for each of the drug users who had died in British Columbia since 1993, the vast majority of whom were in the Downtown Eastside. But the event was more than this. Drug users also occupied parts of East Hastings Street—the main street running through the neighborhood where all the commuter buses ran—and stretched a steel chain across the street with a sign on it that read "THE KILLING FIELDS." With this event the users of the Downtown Eastside began to respond to the demand of their world. Motivated by an ethics of dwelling—the desire to rebuild a world that had become what Martin might have called a void—the users and inhabitants of this neighborhood began the long and difficult political process of transforming their "Death Zone," their "KILLING FIELDS," into a world where they could once again dwell.

This event, which is symbolized and named by the absolute inability to dwell in a world, was motivated by the ultimate final straw of an ethics of dwelling—that is, death—and marked the recognized beginning of a new politics of worldbuilding. In just a few months after this event the by now globally famous Vancouver Area Network of Drug Users (VANDU) would be formed, and this union along with the SRO organization and other allied organizations would begin a process that has resulted in such things as the first and only legally sanctioned safe injection site in North America and a trial heroin prescription project. Most important—as I will describe in more detail in the next chapter—they have completely transformed the Downtown Eastside into an attuned world in which drug users not only no longer die at extraordinary rates but also can now actually dwell in the sense that I have been trying to describe in this chapter. They have, in other words, built a world that is both otherwise and remains open to ever-new possibilities for becoming.

A Demand for a New World

In this chapter I have tried to address what Simon Critchley has called the motivational deficit of contemporary politics. I have agreed with Critchley that this deficit is properly addressed through a reconceptualization of the link between ethics and politics, and argued that this can only be done through an anthropologically informed critical hermeneutics of particular worlds and their situations. I offered the example of anti–drug war agonists to illustrate how an existential imperative arises from a world that has become unbearable, and I have called the response to this demand an ethics of dwelling.

Unlike other recent anthropological renderings of moralities and ethics, the critical hermeneutics approach does not repeat the a priori and transcendental assumptions of metaphysical humanism. In order to show how this is so I contrasted critical hermeneutics with the ordinary ethics approach. Most significantly I argued that, first, ordinary ethics is limited in its equation of ethics with all social activity, which we can understand as a metaphysical humanist projection of the subjectivity of the subject onto a totality called society; and second, ordinary ethics is limited by the assumption that we already know what counts as morality/ethics and that this is restricted, fortuitously, to the already well-established moral concepts and frameworks of our ontological tradition. In response to these limitations I provided a critical analysis that discloses how ethical imperatives may exceed familiar moral concepts despite the fact that the latter are utilized in ordinary everyday language because they are the only moral concepts currently available. In this sense, familiar moral concepts may not best be considered as moral aims, but rather as pointing to or indicating an ethical problem or imperative that cannot yet be neatly conceptualized but nevertheless motivates action. It is the analysis of these ethical problems or imperatives that I am arguing a critical hermeneutics is suited to do.

Dignity is one of those familiar moral concepts that anti–drug war political agonists regularly utilize. I have tried to show that how at least one major player in the international drug policy reform world uses this concept is better conceived as pointing to the existential inability for many people around the globe to dwell in worlds conditioned by the drug war situation. Terrance and Martin made this particularly clear in their articulation of why they were motivated to become politically active in VOCAL, and further described to me how they conceive of this work as providing spaces within which users and nonusers can dwell and as such become open to new possibilities for being-in-the-world. Martin described this experience of dwelling as an "awakening." Both Terrance and Martin, like many other agonists around the globe, look to the new world being created "on the ground" in Vancouver as an example of the kind of politics of worldbuilding they are trying to enact in response to the ethical demand they have felt. I briefly described how the politics of worldbuilding currently underway in Vancouver was similarly motivated by an ethics of dwelling, and in the next chapter I will consider in more detail the results of this politics.

The dominant meaning of the concept *dignity* captures none of this, and yet this is precisely what the director, Terrance, Martin, agonists in Vancouver, and many others have talked to me about and shown me they are doing in their political activity. They are attempting to transform worlds such that those who have found themselves in them no longer have their way of being-in-the-world limited to such a degree that in a very real sense they may be better described as trapped in a world than as dwelling in a world. In other words, by looking to see what the familiar concept of dignity points to rather than taking it as the aim or end of ethical activity, we discover that in this instance dignity points to an ethical imperative that has not only political but also ontological implications. That is to say, the ethics of dwelling that drives the anti–drug war political movement is an ethical motivation for doing a kind of politics that seeks to change the ontological conditions of worlds because those conditions that are currently enacted through the drug war situation have become existentially unbearable. As a result, an ethics of dwelling is a response to the demand to begin to build a new world, one in which it will be possible once again to dwell.

CHAPTER 5

Worldbuilding and Attunement

Worlds are to a great extent what we make them, but never entirely. Usually and for the most part, worlding is non-consciously enacted as worlds continually unfold in the process of us doing whatever it is we do in our everyday lives as we intra-act with one another, things, institutions, nonhuman beings, ideas, ourselves, and everything else. In this sense the continuous process of worlding follows along trajectories that we ourselves may not have started but nevertheless enact. Thus, while each of us participates in the unfolding of worlds, this process always exceeds our capacity to know it, control it, and in most cases even be aware of it. We are world creators and maintainers despite ourselves.

Worlding, though, is never entirely a human endeavor, as nonhuman beings and forces also play an integral role in this process. Humans are only one part of the worlds with which they are intertwined, despite how it might seem and feel. But to deny the part of the human in worlding is just as shortsighted as denying the role of the nonhuman, and perhaps more so since the role of the human remains central to our worlds whether we consider this in terms of something like caring for a loved one, friend, or oneself; housing policy; militarism; or the human shaping of the anthropocene.[1] A tsunami may destroy homes, an asteroid may be more destructive than any nonnuclear warfare, and global warming may change everything, but until these things happen—and in most cases afterward as well—humans continue to world and preferably in ways that increasingly diminish the devastating likelihood and impact of these nonhuman participants. For better or worse humans world, and this fact is central to what I have been calling a politics of worldbuilding.

A politics of worldbuilding begins from this fact that although humans do not fully make the worlds in which they are, and in most cases make worlds without awareness of doing so, they can and do make intentional and creative interventions in the attempt to remake worlds in another light. In other words, despite the fact that existence is never human-centric, only humans can intentionally imagine, experiment with, and create new worlds and begin new worldly trajectories. The fact that such a politics has been a rare occurrence, and its success even less common, does not prove its impossibility but rather its possibility. It has occurred, it is possible. But questions remain. How do we build a world and what can it be like? If the world built on human rights, the world of the a priori, is one of reproductive totality and thus is closed, then how might a world that is characterized by attunement and thus openness come about? How might we need to conceive of and understand such a world and the relations of those existents within it? These are some of the questions I will try to address in this chapter.

Metaphysical Humanism and Responsibility

I began this book by arguing that within the ontological conditions set by metaphysical humanism, worlds and their existents become fixed and quantitated by mathematics, which is understood as the "language of nature" and projected onto them, while humans and their activities, when not themselves quantitated, are secured with transcendental properties such as dignity, rights, and thus a unique and otherworldly moral value. As a result, Reason and Morality, the twin "properties" of humans posited, enacted, and projected through metaphysical humanism, have resulted in what Hannah Arendt calls world alienation. That is, this ontology has led to the alienation of humans from the worldliness of their being, as well as the potentially open possibilities available to them within those worlds. This ontology, therefore, has resulted in a leveling or the closing off of possibility, and as such, a closing off of the possibility of becoming otherwise that might be available if we lived within other ontological conditions.

Thus, as it currently stands, worlds conditioned by metaphysical humanism foreclose the possibilities of disclosive spontaneity while only allowing "normalized" behavior.[2] It is for this reason that Arendt, foreshadowing Foucault, concluded that in the "modern age . . . life, and not the world, is the highest good."[3]

Indeed, for Foucault modernity is characterized by the biopower and politics that is concerned with the life of populations.[4] Although according to the Foucauldian story this concern with life has been central to modernity since its beginnings—and for Agamben[5] this concern can be traced to the Romans—there is much evidence to support the view that contemporary late liberalism, with its proliferation of NGOs and humanitarian interventions, therapeutic technologies and decentralized disciplining, biocitizenship and the normalization of inclusive-exclusion, has become the epitome of biopolitics.[6] As Nikolas Rose has so aptly put it, politics today is largely a politics of life itself.[7] But this life is an extremely limited and narrowly defined life perhaps best understood as the expression of the fantasy of a totalized a priori being characterized by such values and capacities as rights, dignity, and responsibility. Indeed, this triumvirate has come to delimit the very possibilities of being morally and politically human today. As if by a deal with the devil, we have found ourselves in a political context where there has been widespread acceptance that in order for something called the dignity of a person to be recognized she must first exercise such dignity by being a responsible person who, in turn, will then have her human rights recognized. This closed circle that begins with dignity and ends with rights is drawn along the trajectory of individual responsibility, a capacity that is said to be "natural" though we have plenty of evidence suggesting it is a trained and disciplined one.[8] In the closed late-liberal context of the politics of life itself, which is just the latest instantiation of the politics of the a priori I have been writing about, responsibility as a disciplined capacity misrecognized as a "natural" capacity is the key to a politics that has forgotten the world and turned life into "the highest good."

Responsibility today primarily indicates a capacity to be answerable or accountable for one's actions, words, and thoughts. To conceive responsibility as such is to conceive of human agency as efficient cause.[9] This conceptual link between responsibility and causality was already underway with Aristotle's conception of responsibility as voluntary action,[10] but it became solidly entangled as one of metaphysical humanism's primary moral concepts only with Kant's notion of responsibility as *causa sui*. For Kant the primary question of morality was how a human being could be conceived as a free being in a world determined by the mechanisms of natural law.[11] If everything in nature had a prior cause that could ultimately be traced back to the creation by God, then how could we conceive of the human being as a free and rational being—that is, as a moral being? Kant's answer: humans could only be moral beings if conceived as a *subjectum*, a spontaneous origin, a giver of law to itself analogous to God as lawgiver to nature. It is important here to note that such a lawgiver—this *subjectum*—is also a self-controlled being. For to be autonomous—a rational lawgiver to oneself—one must never act heteronomously, as Kant would put it—that is, influenced by anything other than the moral law one gives to oneself—and thus must be a being that exercises the kind of self-control necessary to avoid the influences of such things as desire, self-interest, and social pressure.[12] For Kant, then, humans could only be moral beings as unique beings with the capacity to exercise the kind of self-control necessary to freely and spontaneously cause action—moral beings, that is, with the capacity to act *causa sui* and as such to be responsible for their action. To be a moral human person, then, is to be a self-controlled and self-responsible cause of action.

This conception of responsibility as self-controlled and spontaneous causality has become central not only to the politics of the a priori and its concern with life, but also, and not unrelatedly, to contemporary legal and moral discourses and practices. As a result, whether in the realm of politics, law, or morality, responsibility indicates a self-reflective and rational capacity to evaluate, judge, manage, and control oneself. Ultimately, to be responsible today is conceived in terms of being a kind of person who is normatively self-managed no matter one's past experiences or current living, social, or political conditions, not to mention one's hopes or expectations, or lack thereof, for the future. In other words, to count as a responsible person today is to be counted as a person who is already separated from a world. For to render responsibility as answerability and accountability is to forget and move from a world and turn to an assumed and a priori humanness—a *subjectum*—that stands over and against any possible world. Thus, in the context of the politics of the a priori and the metaphysical humanism it enacts by means of the biopolitical concern with life, responsibility has become a key concept for articulating the world alienation of which Arendt wrote. As such, responsibility as answerability and accountability has lost any semblance of responsibility as respond-ability.[13]

In the rest of this chapter I will attempt to recover a notion of respond-ability through the concept of attunement. To do so I will trace the ongoing politics of worldbuilding currently enacted in the Downtown Eastside of Vancouver, where a world is emerging that is perhaps best described as attuned to itself. But before I can get to that world I will begin with the more familiar (bio)politics of the a priori in order to more clearly draw out how a move from responsibility to attunement is possible. One of the most significant manifestations of metaphysical humanism today is that of the so-called biopolitical therapeutic regime by which "life, and not the world, is the highest good," and through which what Rancière calls the police, or "the distribution of the sensible characterized by the imaginary adequation of places, functions and ways of being,"[14] is enacted. Just one example of such biopolitical therapeutic regimes is harm reduction.

In the previous chapter I showed that harm reduction organizations and practice can provide a space of dwelling from which new possibilities become available and, according to people like Terrance, Martin, and the drug policy director, provide spaces for new subjective worlds to come into being. In this chapter, however, I will focus on the tension within harm reduction between its current predominant manifestation as a biopolitical practice of responsibilization and the potential it holds for opening possibilities for new worlds to come into existence. Therefore, I will begin by considering the way harm reduction as a biopolitical practice, to a great extent, enacts a closure of possibilities. This is so, I will argue, because harm reduction as commonly practiced around the globe—or as they say in the public health world, as best practice—is a biopolitical therapeutic regime primarily concerned with a metaphysical humanist notion of life and seeks to realize this concern primarily by means of responsibilization. This enactment of metaphysical humanism and responsibilization is perhaps most obviously discerned in the very organization of most harm reduction services and the kinds of assumptions that go into this organization, as well as the way those who encounter these metaphysical assumptions in practice, in turn, come to embody such assumptions. Thus, there is a tension between the more dominant institutionally disciplinary aspect of harm reduction practice that aims at normalization, and the potential that exists within this practice for opening possibilities for an otherwise. We can understand this tension in terms of the sites of potentiality that exist right here in any world, and in this chapter I will explore this potential and the ways it can be covered over or released. As will become clear, ontological starting points are decisive for what happens at these sites of potentiality.

In the rest of this chapter, then, I will consider this relation between ontological starting points, harm reduction, and responsibilization. I begin with what I call the standard model of harm reduction as an illustration of the enactment of the ontological tradition of metaphysical humanism and how this results in what we call responsibilization. I then briefly and critically engage a recent and influential alternative ontology offered by a prominent social theorist and consider its shortcomings in taking up a Levinasian conception of responsibility. Finally, and in response to this critique, I turn to the unique case of Vancouver and the enactment of what I call a politics of worldbuilding. In this final section I show that the approach taken in Vancouver differs significantly from the standard harm reduction model—in contrast to the linear and individualized approach taken by the latter, Vancouver agonists are in the process of creating a new world that is primarily characterized as being attuned with itself.

Such attunement, in contrast to the closed normalization of responsibility, ultimately allows a world to remain open such that new possibilities regularly emerge for those who dwell there. The result, I will argue, is that the politics of worldbuilding currently underway in Vancouver reveals an alternative to the closed normalization of responsibility because it begins from and enacts another ontology. This politics may in fact allow us to leave behind the concept of responsibility altogether as a remnant of an ontology that no longer holds much social, political, or intellectual validity despite its continuing hegemony. Ultimately, I hope to show that the politics of worldbuilding in Vancouver reveals that such alternative ontological starting points, and the other worlds that can be built from them, open new possible futures in ways that the temporalities of metaphysical humanism and its concepts such as responsibility cannot, and thus provide new paths for the rethinking of political action.

Responsibilization and Harm Reduction

"Meeting them where they are at" is one of the pillars of harm reduction, which can be defined as the "policies, programmes and practices that aim to reduce the harms associated with the use of psychoactive drugs in people unable or unwilling to stop. The defining features are the focus on the prevention of harm, rather than on the prevention of drug use itself, and the focus on people who continue to use drugs."[15] Harm reductionists consider this "focus on people" and the "meeting them where they are at" approach to be quite progressive. It is not uncommon that harm reductionists contrast their approach, which they see as tolerant and nonjudgmental toward drug users and use, with what they call behavior change approaches such as abstinence-based therapy, which are considered judgmental, conservative, and ultimately unrealistic. This contrast may work at the surface level, as it were, of the use of drugs or not. But it does not take account of the ways certain kinds of moral values and virtues, for a lack of a better term, are worked on, altered, and embodied by means of the tolerant and nonjudgmental harm reduction practices. In what follows I will consider this latter phenomena by addressing the responsibilization that is at the very core of the harm reduction approach.

Of course pointing out that responsibilization is at the core of harm reduction is nothing new, as several critical studies have already done so.[16] Indeed, in previous work I have pointed to some similarities in responsibilization practices between abstinence-based therapeutics and harm reduction.[17] What I hope to do in this section is not so much argue that responsibilization occurs in harm reduction practices but to suggest that it occurs because of the deep ontological assumptions enacted by the harm reduction approach—assumptions which, as I've been arguing throughout this book, it shares with various hegemonic social and political projects of modernity.

For the standard model of harm reduction, "meeting them where they are at" indicates what is often called "the reality" that many people who use drugs are not ready or willing to stop their drug use. "Where they are at" indicates where an individual user is "at" in terms of her own desires and capabilities. The "where" and the "at," then, do not indicate a relationship to anything other than one self and the contained attributes of that self. Beginning from this assumption of the isolated individual, the standard model of harm reduction offers services such as syringe exchange, condom distribution, and substitution therapy with the primary aim of reducing harm that this individual can cause others or that others may cause him. Since harm reduction makes no formal attempt to help users stop using, the occasionally stated, but in most cases not stated, goal is to train users to become better managers of themselves and in so doing to take more responsibility for their own health and the effect they may have on others' health.

I do not want, however, to create the image that harm reducers do not recognize the various ways drug users are intimately connected to their worlds and the effects this has had on their drug use. Poverty, unstable family environments, lack of opportunities, and police oppression are all recognized as potential factors in why people begin and continue to use drugs. But these are viewed as just this, factors, things out there that have *happened to* and thus shaped this individual. In this closed space of things, persons, and happenings—a space often referred to as society or community—individuals move about, and as they encounter other things and persons they are more or less affected by these encounters. The cause and effect imaginary here is something akin to the Humean billiard table. Harm reductionists hope to provide yet another knock-on effect through their encounter with users.

These encounters normally occur at a fixed location, at a mobile unit, or through peer outreach work. The latter two, in fact, are also usually located at one or a few fixed spots on a scheduled, rotating basis. In this sense, harm reduction services fit into the predefined space of society or the community and in so doing offer just one more possible encounter in this closed space. The hope is that the effects of this other possible encounter will counteract the other potentially harmful encounters users will likely have. The fixed or semi-fixed location of the standard harm reduction model, then, provides a relatively safe place for users to go, and the opportunity to change themselves by being there. Again, this change is best described in terms of self-management and increased responsibility.

This model of harm reduction is far and away the dominant model and can be found nearly every place that harm reduction is practiced. It is not surprising, then, that in my research in places like Honolulu, New York, St. Petersburg, Denpasar, and Copenhagen, as well as other cities I have visited or read about, this is precisely the model that is enacted. Each one of these cities offers harm reduction services out of fixed or semi-fixed locations. But the point to be made is not so much the fixity of the services but the fact that this fixity is regularly an isolated and contained one. That is, these locations are typically found in areas of the city where either very little of anything else is actually taking place—for example, the back road behind one of the main hospitals in St. Petersburg where a center is located—or in a part of town hectic with other activities completely distinct from, and in many cases, completely opposed to, harm reduction practices—for example, in the middle of a busy street in the Lower East Side of New York, or in a residential neighborhood in Denpasar. Fixity in and of itself is not the problem. But isolated and contained fixity is.

This is so because such contained isolation spatially enacts the same metaphysics of individualism that supports the isolated individual model of the person that underpins the assumption that "where a user is at" is indicative of that person's ability or *will*ingness to stop using drugs. Thus, whether we focus on the location of a service center or the conception of a person, both work together to make the assumption "that the world is composed of individual entities with individually determinate boundaries and properties"[18] seem that it is in fact the case. The way these different practices work together to support and bring into being a certain kind of reality becomes even clearer when we consider the activities that occur at these fixed locations of harm reduction. Furthermore, through these practices *responsibility* emerges as one of the primary value terms that signify, and thus further congeals, this reality.

The central activity of harm reduction is the syringe exchange program. This program provides the opportunity for drug users to bring used syringes to the exchange in order to receive clean and unused syringes in return, along with other necessary "works" such as cotton, sterile water, and bottle caps. In most cases the exchange is one for one, such that if, for example, someone brings in thirty used syringes, she can receive thirty new ones in return. In some locations, such as the exchange where I worked in New York, there is some leeway on this rule such that if a sufficient reason is given for why a person needs more syringes than she brought in, she is able to receive a certain number more. What counts as a sufficient reason is already predefined and listed on the form that needs to be filled out by the exchange worker during each exchange. Some possible reasons are: (1) a planned upcoming trip during which there will be no access to clean needles; (2) the user lives far from the center and so the distance makes it inconvenient to come regularly; and (3) fear of carrying used syringes. Notice that each of these reasons are directly tied to the fact of the fixity of the center, which, as pointed out above, is normally in an area of town not particularly convenient to access for many users. In some locations, such as in St. Petersburg, there are limitations on the number of syringes one person can receive on any given day. At the center in St. Petersburg this number is one hundred. This limitation is imposed so that users cannot collectively assemble their used syringes and take turns returning them and getting new syringes for the collective. That is, the limitation is imposed in order to "force" each individual user to take responsibility for his safety and health and come to the center on his own. Getting users in the door, then, is considered the first step on the road to self-management and responsibilization.

Thus, in addition to the access to clean syringes such exchange provides, and therefore the potential harm it reduces by preventing the spread of infectious diseases, the exchange also provides an encounter through which individual users are disciplined to become better self-managers and more accountable for their actions. They must travel to a fixed location where they have been registered, often risking encounters with police who are aware that users are going to this location and will have pockets or a bag filled with a good number of used syringes that still have heroin residue in them, and very possibly other illicit items and substances in these pockets or bags. They must make this risky trip during certain preset times, which normally are those of a typical business or institutional hours. Additionally, what they are able to receive from the center in terms of items and numbers is preestablished by the center and may not reflect the needs of the user himself. Finally, any attempt to deviate from these guidelines is met with a demand for an account of why this individual might be allowed to deviate. All of this fails to take into account the fact that during these exchange encounters it is not uncommon that users will be asked whether they have recently been tested for HIV or hepatitis C, or would like some kind of counseling, or if they would like training in overdose prevention, or any number of other similar questions. Ultimately, then, users who come to a syringe exchange cannot help but get the message that they must become more accountable and responsible for their actions, and a good way to do this is to become better self-managers of their behavior, thoughts, emotions, and time.

A similar message is communicated through other activities that commonly occur in harm reduction centers. This is illustrated well in the center where I worked in New York City. In addition to the syringe exchange this center also offers a number of therapeutic activities—from group talk therapy to yoga—that take place in the "hangout space." A weekly schedule of these activities is posted near the front door, next to the "house rules" sign, by the reception desk. As one looks at the schedule to find the time of the activity one wants to attend, it is difficult not to notice that no cursing, no arguments, and no dealing, among a number of other restrictions, are all prerequisites not only for joining an activity but also for being in the space at all. To be in the center, then, is to be a certain kind of person who can manage her being that kind of person.

This, of course, does not go unnoticed by a number of users who frequent the center, and the restriction on cursing is the least of their concerns. Quite a few of these "regulars" have been around since the opening of the center in the mid-1990s, when it was founded as a collective of user and AIDS activists who sought not only to reduce the harm of drug use but also to provide a space where "users could be users," as I was told by one of them. Back then, so the story goes, the center was a space where users could discuss, debate, and argue with one another over their needs and desires—political, economic, social, health, or otherwise. It was a space where spontaneous concerts or poetry reading or art projects would occur. It was a space that was theirs, where they didn't have to become something they weren't; rather, the space became that which they made it.

Today many of these same people, and many of the more recent "participants," as they are called, no longer make the space but are made by it. The center, so I was told several times, has been taken over by college-educated therapists and managers, and in so doing has become institutionalized. The "hangout space," once open to become whatever it was the users who were there wanted to make of it, is now primarily where the therapeutic activities occur. And when the "hangout space" is free to be used for hanging out, it is dominated by a big television that plays recent Hollywood hits at a volume that takes over the space. It has become, to a great extent, a waiting room for the next therapeutic session. It has become a place where most activities that occur there are aimed at the learning of better self-management, accountability, and responsibility, or a place where one can wait until he is able—according to the schedule or his "choice"—to begin this self-work.

It is not uncommon that at least one of these therapeutic sessions would be aimed at "participants" gaining some skills—usually "emotional" and self-management skills—for entering the labor market. Such a weekly session also takes place in the center in Honolulu.[19] What is particularly noticeable in these sessions is that a good deal of emphasis is put on the distinction between "good" and "bad" labor. For example, sex work or bartending is considered "bad" labor, the kind of work that denies one's dignity or self-respect. The message of these sessions is that "participants" must take responsibility for themselves and do the kind of training necessary to break away from the trappings of these "bad" jobs and make oneself into a person capable of getting a "good" job. The unfortunate limitation of these sessions, however, is that the only kind of training provided is for peer work within the center itself or the HIV-prevention organization with which it is affiliated. Such sessions, then, limit possibilities for labor to such an extent that to be considered a responsible worker, one must—considering the lack of education and training common among participants—become a worker within the very institutionalized and closed model of harm reduction that claims to offer possibilities to escape the world of drug use and the stigmas that go along with it. This not only limits possibilities of learning to labor in an "acceptable" way (e.g., not doing sex work) but further limits the skills one actually acquires to such a narrow set that one remains, as it were, trapped in the excluded zones rendered barely inhabitable by the drug war. Peer work may be considered a "good" job done by responsible workers, but it is a job that provides little possibility to transition to one entirely outside of harm reduction in particular or the biopolitical therapeutic industry in general.

In this section I have tried to show how what I am calling the standard model of harm reduction—and particularly its emphasis on responsibility—enacts and reproduces the contemporary form and values of metaphysical humanism. The forgetting of the world that further characterizes this practice results in precisely the kinds of labors and projects that Hannah Arendt predicted and Foucault elaborated—that is, an unswerving focus on life and normalization. Recall that the primary focus of the standard model of harm reduction is preserving life by reducing the potential harm of drug use. The harm reduction project enacted is the maintenance of the health and life of individual humans through interventions on the being of those individuals, but not through any significant intervention in the worlds of these individuals. As we saw, the most significant intervention into the life of individual drug users is not necessarily in terms of the provision of syringes, for example, but in the disciplining of self-management, accountability, and responsibility. In this standard harm reduction model, then, we see a clear example of how the biopolitical focus on life, and the turning away from the world that accompanies this focus, results in the normalization and responsibilization of individuals in locations that have become institutionalized. It is a model that enacts a distribution of the sensible that Rancière calls the police.[20] That is to say, the biopolitical focus of harm reduction is entirely on preserving life and in the process making individuals into a particular kind of being—a being that fits into a prior conception of what counts as human that, as such, fits into a certain order of things; a being that is fit into a preconceived world rather than recognized as intertwined with and of a world, and thus capable of becoming attuned to that world, which becomes otherwise as such attunement occurs.

What is the difference between being fit into a preconceived world and being intertwined with and of a world? How might this ontological difference allow for ethics and politics that differ from that of metaphysical humanism? Recently some have argued that beginning from a different ontology can lead to different social and political ways of being and becoming. In the rest of this chapter I would like to show how this in fact may be the case. But before turning to the example of what I will call the Vancouver model of harm reduction, I will first consider one of the more original, insightful, and influential contributions to the so-called ontological turn and its possible ramifications for social, ethical, and political theory.

Barad, Levinas, and Responsibility

It has become trendy in academia to eschew perspectives that focus on humans. Many of these studies rightly emphasize the shortcomings of humanism and attempt to provide an alternative to its human-centrism.

These come in various guises, ranging from new and vital materialisms to object-oriented ontology. What becomes clear when reading many of these "alternatives," however, is that despite their claims of offering something new, they nevertheless continue the leveling of all existents that is characteristic of metaphysical humanism. If one of the most pernicious consequences of metaphysical humanism is the leveling of all existence by means of the projection of humanness onto all that is, then many of these "alternatives" similarly level existence by means of projecting certain presumed qualities of objects or matter or what have you onto all that is. Thus, whether we continue the old projections of metaphysical humanism or enact new ones with the variously new realisms, we continue the project of leveling with yet another flat ontology.

But perhaps an even more dangerous consequence of some of these "alternatives"—and dangerous because unrecognized and adamantly denied—is that they tend to continue metaphysical humanism in another form. Whether it is forests thinking or chemical systems choosing a path of development,[21] one thing that is not difficult to find in the writings of the so-called posthumanists is the language traditionally reserved for human capacities now assigned to nonhuman beings. I imagine that one possible response of posthumanists would be that such language is intentionally used to disrupt assumptions of human exceptionalism. That is, of course, a perfectly reasonable response. But as I showed in Chapters 1 and 2, concepts tend to have a proclivity that resists the performative openness argued for by Butler and others, such that their accumulated historical use tends to make them stick to or slip back to or remain anchored to (or whatever metaphor you prefer) the range of possible meanings and practices they have acquired, as well as the institutions of power that have supported these meanings. Chemical systems, for example, may in fact spontaneously and inexplicably develop in certain ways under certain conditions of disequilibrium, but to refer to this as choosing—and to do so in a way that clearly draws on notions of human choice—at the very least resembles too closely the kind of metaphysical humanism that many posthumanists claim to be arguing against.

Perhaps the worst violator of slipping metaphysical humanism in through the backdoor of posthumanism is Karen Barad in her highly influential and deeply interesting *Meeting the Universe Halfway*. Here I am not referring to her reliance on quantum physics as providing the key to understanding the nature of reality. For unlike most posthumanists who have turned to science or mathematics as offering a nonhumanist approach to reality—despite the fact that these are perhaps the two most obvious metaphysical humanist practices—Barad, for the most part, tempers and alters her use of quantum physics just enough so as *not* to make this the most obvious contradiction of her own point. Rather, I am referring to her conclusion that the agential realism approach she offers results in "an ethical call . . . to take responsibility for the role that we play in the world's differential becoming."[22]

In the posthumanist world of agential realism, Barad claims, all existents must take responsibility for this becoming. Not only humans, but brittle stars, photons, and everything else is responsible for the world's becoming in Barad's view. As she puts it, "The becoming of the world is a deeply ethical matter."[23] It seems that it is not enough that politics and art have taken a deeply ethical turn[24]—and often with moralizing consequences[25]—but now existence itself is ethical through and through. Indeed, as Barad further explains, ethicality "is part of the fabric of the world; the call to respond and be responsible is part of what is. There is no spatial-temporal domain that is excluded from the ethicality of what matters."[26] Not unlike the ordinary ethicists I discussed in the previous chapter who project metaphysical humanist notions of morality onto social life and argue that the social is ethical through and through,[27] Barad projects one of the twin pillars of this ontology—that is, Morality—onto all of existence. Indeed, this projection takes on a neoliberal tinge as we are told that questions "of responsibility and accountability present themselves with every possibility."[28] Just as the neoliberal free agent is personally responsible for every one of her actions, thoughts, and desires, so, too, the agent of agential realism is responsible and accountable to "each moment" of becoming.[29] All of existence, so it would seem, must take on the heavy burden of a neoliberal-like responsibility and accountability.

Along with this metaphysical humanist leveling, Barad, furthermore, maintains a privileged and exceptional place for humans in her supposedly posthuman world. For, although all existents have responsibility and are accountable "for the becoming of the world," humans must take on more responsibility than any other being. Here we return to human exceptionalism. Indeed this is not an uncommon result of posthumanist "alternatives," and certainly not unexpected considering the prevalence of human-centric language projected onto other existents in these works. Thus, for example, the political theorist Jane Bennett concludes her *Vibrant Matter: A Political Ecology of Things* with a confession of sorts that she is unable to articulate any normative implications of her vital materialism and so falls back on what she calls a "Nicene Creed for would-be vital materialists."[30] The fundamental content of this creed, as it turns out, is that "a careful course of anthropomorphization" is the best way to combat the possible hubris of anthropomorphism. In the end, then, the best this vital materialist political theory can offer is a warning that we ought (and I intentionally use this term) to anthropomorphize a bit more carefully. This is certainly not a compelling alternative to metaphysical humanism.

And neither is Barad's adoption of Levinas and his central concept of responsibility for the Other, which Barad reads as a rejection of the metaphysics of individualism.[31] This, however, is a fundamental misreading of Levinas. For as François Raffoul puts it, Levinas does not reject the metaphysics of individualism by which responsibility emanates from an autonomous and free subject, but rather reverses and thus remains within the logic of this metaphysics.[32] It is true that Levinas has moved beyond the long tradition of responsibility as the accountability of an autonomous and free subject—a tradition that began with Aristotle's conception of responsibility as voluntary and solidified with Kant's grounding of responsibility in an autonomous (i.e., self-legislating), accountable, and ultimately self-responsible agent. But he has done so only by reversing the terms: thus, for Levinas responsibility begins with the demand of the Other and not with the self; the subject is structured by this demand and does not precede it; and therefore, this subject is held "hostage" by the Other rather than free in its action. With Levinas, then, we do not escape the metaphysics of individualism as much as invert its central elements.

So what is this Levinasian responsibility that Barad misreads and adopts? For Levinas it may be the case that everyone is obliged with responsibility, but the key claim that Levinas makes is that one always bears full responsibility for the Other. Responsibility for Levinas is always focused and centered; it is always "my" responsibility for the Other, not, as we might hope, mutual responsibility for one another. Indeed, such mutuality is impossible for Levinas, as the Other is always infinitely separated from oneself along what he called "the curvature of intersubjective space."[33] This is an infinite curvature that, like Descartes's infinite curvature between the human subject and God, forecloses any possibility for mutuality, reciprocity, or being-with. Not only does this infinite curvature, or this "relation without relation," leave us with an impossibility of being-together-with an Other, but as Maurice Blanchot argued, this "relation without relation" relies on the starting point of two terms or existents that each have "outside this relation, their own reality and determinations . . . [and] exist as a distinct, objective reality, or as a Self-subject."[34] It is this metaphysically individualist notion of responsibility that Barad adopts as the main ethical and political conclusion for her "posthuman" and supposedly "non-individualist" agential realism.[35]

Barad, however, is enticed by Levinas's notion of proximity, which he characterizes as "difference which is non-indifference," and which he equates with responsibility.[36] Barad reads proximity as similar enough to her notion of entanglement, which is the intimate intra-action of existents even if separated by large distances, such that she can make a case that entanglement, like proximity, is responsibility. But she does not account for the infinite curvature of intersubjectivity that Levinas places as the condition for his conception of responsibility for the Other. Intra-acting entanglement may, à la quantum physics, entail that all existents that are entangled respond to one another even if separated by great distance. For Levinas, however, there is no response of the Other to the one who is responsible; the infinite curvature between the two establishes an essential and insurmountable division that not even a quantum leap can overcome. Indeed, in *Otherwise Than Being* Levinas seems to go even further in this infinite non-mutuality of being when he writes of the subject being held "hostage" by the Other. For Levinas, to be held hostage by the Other entails that this "persecuted" subject is rendered an "*I* [that] means *here I am*, answering for everything and for everyone."[37] Ultimately, then, not only must the subject of the "relation without relation" remain infinitely separated from the Other, but this individual entity with "determinate boundaries"[38] is held hostage by the Other, and as such rendered responsible for everything and everyone. As a result, so it seems, the Levinasian subject isn't so much agential as imprisoned. Indeed, in Levinas's attempt to create an ethics that would not subsume the Other to the Same of the freely acting subject, he has simply inverted this persecution of traditional morality so that the responsible subject now becomes a captive of the Other.[39]

In adopting a Levinasian notion of responsibility and trying to fit it with her quantum-inspired ontology, then, Barad only repeats in a differential form the very metaphysical humanist and individualist perspective she attempts to escape. Indeed, by adopting the central concept of perhaps one of the most individualist of all moralist thinkers, Barad risks espousing an ethical politics that isolates the human more than ever from the rest of existence and, as pointed out above, resonates well with the demand of endless responsibility that is now central to neoliberalism. This is a resonance that has echoed over the *longue durée* of the metaphysical humanist ontological tradition, a reverberation that helps maintain this tradition and limits its concepts, such as responsibility, within the kind of conceptual proclivity I wrote of in Chapter 1. For this reason it is difficult to imagine that Barad's onto-ethical politics will bring about anything other than a repetition of the same old humanist politics—except perhaps, as Bennett might put it, a bit more carefully considered.

If recent attempts to rethink ethics and politics through the rethinking of ontology have tended to do little more than repeat in a differential manner some of the most basic assumptions of metaphysical humanism, must we conclude that such a project is doomed to fail and is best set aside? In the next section I will try to make the case that we need not give up yet. But in order to move forward it is imperative, so I hope to show, to move beyond mathematics, physics, and the other natural sciences that have informed much of the ontological turn thus far, and as a result done little more than maintain a metaphysical humanist tradition. In the next section I argue that this moving beyond is possible not by turning to "our best" scientific explanations of reality, but instead by turning to the worlds where we find ourselves.

Vancouver

While having a conversation with the director of one of the main organizations addressing the situation of the drug war in Vancouver, I mentioned how impressed I was that this organization, in alliance with several others, had been able to "build a parallel world" in the city's Downtown Eastside. The Downtown Eastside, so it seemed to me, had become a parallel world in the sense that it is a world which at first glance looks just like most other North American, urban, and poverty-stricken ones, but after a closer look it quickly becomes obvious that this, in fact, is quite a different world. Furthermore, this new world was built in the sense that I connected creative building with dwelling in the previous chapter. For human political actors, who did not seek to enframe their world with an a priori but rather sought to address the demand imposed on them by their world, built this parallel world by means of intentional and experimental intervention with the aim of making it once again one in which dwelling is possible. The director immediately sat up in his seat and his facial expression changed, seeming to indicate a sense of recognition mixed with pride; he replied, "Yes, that's exactly what we have done. No one's really put it that way before, but that's what we've done." This struck me as just a bit strange, and in fact I am still not entirely sure he was being honest with me, since it seems so obvious that this is exactly what has happened in this down-and-out zone of exclusion that was once the center of historic Vancouver.

As I wrote in the previous chapter, by the late twentieth century the Downtown Eastside of Vancouver had become the front line of the city's drug war. By 1997 an estimated six to ten thousand drug users, over half of whom were HIV-positive, were concentrated in just a few square blocks; over six thousand persons lived in single room occupancy (SRO) hotels; a constant police presence resulted in regular and random harassment and arrests; and the death toll mounted.[40] This neighborhood had become a world in which the people who lived there could no longer dwell. This world had become uninhabitable and unbearable. Hundreds of people a year died of overdose in the Downtown Eastside, and it was this fact of trying to survive in what was referred to as a "Death Zone" in the minutes of one of the first users union meetings in 1998[41] that motivated some to begin a politics of worldbuilding.

When the various SRO organizations and the new users union first began to mobilize to address the fact of the unbearableness of this world, much of their activity focused on the establishment of harm reduction services along the lines of the standard model I described above. Soon, however, this coalition of worldbuilding agonists began to experiment with a new model of harm reduction. At the core of this effort was the realization that "where a user is at" is in a world, and therefore, this creative experimentation in politics necessitated a shift of focus from individual drug users to the world with which drug users happen to be intertwined. With this shift—so I will argue—there was an accompanying shift from a concern with self-management, accountability, and responsibility to something we might call worldly attunement.

Elsewhere I have argued that attunement in the ontological sense is that force of existence that allows relationships to assemble.[42] When speaking of the existent we call human, attunement is what allows it to be a being that is initially and always a being-in-relationships. Because of attunement humans are always and inseparably intertwined in diverse relations with other humans and nonhumans that come to be a world. Similarly, attunement allows all nonhuman things to assemble and come to partially constitute worlds, and in so doing to be always and inseparably intertwined in diverse relations, just one of which is with what we call humans. Worlds come into being and maintain this being because existents become attuned and maintain this attunement in certain ways.[43] I have argued elsewhere that what we call ethics is best understood as human participation in this maintenance of attunement; we can call it an ethics of perseverance or fidelity with the aim of existential comfort.[44]

James Laidlaw has been critical of this notion of existential comfort.[45] He is right, of course, to draw critical attention to this odd notion that ethical activity is aimed at existential comfort rather than either doing rightly or being good, as much traditional moral theory and contemporary anthropological accounts of moralities or ethics tend to argue. Unfortunately, Laidlaw's critique rests on a fundamental misunderstanding of what I intend by existential comfort. This misunderstanding, no doubt, is the result of a lack of clarity on my part, so I will here try to specify what I mean by this comfort. This notion of existential comfort developed out of an attempt on my part to phenomenologically describe moments of everyday ethical dilemma and reflection—what I called moral breakdown—and the consequent motivation and aim of ethics, without relying on notions of, for example, the good or the right or freedom passed on to us by philosophers.[46] Because of this it is important to recognize that the concept of moral breakdown in no way entails a "rupture, cut off from everyday life and relations of power"[47] as Laidlaw puts it. Rather, breakdowns are a part of ordinary social life, and the concept is only meant to indicate that ordinary social life is occasionally disrupted (but not ruptured) by "moments" when we become more or less reflective or experience more of a dilemma than usual. It is difficult for me to see how this is any different from Laidlaw's notion of reflective freedom that he develops.[48] In fact, we both use the same quote from Foucault linking thought, reflection, and freedom to describe this ethical moment.[49] The difference, however, is that my task, as a phenomenologically inspired anthropologist, was to analytically describe the experienced phenomenon of reflective freedom, which is what the concept of moral breakdown was meant to do.

Furthermore, as I have clarified elsewhere,[50] there is no reason to assume that a moral breakdown must be so extreme that it results in "full" reflective awareness; instead, as Jason Throop has argued,[51] such breakdowns can be understood as nonconscious, mooded, affective processes of working through an ethical dilemma in the midst of everyday life. In this sense, we can think of moral breakdowns variously occurring along a spectrum of reflection depending on, for example, the intensity of the disruption that initiated the breakdown. Therefore, to read the notion of moral breakdown as somehow transcending or "outside the flow of" the everyday[52] (I really wouldn't even know what that means) is a significant misreading of the concept. Rather, it simply indicates that some "moments" or interactions or what have you are more "problematic" than others and need to be "worked out" in more explicit ways than does most of everyday life. Thus, in the "moral breakdown" article I wrote that an ethical subject "stands uncomfortably and uncannily *in* the situation-at-hand. The ethical subject is still being-in-the-world (he or she can never step out of that) but the mode of that being-*in* has significantly changed."[53] This was written precisely in order to clarify that the ethical subject experiencing a moral breakdown remains very much in the everyday—or what is now more often called the ordinary—and I italicized the "in" so as to be especially clear about this. Experiencing a moral breakdown, then, does not—somehow—force one "out of" the everyday or ordinary, but rather shifts the modality of how this ordinary is experienced. As I put it in that article, the modality of the experience of being "in" shifts, but the ethical subject remains always being-in-the-world, which is, to be rather simplistic, merely a phenomenological term for describing ordinary life.

Indeed, this idea that certain moments of ordinary life are more ethically problematic than others has become rather commonplace within various anthropologies of moralities and ethics since I first introduced the concept of moral breakdown. Thus, when I first began to develop this concept I engaged with Joel Robbins's notion of moral torment,[54] which I understood to be a temporally extended experience of a breakdown. Since then a number of other anthropologists have emphasized the importance of these ethically "problematic" moments—for example, Faubion's themitical/ethics distinction,[55] Mattingly's moral laboratories,[56] Keane's stepping back[57] (in fact, "stepping away" is a phrase that I have used for over a decade now to describe ethics and breakdown), or Lambek's tacit/explicit ethics distinction[58]—all of which, at least on my reading, are not all that very different from a moral breakdown, at least in *form*. Perhaps it is high time for anthropologists of moralities and ethics to acknowledge this fundamental similarity (despite some minor differences) instead of continuing to insist that every new articulation of this ethical "moment" is somehow much more analytically appropriate than the last.

But I digress. This digression was necessary, however, to get to why Laidlaw's critique of existential comfort rests on a fundamental misunderstanding. To return to existential comfort, I have argued several times, is a way to understand the outcome of ethical activity without relying on notions of the good or the right. So it would be a gross misinterpretation to conceive of existential comfort, as Laidlaw seems to, as "comfortable confidence of being able routinely to do the right thing,"[59] or as a psychologized, or even and especially a bourgeois, sense of feeling comfortable. Rather, by existential comfort I intend an effortless absorption in a world as one's everyday way of being.[60] But we need not think of such effortless absorption in terms of a confident ease. For if one's world and everyday way of being is one that is normally and routinely marked by a sense of moral inadequacy or questioning, as Laidlaw argues is the case for Jainism, as well as "varying other cultural traditions,"[61] then I would argue that this very sense of inadequacy would constitute Jain existential comfort. That is, to be an existentially comfortable Jain is normally to be and feel morally inadequate. In fact, this seems to be a conclusion that Laidlaw makes himself when he writes that the "more you are a good *lay* Jain, the less you can be a true *Jain*."[62] The difference, it seems to me, is that while Laidlaw has no hesitancy repeating the traditional moral vocabulary to anthropologically understand ethical experience—notice he here refers to the "good" lay Jain—I am trying to move beyond what I see as the limitations of this traditional conceptual apparatus by rethinking some of its key concepts in terms of ecstatic relationality (e.g., existential comfort, moral breakdown, dwelling and attunement) in order to open anthropological, theoretical, and practical possibilities for phenomenologically describing what moral and ethical experience is and could be. Indeed, Laidlaw's example of Jain moral inadequacy understood in terms of existential comfort highlights the etymological root of comfort that helps us see it as a possible ethical concept. That is, the Latin root of comfort would be something like strength together, or communal fortitude, or perseverance, revealing to us how existential comfort as the aim of an ethics of perseverance or fidelity is not only something always achieved with others, but also a modality of being that is not necessarily anything like a "good."[63]

If a moral breakdown as just described demands an ethics of perseverance or fidelity with the aim of existential comfort, then another kind of ethics is demanded when worlds breakdown. For worlds become uninhabitable and unbearable when attunement can no longer be maintained. From the breakdown of a world, out of its unbearableness, a demand for another kind of ethics emerges; this is an ethics of dwelling, which motivates one to act politically—that is, to act in order to begin a process of worldbuilding. Although motivated similarly, the politics of worldbuilding differs from the politics of sociality about which Anne Allison has written. Inspired by Marc Abélès's notion of a politics of survival, Allison argues that politics in Japan today, and increasingly around the globe, focus not on living together but surviving.[64] This "biopolitics from below,"[65] I would argue, is not entirely different from the biopolitical practices I described above in terms of the standard harm reduction model. Although Allison puts more emphasis on such "service programs" as zones of possibility[66] than do those working in most of the harm reduction centers I have spent time at, nevertheless, both are framed in terms of life and survival in the time of war. The ethics of dwelling and the politics of worldbuilding of which I am writing, however, are not concerned with survival in this world of war—except perhaps as triage—but rather are focused on building new worlds in which that war no longer exists.

Such an ethics of dwelling as a politics of worldbuilding is underway in Vancouver. It is not clear, however, to what extent this is recognized outside the city. Certainly Vancouver has become a beacon of hope for harm reductionists and anti–drug war agonists around the globe, but this is primarily so because a coalition of users, harm reductionists, and SRO organizations were able to establish the first and only legally sanctioned safe injection site (Insite) in North America. The fact that this accomplishment—certainly a tremendous one—is what Vancouver is primarily known for says more about the assumptions and focus of those who remain within the limits of the standard harm reduction model than it does about what Vancouver has actually become. For while the establishment of Insite is a central aspect of the new world that has emerged out of the breakdown of the Downtown Eastside, it is just one aspect of this new world within which it is now possible for drug users to dwell. This new world, created primarily by users and allied organizations who became motived by an ethics of dwelling to enact a politics of worldbuilding, consists of art galleries and studios, a bank, a grocery store, a dentist office, a community center, and a network of social enterprises where users can be trained for employment that includes two cafés and various stores.

This is a new world attuned to itself and as such always open to an otherwise. For to be attuned to itself a world must always be open to becoming something it is currently not. Attunement entails a process of becoming. What does this mean and how is it different from the standard harm reduction model? Consider the following. One October morning I was standing outside one of the social enterprise cafés talking with its manager and the director of the First Nations program of one of the neighborhood organizations. The manager was telling me about how the social enterprises provide possibilities for individuals to become connected to the neighborhood while also gaining skills that could provide opportunities outside the neighborhood. Just then the director interjected and began telling me that unlike most service programs around the globe, Vancouver's is unique in that they have built what he called a structure—but for reasons I outlined in Chapter 3 I will call a world—in which any one of the programs within this world serves as an entry point for the others. The director went on to draw a distinction. As he put it, normally if one is seeking harm reduction services then she can only find these services at a particular location run by a particular organization that is generally disconnected from other kinds of programs and services. The director called this common way of providing and finding services linear because there is only one entry point—the harm reduction clinic—and it provides only one kind of service.[67] This linear track is characteristic of the standard harm reduction model I described above. Vancouver's Downtown Eastside, on the other hand, is a world of what he described as networked services and social enterprises into which one can enter at any point and be referred to, learn about, and take advantage of any number of other available possibilities.

The director continued and gave me the following example of how this emergence of possibilities happens. The bank, he said as he pointed to it across the street, can be an entry point for a range of possibilities that are not predefined as necessary aspects of what we normally consider a bank to be. This bank is a space where tellers come to know local customers quite well, as they all tend to be people from the neighborhood. Over time they hear their stories, see them in the streets and the cafés or at the community center, and thus relationships develop. It is not uncommon, then, that someone might confide in a teller about some difficulties she might be experiencing, or the teller might simply be able to see that she is acting differently than usual—and thus the teller can suggest she go across the street to the detox center, for example, or to the dentist, or suggest she seek employment at one of the social enterprises within the neighborhood. The bank, then, becomes an entry point into a range of possibilities that emerges from a world that is attuned to the ways of being and becoming of itself. It is a clearing, or site of potentiality, from which a world opens itself to one of its inhabitants and in so doing potentially opens itself to becoming a new world as the eventual feedback consequence of this original opening can never be known. This is attunement as a process of becoming.

It should be noted that this attunement is not the result of what we might call a "neighborhood effect" or a "small town effect" by which, through regular interaction, people come to know and sometimes help one another. Rather, this attunement emerges out of the very being of this particular bank. This bank, unlike most banks around the globe, is not there as simply a place to keep one's money so that the bank can make profit, and where human interaction occurs as a consequence. Unlike most other banks, this bank is not narrowly defined in its being and possibilities. This bank was conceived, designed, and built to become part of the Downtown Eastside world as a space where human and worldly intra-action could happen so that other possibilities would emerge.[68] This openness onto the world is the very point of the bank's being there. The money is just one, but not the most significant, aspect of this.

As such, the bank is first and foremost there as an opening onto a world specifically designed and attuned to those beings that dwell there. Unlike other banks in nearby neighborhoods, there are no security guards at the doors to keep out "undesirables." The bank is open to anyone no matter how they dress, smell, look, or sound. Indeed, some even ride their bikes through the front door and right up to a teller's counter. And while identification is necessary to open an account, it can be a photocopy, and unlike most other banks no address is required. This openness is central to how this bank is part of an attuned world. For in a neighborhood with many homeless and/or transient persons who also may use drugs or do sex work, and some of whom have obvious physical and mental handicaps, such criteria that would normally exclude them from other banks do not pertain here.

The order of priority at this bank differs from most others. Here the profit of the bank is secondary to the availability of money for those who dwell in the neighborhood. For many of those who use the bank, money is scarce. Other than the regular but minimal state-based assistance many of them receive, income is often sporadic. While some may work in the neighborhood social enterprises, which brings in a fair and steady wage, many still rely on such things as sex work, panhandling, and occasional day jobs for income. If it were not for the openness of the bank to any and all who dwell in this world, any actual checks they might receive, such as those from the state-based assistance programs, would normally be cashed at a check-cashing establishment, where the customers would be charged a hefty fee from their already-meager income. Instead, the bank charges only a five-dollar monthly fee that covers all transactions. Indeed, the simple availability of the bank in and of itself already provides a range of possibilities that would normally not be available to many of those in the neighborhood. Without this bank many would not be able to use the services of other, big commercial banks, and would be left with their cash in hand. For those who often live in precarious housing, or are homeless, or have addiction problems, having all your cash on hand can be problematic. The availability of the bank, then, opens up the possibility of, for example, not having one's money stolen from your room, or not spending it on a binge, or even saving a small amount each month. As the globe continues to be dominated by a market economy, money remains central to one's survival, and this bank has opened the possibility to the residents of the Downtown Eastside of at the very least surviving in the money-based economy. This was a possibility that for many simply did not exist prior to the establishment of this bank that was designed and built to be attuned to the world of the Downtown Eastside.

But it is not only the services of the bank, and the human interactions between the tellers and customers that are attuned to this world, and as such open possibilities, for so, too, is the architectural space and technology of the bank. The lobby, for example, unlike in other banks, is not simply a place to fill out deposit slips or wait to meet a teller or service representative; it is also a space for people in the neighborhood to hang out, drink the free coffee, and use computers and the Internet provided to anyone free of charge. The bank lobby is a clearing where it is possible to learn about what is happening elsewhere in the neighborhood—for example, political rallies, concerts, yoga sessions, or art exhibits—by talking with others or reading the announcements posted. It is also an opening onto the globe as one can interact with others anywhere or learn about anything via the Internet. The bank lobby, then, is a clearing out of which possibilities of learning, acting, and becoming are opened. And just in case this is not enough, the lobby is also a space where anyone can go and get a safe crack pipe from a vending machine—likely the only bank anywhere that offers such an option.[69] This bank, then, opens possibilities that go way beyond those of the linear or standard harm reduction model, and certainly way beyond those of any commercial bank—and these possibilities only become available because it is attuned to a world that is already attuned to itself.

The bank is not the only clearing in this world. Consider the life trajectory of Joan, a thirty-three-year-old woman who was born in the Downtown Eastside and has become who she is today because of the attunement of her world to itself, and the clearings available to her because of this attunement. Joan grew up living in the SROs and family-housing units in the neighborhood with her heroin-using mother, and she started using various drugs herself in her early teens. At one point she realized she wanted to find a job but didn't know how to do so since her background didn't provide her with the kind of skills and education sought by most employees. As is the case for most drug users around the globe, the larger world of Vancouver that Joan had been thrown into excluded her from most possibilities of becoming otherwise. Even if Joan had wanted to enter rehabilitation and attempt "to get clean," as would be expected by most employers, her past as a "former addict" who lacked education and experience would likely limit her possibilities to surviving on the margins of precarity. In a very real way Joan not only felt as if she had no options, but she was in fact trapped in a larger world that excluded her simply because she put certain substances into her body. She was, as Martin put it, trapped in a void in which she was damned if she did and damned if she didn't—that is, whether she became a "former addict" or continued to use mattered very little in the larger world structured by the drug war situation, for the "contamination" of using drugs can never be washed away in a world so structured.

Luckily, Joan had also been thrown into a parallel world created by a particular enactment of a politics of worldbuilding, and this world had clearings that opened possibilities for Joan. Thus, she turned to the people working in the office of the housing unit where she was living at the time. They had known Joan since her childhood, could see that she was ready and willing to work, and therefore helped her get her first job in their office. Soon, however, everyone realized that such a job did not suit well Joan's creative interests, and so they helped connect her to an arts and crafts shop within the network where she could do her art and interact with people more regularly. What was important here, why this is an example of a world attuned to itself, is not that Joan was able to find work through a network of acquaintances, as that makes this sound like a story of nepotism. Rather, this world is attuned to itself because it does not come with a predefined notion of who is included and who is excluded. As with the bank, so, too, with finding work in the social enterprises of this neighborhood—there is no criteria of how you look, smell, or talk, for example. If one is willing and able to work, a job will be found. Joan's use of drugs and lack of experience was not seen as an impediment, but rather as simply one aspect of who she is, and so the world of which she is a part would need to attune to her as she would to it.

When I met Joan she had already been working in the arts and crafts shop for several years, a place where she could not only earn an income but also develop her creative interests. In fact, the shop is a place where local artists go in their spare time to use the facilities to create. By the time we met, Joan had not used drugs for a couple of years. This came about because she got pregnant and decided that she did not want to be a mother who used. Unlike the case with most menial jobs that Joan might have been able to find as a drug user in the larger world of Vancouver, Joan did not have to worry about how time spent on detox and kicking her habit might affect her job status at the arts and crafts shop. In fact, because the shop is a part of the networked and attuned world of the Downtown Eastside, the managers not only gave her as much time and flexibility she needed but also helped her access various support services in the network. In this attuned world of the Downtown Eastside drug use is not an impediment to having a job; however, if one chooses to stop using, one's job, in turn, is not an impediment to "kicking."

Today Joan lives with her husband and two-year-old son in social housing that is a part of a new high-rise condominium of mixed social and private housing, a project initiated and fought for by the alliance of organizations engaged in this politics of worldbuilding as they battle against encroaching gentrification. In the early 1990s a well-known department store chain went out of business across Canada, and as a result its city block–sized location in the Downtown Eastside was left empty. For several years the city, developers, and agonists went back and forth over what should be done with this space. For many in the Downtown Eastside this struggle became emblematic of the larger fight for adequate housing, fair drug policy, and a neighborhood in which people could once again dwell. Some agonists occupied and squatted in the building, and then set up a tent city on the site for three months. A number of protests took place. Eventually the city worked with some of the SRO organizations to design a mixed social and private housing complex that includes two hundred social housing units. In fact, because the negotiation process took so long, an additional two hundred units were also provided by the city at another nearby location, resulting in four hundred units as a result of the political activity centered on this one building.

Although different entrances separate the social and private units, and thus maintain an exclusion from the "private" world of "normal" Vancouver, the atrium of the complex is a space where the residents of all units (as well as others from the neighborhood) come together. In this space, overlooked by a thirty-by-fifty-foot photographic mural depicting the 1971 Gastown Riots that took place in this neighborhood, and during which mounted police charged in to break up a sit-in protest of marijuana laws—an image that reminds all in the atrium of the much longer history of the drug war situation in this neighborhood—people gather. Coming in and out of the grocery and drug stores that line the atrium, or coming in off the streets, people recognize one another and stop to chat; tables with information about the neighborhood—political or artistic events, for example—regularly are set up; weekly arts and crafts events take place; or people just rest on benches. Here is a space on a border between two worlds—the larger world of Vancouver where people do such things as go to their jobs and pay their mortgages and buy groceries for their families, and the world of those caught up in the drug war situation. On this border worlds come together, even if only for a moment as, for example, one person looks to buy a necklace designed by a person who also uses drugs, and in that moment they begin to talk.

It is here, on this border, that the hermeneutic nature of worlds and politics become most obvious. In this intertwining something like interpretation and understanding and becoming occur. Echoing the drug policy director in the prior chapter, I once heard one of the leaders of an SRO organization tell an intern with this organization that such hermeneutic moments and spaces provide what he called dignity, but I am calling dwelling, for people in the neighborhood because they provide clearings through which persons can become a part of a world and do so together. It was this togetherness in a shared world that the leader emphasized to the intern, for as he put it, it is only in this way that change becomes possible—change, that is, not only for the drug users, but for all persons, and thus for the worlds they share.

Notice that such dwelling is possible because of the space designed for such interaction, within a parallel world built for just such purposes. In fact, when the leader told this to the intern he was speaking of the social enterprises, not the atrium. But what he said pertains not only to the social enterprises and the atrium, but also to the world of the Downtown Eastside in general. For as I have tried to make clear in this section, the politics of worldbuilding that has brought this world into being is concerned first and foremost with making a world that is attuned to itself and its inhabitants—a world that is always open to an otherwise because its only foundational ground is groundless openness. The hope of this politics is that it is not only the world of the Downtown Eastside and its inhabitants that become otherwise but—through such interactive moments as those that occur on this border in the atrium—so, too, the other worlds that come to this space will also, in time, become otherwise. Several residents of the complex I spoke with agreed with the woman who eventually bought the necklace in the atrium: "I think most of us are aware of the experiment we are taking part in here. It can be uncomfortable at times, but that is how you change, I think. You get pushed out of your comfort zone and realize that things can be different, and that's okay."

This woman did not buy her necklace from Joan, but this is the space that Joan walks through every day on her way home, and she, too, will stop and talk to the jewelry maker, whom she knows from other artist venues in the neighborhood—and perhaps she also will talk to this woman or other residents of the complex. This is Joan's world, where she continues to work in the arts and crafts shop, as well as in one of the neighborhood art galleries, and continues to do her art. This is the world where she lives with her husband and child in a building designed and built for people who have lived lives like hers. This is a world where she can dwell without her past making such dwelling impossible. This is a world that doesn't exclude one who is the daughter of a drug user, or a drug user herself, or a former drug user; rather, it is a world that is open and attuned to whatever it is one might be as an existent intertwined within it. The person Joan has become, then, is in a very real way a result of the possibilities for becoming available within this attuned world created through the politics of worldbuilding underway in Vancouver.

This is not a world defined by the closed normalization of biopolitical metaphysical humanism, and neither is it a practice of harm reduction focused on responsibilization. Rather it is a world characterized by attunement, in which clearings become available that open possibilities for both the world and its inhabitants to become otherwise. In this world, for example, it is possible for banks to become social centers, craft shops to become places for young artists to do art in their free time, vacant lots to become community gardens with a sweat lodge, and sidewalks to become impromptu flea markets. As these spaces open and become otherwise, so, too, do those who inhabit them, as worlds and existents mutually attune.

I do not want to create too rosy a picture. This world is not a utopia. Many problems remain: people still suffer, disagree, argue, and fight with one another; people still sleep on the streets; violence against women remains; overdoses still happen; and most inhabitants of this world are still excluded from the larger world of Vancouver. But what is being created in the Downtown Eastside is a world in which one is not by definition excluded simply because of what one does with or puts into his body, or simply because of how one looks, smells, or moves through space. It is not perfect, but it is also not a world grounded on predefined and exclusionary notions of who and what counts as "normal." This alone makes the creation of this world—one groundlessly grounded by openness to being and becoming otherwise—a radically transformative political accomplishment.

Opening Possibilities

Jacques Derrida writes of the impossibility of knowing beforehand what or who will arrive with any event, but yet we have a responsibility for whatever or whoever does.[70] I have tried to write in this section of attunement in a similar manner. For in any world it is impossible to know beforehand what or who will arrive next—there is no rule or law that governs "the next." A world governed by the a priori falters in the face of this unknown and responds—sometimes violently—by attempting to turn the unknown into a pre-known. A world attuned to itself, on the other hand, responds to whatever or whoever may arrive; it adjusts as needed. The creation of such attuned worlds is perhaps the political imperative of our times, and those in the Downtown Eastside have shown us how it could be done.

The creation of this world became possible because of the simple shift by a few political agonists from metaphysical humanism to a world. This is a simple shift that allows us to witness in the Downtown Eastside of Vancouver a politics of worldbuilding that has allowed an entirely other kind of world to emerge, because the politics began from an entirely other ontological starting point. This is an ontology that begins with the assumption that openness and potentiality *are* right here and now, even if presently absent. When a politics begins to build a world that reveals these openings and potentialities, spaces, things, people, worlds are no longer limited and closed. A bank becomes more than a place to put money, a waiting room becomes more than a place to wait, a luxury apartment complex becomes more than privatized housing. Spaces, things, persons—existents—are no longer closed but become and always remain open. This ontological shift, this political event, I contend, provides us with something like hope. Indeed, in times such as those we are currently enduring—in times, that is, of political and social disappointment, as well as potential existential extinction—building such attuned worlds is our only political hope. Ultimately, then, the provocation Vancouver provides us is to ask the question of when and how this politics of worldbuilding will be taken up by other political projects related and unrelated to the drug war situation—political projects, that is, through which being is never limited but is always open to possibilities that become available through any entry point into an attuned world.

Epilogue: Critical Hermeneutics

> A critique is not a matter of saying that things are not right as they are. It is a matter of pointing out on what kinds of assumptions, what kinds of familiar, unchallenged, unconsidered modes of thought the practices that we accept rest . . . We must free ourselves from the sacralization of the social as the only reality and stop regarding as superfluous something so essential in human life and human relations as thought.
>
> —MICHEL FOUCAULT

> The practical task of our age: to remove everything that tends to place itself in front of the emergence of things into their world.
>
> —REINER SCHÜRMANN

This book has been an attempt to offer a framework for an experiment in politics that would allow human and nonhuman existents to emerge into worlds that always remain open to possibilities for an otherwise. The epigraphs of this epilogue—one by a prominent critical theorist and the other by a hermeneutist—help shed light on this framework. For in taking up the practical task of discerning an alternative politics from the words and practices of the anti–drug war movement it was necessary to move between critique as an ungrounding and analysis as an opening. The critique of pointing out the ontological assumptions that underlie our political-moral discursive practices was necessary to remove that which places itself in front of—or forecloses—possibilities for an otherwise. A critical hermeneutics cannot simply tear down and destroy; it cannot simply unground. It must also create by disclosing the openings that are already there. It is for this reason that a critical hermeneutics is necessarily an anthropological task. This is so not for the rather simplistic reason often repeated that ethnography complicates matters and provides more robust understandings. Rather, it is because the anthropological endeavor—which always begins in situations and worlds—can become particularly attuned to the potentialities of worlds that even the regular inhabitants of those worlds may not recognize. The result of this anthropological endeavor is not, then, an ethnographic description of what is, but rather a critical hermeneutics of what *can be* as a practice of the not-yet.[1] If Foucault described his work as a history of the present, then perhaps we could describe a critical hermeneutics as a history of the future.[2]

This critical hermeneutics must begin from the ontological assumptions that enframe existence today so that we can begin to work out of them. This is so not only because these ontological starting points ground the ways of being, acting, thinking, speaking, and so on of human and much nonhuman existents today, but they also, as a result, ground our modes of analysis. Indeed, first metaphysical individualism and then metaphysical humanism arose and became dominant in large part through the methodological and analytical practices of mathematics, the natural sciences, and eventually the social sciences that attempted to mimic the former. The container view of space, individual entities bounded and defined, the functionality and instrumentality of all beings, the subject/object distinction, and finally the subjectivization of all existence, none of these "truths" of reality would have the dominance they have today without them also being central to the very methodological and analytical practices of our intellectual endeavors. It is no wonder that not only our intellectual practices but so, too, political, moral, and everyday practices tend to repeat, reaffirm, and maintain the ontological tradition that has arisen from such practices. As we have seen, the conceptual practices of this tradition result in the conditions of repetition and totality; and this comes as little surprise considering that the primary grounding concepts of this tradition are characterized by closure, boundedness, and totality.

If we wish to break out of the limitations of this ontological tradition; if we wish to be politically, morally, and socially in worlds of openness and possibilities—that is, if we wish to be in worlds primarily characterized by "why not" rather than "no"—then we must begin with different practices that invoke different concepts, which will eventually build both different worlds and different ontological traditions. For Gadamer hermeneutics is a theoretical analytic for the disclosure of the limiting conditions of our ways of being-in-the-world.[3] But hermeneutics is more than the critical disclosure of limits, for in this disclosure there is always an opening to something otherwise—that is, the disclosure of a limit always opens new possibilities for thinking, saying, doing, or being. Hermeneutics, then, is essentially a theoretical analytic of becoming.[4] In this sense, to do hermeneutics—whether of a text such as a poem or novel, or of a concept, or a history, or a political practice, or what have you—is to open possibilities.[5]

This is so because for Heidegger, Gadamer, and many of those who build off their work, existence itself is a hermeneutic process. In this sense, to do hermeneutic analysis is in fact to participate in the becoming of being; it is, as it were, to enter the hermeneutic circle of existence. "Parts" and "wholes," or as I would prefer it, aspects and assemblages, continuously attune in a process of "understanding," meant here in its etymological sense of "standing in the midst of."[6] To "understand" in this sense is to participate in the becoming of that which one is a part. Here we see the import of the hermeneutic circle, and why how we enter this circle is vital for our participation in its becoming. Entering the circle so as to participate in the "understanding" of its becoming is a practice of what Heidegger called thinking. Reiner Schürmann describes this thinking as "simply the echo—response and correspondence—to any aletheiological constellation as it has already established itself, each time."[7] For Schürmann such thinking is necessarily an-archic because it is thinking necessarily done without a priori principles or grounds. It is thinking that begins, that is, from the radical finitude of existence. Restated in terms used in this book, thinking is the an-archic process that arises from becoming attuned to the conditions of situations and worlds. Thinking, then, is the first step in coming to understand—and I mean this primarily in terms of participating in, but also in terms of comprehending—a situation or world, so as to become able to act in that situation or world.

Here we see the significance of Heidegger for Foucault, who described Heidegger as an "overwhelming influence" and claimed that his "entire philosophical development was determined by my reading of Heidegger."[8] For Foucault thought was essential to ethics; it is the first step of constituting "the human being as an ethical subject."[9] And as with Heidegger, so, too, for Foucault, as we see in the epigraph to this chapter, thinking is critical thinking in the sense of disclosing the grounding assumptions of our ways of being-in-a-world. This critical hermeneutics is, as Schürmann argues, necessarily an-archic because it begins not with a priori principles but by entering the situation or world to be thought. Here we see the hermeneutic influence on Foucault. For just as with Foucault, so, too, with critical hermeneutists such as the late Heidegger, Schürmann, and Caputo, critical and an-archic thought is the first step of an ethics that is also political because it is an ethics for becoming otherwise.[10]

Acting with a critical hermeneutic sensibility is similarly an-archic. That is, it is acting without grounding principles, or acting without an a priori. Such acting is "acting according to presencing";[11] or again in the terms of this book, it is experimental acting as a response to being intertwined with a particular situation or world. As one of the Vancouver agonists told me, the politics they do is not enacted as a blueprint, but rather as a response to particular problems as they arise in the world of the Downtown Eastside. This an-archic political acting does not add value to a situation or world in order to render it understandable according to a predetermined mode of comprehending. It does not, as does the politics of the a priori, project pre-known value concepts such as rights, dignity, or responsibility onto a world so as to make it understandable because it now mirrors what one thinks of oneself. Rather an-archic acting—the kind of ethical and political acting I have tried to delineate throughout this book—is only possible by acting along with and in response to the demands of particular situations and worlds, and thus begins—for those who do politics as much as for those who do intellectual analysis—with thinking and experimentation. As the Vancouver agonist put it, when a problem arises and their world makes a demand, "they figure it out."

Ultimately, then, what I have tried to lay out in this book—and only in a preliminary manner—is that if we hope to address the political disappointment of our time, we must begin from different ontological starting points than those that have grounded the ontological tradition that has now reached its point of exhaustion. These new starting points need not be created ex nihilo, but rather can be disclosed as potential in the situations and worlds in which we now find ourselves. I have tried to show that a critical hermeneutics provides a way to such disclosure, and I illustrated this through a critical hermeneutics of the contemporary anti–drug war movement, where I have discerned something potentially new in the midst of that which appears quite familiar. What I hope became clear through this critical hermeneutics is that when we analyze and act—and again I mean this both intellectually and politically—that is, when we think and act without the grounding limitations of the a priori, then we may begin to notice "the many ways, changing with time, in which things enter into mutual relations. There is nothing stable in this 'unfolding.' Nor is there anything that would allow for a normative discourse, legitimating action, to be construed. We *think* by 'complying' with [situations and worlds]. We *act* in the same way."[12] In this way, as John Caputo describes the task of what he calls radical hermeneutics, we are not "blinded and hamstrung by wooden maxims and methodological constraints when what the matter . . . requires is plasticity, inventiveness, suppleness, the ability to play along with the matter."[13] Ultimately, then, what I hope to have shown is that whether as intellectual or political endeavor, or as a combination of the two, possibilities for an otherwise only present themselves when we attune ourselves—our thinking and acting—to the openness that is radical finitude.

ACKNOWLEDGMENTS

The research and writing of this book were made possible through funding provided by a Vidi grant from the Dutch Science Foundation, a Starting Grant from the European Research Council, and the Institute for Advanced Study, Princeton. I thank everyone at the University of Amsterdam who helped administer the first two grants and provided much needed and helpful support along the way. Special thanks for this go out to José Komen and Janus Oomen. I also thank everyone at the Institute for Advanced Study who helped me take advantage of that wonderful work environment to the best of my abilities.

All texts are collective efforts even if, in the end, only one name appears on the front cover. This book is no different, as many people in various ways have helped make it possible. I thank the following persons for important conversations around the topics and ideas explored in this book or for reading various versions of it, whether in part or in whole, all of whom have been essential to its outcome: Jason Throop, Oskar Verkaaik, Patrick Neveling, Talal Asad, Martin Holbraad, Robert Desjarlais, Elizabeth Povinelli, Charles Stewart, Thomas Schwarz Wentzer, Rasmus Dyring, Alessandro Duranti, Michael Jackson, Niko Besnier, Oliver Human, Didier Fassin, Joan Scott, Anne Allison, Jonathan Lear, Cheryl Mattingly, James Laidlaw, Henrik Vigh, Kabir Tambar, Ghassan Hage, Miriam Ticktin, Joe Hankins, Brian Goldstone, Elinor Ochs, and Joel Robbins. I also thank Natalie Frigo, Eric Werner, and Mark Francis for their friendship, which over the years has been life preserving, intellectually stimulating, and, most important, just plain fun. For their ceaseless support I thank my parents: Sandy, David, and Janelle. The final version of this book took shape thanks to the editorial guidance of Richard Morrison and the helpful comments of the reviewers. I also thank all those whom I may have forgotten.

This book would not have been possible without the help and support of what I have come to call the anti–drug war movement. I thank everyone who is a part of it not only for their help with this research but also for their tireless fight to end this war on people. I would, however, like to single out a few individuals and organizations who were particularly helpful in the research that led to this book: Matt Curtis, Daniel Wolfe, Mark Townsend, Russell Maynard, Sarah Evans, VOCAL-NY, the Portland Hotel Society, and the Danish Drug Users Union.

Finally, I thank Sylvia Tidey for standing with me through all the ups and downs of this book coming into being. At the most obvious level, our many conversations about, and your tireless readings of, the manuscript helped me shape and hone many of the thoughts articulated in this book. For that alone you were vital to it. But ultimately what has been more important is the encouragement and support you always provided, the love you gave, the shit you put up with, and the faith you had in me and this project. You know well that this book would not have happened without your being there, and I'm not sure how I'd be today without you either. Thank you.

Parts of this book have appeared either partially or as earlier drafts in the journals *Cultural Anthropology* (Chapters 2 and 3); *Journal of the Royal Anthropological Institute* (Chapter 4); and in the following edited volumes: *Moral Engines: Exploring the Ethical Drives in Human Life*, ed. Cheryl Mattingly, Maria Louw, Thomas Wentzer, and Rasmus Dyring (New York: Berghahn Books) (Chapter 4); and *Competing Responsibilities: The Ethics and Politics of Contemporary Life*, ed. Susanna Trnka and Catherine Trundle (Durham, N.C.: Duke University Press) (Chapter 5).

NOTES

INTRODUCTION

1. Simon Critchley, *Infinitely Demanding: Ethics of Commitment, Politics of Resistance* (London: Verso, 2007).

2. "Becoming otherwise" is a conceptual phrase likely most familiar to anthropologists through the work of Elizabeth Povinelli. It should be recognized, however, that "otherwise" is a concept with a much longer and broader history in the hermeneutic tradition and continental philosophy in general. See for example Povinelli, *Economies of Abandonment: Social Belonging and Endurance in Late Liberalism* (Durham, N.C.: Duke University Press, 2011); Elizabeth A. Povinelli, "The Will to Be Otherwise/The Effort of Endurance," *South Atlantic Quarterly* 111, no. 3 (2012): 453–75. For examples of the otherwise from hermeneutics and continental philosophy see John D. Caputo, *Radical Hermeneutics: Repetition, Deconstruction, and the Hermeneutic Project* (Bloomington: Indiana University Press, 1987); Reiner Schürmann, *Heidegger on Being and Acting: From Principles to Anarchy* (Bloomington: Indiana University Press, 1990); Giorgio Agamben, *The Coming Community*, trans. Michael Hardt (Minneapolis: University of Minnesota Press, 2009).

3. Giorgio Agamben, *Means without Ends: Notes on Politics*, trans. Vincenzo Binetti and Cesare Casarino (Minneapolis: University of Minnesota Press, 2000).

4. On the necessity of creating new worlds see Jean-Luc Nancy, *The Creation of the World or Globalization*, trans. François Raffoul and David Pettigrew (Albany: State University of New York Press, 2007); Jean-Luc Nancy and Aurélien Barrau, *What's These Worlds Coming To?* trans. Travis Holloway and Flor Méchain (New York: Fordham University Press, 2015). Furthermore, Simon Critchley similarly writes of politics in terms of invention and creation, although, as will become clear in Chapters 4 and 5, his reliance on a Levinasian Other is argued against in this book. See Simon Critchley, *Ethics-Politics-Subjectivity: Essays on Derrida, Levinas and Contemporary French Thought* (London: Verso, 2009), 276–77.

5. I borrow this term from Elizabeth Povinelli. See Povinelli, *Economies of Abandonment.*

6. I would argue that Soviet-style socialism, for example, enacted the same ontological tradition. The shared ontological grounds of socialism and liberal capitalism are obvious once considered, and include shared notions of contained space, linear time, bounded individuals, the priority of the One, and the subject/object distinction, to name a few.

7. Ernesto Laclau and Chantal Mouffe, *Hegemony and Socialist Strategy: Towards a Radical Democratic Politics* (London: Verso, 2001), 167; Schürmann, *Heidegger on Being and Acting*.

8. Cf. Stephen K. White, *Sustaining Affirmation: The Strengths of Weak Ontology in Political Theory* (Princeton, N.J.: Princeton University Press, 2000).

9. Lee Braver, "On Heidegger, Wittgenstein, Derrida," interview by Richard Marshall, *3:AM Magazine*, August 24, 2012, http://www.3am magazine.com/3am/on-heidegger-wittgenstein-derrida/.

10. James Laidlaw and Paolo Heywood, "One More Turn and You're There," *Anthropology of This Century* 7 (May 2013): http://aotcpress.com/articles/turn/.

11. Terry Eagleton makes a similar claim regarding ideology. See Eagleton, *Ideology: An Introduction* (London: Verso, 2007), 63.

12. Cf. Schürmann, *Heidegger on Being and Acting*.

13. Talal Asad, "The Idea of an Anthropology of Islam" (Occasional Paper Series, Georgetown University Center for Contemporary Arab Studies, March 1986), 1–23; Charles Hirschkind, "Heresy or Hermeneutics: The Case of Nasr Hamid Abu Zayd," *SEHR* 5, no. 1 (1996): https://web.stanford.edu/group/SHR/5-1/text/hirschkind.html.

14. Saba Mahmood, *Politics of Piety: The Islamic Revival and the Feminist Subject* (Princeton, N.J.: Princeton University Press, 2005), 115.

15. Timothy Morton, *Hyperobjects: Philosophy and Ecology after the End of the World* (Minneapolis: University of Minnesota Press, 2013), 75; Martin Heidegger, *What Is a Thing?* trans. W. B. Barton, Jr., and Vera Deutsch (Chicago: Henry Regnery, 1967), 102–3.

16. Hannah Arendt, *The Human Condition* (Chicago: University of Chicago Press, 1998), 9–10.

17. Ibid., 9.

18. William E. Connolly, *The Fragility of Things: Self-Organizing Processes, Neoliberal Fantasies, and Democratic Activism* (Durham, N.C.: Duke University Press, 2013), 59–60.

19. Ibid., 219n.

20. Ibid., 156.

21. Martin Heidegger, "The Age of the World Picture," in *The Question Concerning Technology and Other Essays*, trans. William Lovitt (New York: Harper & Row, 1977), 115.

22. Karen Barad, *Meeting the Universe Halfway: Quantum Physics and the Entanglement of Matter and Meaning* (Durham, N.C.: Duke University Press, 2007), 107.

23. See Soumhya Venkatesan, "Ontology Is Just Another Word for Culture," *Critique of Anthropology* 30, no. 2 (2010): 152–200.

24. Cf. Martin Holbraad, "Ontology Is Just Another Word for Culture," *Critique of Anthropology* 30, no. 2 (2010): 152–200.

25. Cf. Akhil Gupta and James Ferguson, "Beyond 'Culture': Space, Identity, and the Politics of Difference," *Cultural Anthropology* 7, no. 1 (1992): 6.

26. Barad, *Meeting the Universe Halfway*, 46.

27. Dana R. Villa, *Arendt and Heidegger: The Fate of the Political* (Princeton, N.J.: Princeton University Press, 1996), 176–80; Schürmann, *Heidegger on Being and Acting*, 113.

28. Barad, *Meeting the Universe Halfway*, 46.

29. Villa, *Arendt and Heidegger*, 176; Barad, *Meeting the Universe Halfway*, 97.

30. Villa, *Arendt and Heidegger*, 176.

31. Qtd. in ibid.

32. Heidegger, "Age of the World Picture," 128.

33. Villa, *Arendt and Heidegger*, 177.

34. Heidegger, "Age of the World Picture," 132.

35. Villa, *Arendt and Heidegger*, 183.

36. Heidegger, "Age of the World Picture," 132.

37. Martin Heidegger, "The Question Concerning Technology," in *Question Concerning Technology*, 27.

38. Arendt, *Human Condition*, 261.

39. Heidegger, "Question Concerning Technology," 27.

40. Villa, *Arendt and Heidegger*, 192.

41. Ibid., 173.

42. Arendt, *Human Condition*, 318.

43. See for example Jacques Rancière, *Dissensus: On Politics and Aesthetics*, trans. Steven Corcoran (London: Bloomsbury, 2010).

44. Wendy Brown, *Politics out of History* (Princeton, N.J.: Princeton University Press, 2001).

45. An obvious exception would be the work of Didier Fassin.

46. Hans-Georg Gadamer, *Truth and Method*, trans. Joel Weinsheimer and Donald G. Marshall (New York: Continuum, 1997), xxxvii–iii.

47. Caputo, *Radical Hermeneutics*; Schürmann, *Heidegger on Being and Acting*; François Raffoul, *The Origins of Responsibility* (Bloomington: Indiana University Press, 2010); Michael Marder, *Phenomena-Critique-Logos: The Project of Critical Phenomenology* (London: Rowman & Littlefield, 2014).

48. Raffoul, *Origins of Responsibility*, 3, 19, 81.

49. Caputo, *Radical Hermeneutics*, 37; Schürmann, *Heidegger on Being and ting*.

50. See for example Stuart McLean, "Stories and Cosmogonies: Imagining Creativity beyond 'Nature' and 'Culture,'" *Cultural Anthropology* 24, no. 2 (2009): 213–45; Povinelli, *Economies of Abandonment*; Anne Allison, *Precarious Japan* (Durham, N.C.: Duke University Press, 2013); Jarrett Zigon, "Human Rights as Moral Progress? A Critique," *Cultural Anthropology* 28, no. 4 (2013): 716–36; Brian Goldstone, "Life after Sovereignty," *History of the Present: A Journal of Critical History* 4, no. 1 (2014): 97–113; Ghassan Hage, *Alter-Politics: Critical Anthropology and the Radical Imagination* (Melbourne: Melbourne University Press, 2015).

51. See for example White, *Sustaining Affirmation*; Barad, *Meeting the Universe Halfway*; Jodi Dean, *Democracy and Other Neoliberal Fantasies: Communicative Capitalism and Left Politics* (Durham, N.C.: Duke University Press, 2009); Jane Bennett, *Vibrant Matter: A Political Ecology of Things* (Durham, N.C.: Duke University Press, 2010), xv; Connolly, *Fragility of Things*.

52. For an excellent critique of this lack of critique see Lucas Bessire and David Bond, "Ontological Anthropology and the Deferral of Critique," *American Ethnologist* 41, no. 3 (2014): 440–56.

53. Ghassan Hage makes a similar point but argues that such disclosure is only possible if we adopt an "ethos of primitivist anthropology," a notion I entirely reject if for no other reason than its implication—despite the author's claim to the contrary—that it is (best?) to be done among so-called primitives. Such an implication seems to be borne out by the fact that the vast majority of those who are associated with the ontological turn in anthropology do their research with societies that not long ago would have been labeled "primitive" by the discipline. See Hage, "Critical Anthropological Thought and the Radical Political Imaginary Today," *Critique of Anthropology* 32, no. 3 (2012): 305–6; and *Alter-Politics*; see also below for Derrida's critique of Levi-Strauss projecting "goodness" onto the so-called primitive.

54. Mario Blaser, "Political Ontology," *Cultural Studies* 23, no. 5 (2009): 873–96.

55. Hage, "Critical Anthropological Thought and the Radical Political Imaginary Today," 303; and *Alter-Politics*.

56. Terry S. Turner, "The Crisis of Late Structuralism: Perspectivism and Animism: Rethinking Culture, Nature, Spirit, and Bodiliness," *Tipiti* 7, no. 1 (2009): 3–42.

57. See for example Eduardo Viveiros de Castro, "Introduction: The Untimely Again," in *Archeology of Violence*, by Pierre Clastres (Los Angeles: Semiotext[e], 2010), 9–52.

58. Bessire and Bond, "Ontological Anthropology and the Deferral of Critique."

59. For an important critique on the anthropological tendency—as exemplified in Levi-Strauss—of projecting "goodness" onto the so-called primitive see Jacques Derrida, *Of Grammatology*, trans. Gayatri Chakravorty Spivak (Baltimore: Johns Hopkins University Press, 2016), 109–52. This tendency seems to be making a comeback of sorts within the so-called ontological turn of anthropology—a turn that is strongly influenced by the work of Levi-Strauss—but this time it is not so much "goodness" being projected—though that is certainly part of it—but rather alternative worlds, as if only among the "primitive" can potential other worlds be found. This book is in large part an attempt to show that this is not so.

60. By *responsive process* I intend an ontological claim that all beings are in a constant process of responding and adjusting to that with which they have become intertwined. In this book I articulate this responsiveness as attunement. For a similar philosophical anthropology of responsiveness, although one much more grounded in a humanist first-person perspective than the responsive attunement of which I write here, see Thomas Schwarz Wentzer, "'I Have Seen Königsberg Burning': Philosophical Anthropology and the Responsiveness of Historical Experience," *Anthropological Theory* 14, no. 1 (2014): 27–48; Rasmus Dyring, "Freedom, Responsiveness and the Place of the Ethical: Toward a Philosophical Anthropology of Ethics" (Ph.D. diss., Aarhus University, 2015).

61. The classic articulation of this is Martin Heidegger's *Being and Time*, trans. Joan Stambaugh (Albany: State University of New York Press, 1996), though it remained central to his hermeneutic project until his death. See also Caputo, *Radical Hermeneutics*; and Schürmann, *Heidegger on Being and Acting*.

62. Perhaps the most subtle and significant of these critiques is that human rights politics relies on and enacts a depoliticization of subjects and of politics itself, rendering alternative political imaginings and projects nearly impossible. This is perhaps most clearly seen in the way human rights has become the underlying political-moral discourse of (military)-humanitarian intervention. Although such interventions tend to be presented as an antipolitical defense of individual victims against the cruel tyranny of undemocratic politics or intolerant cultures, these interventions, nevertheless, enact a specific liberal politics that forecloses the possibility of other forms of political action and subjectivization (e.g., Brown and Žižek). In this way the rights granted to the world's "victims" are returned to the sender of these rights—in many cases the Euro-Atlantic "West"—by means of the intervention of the latter in the name of the former and, as such, are received by the latter as a mandate to enact infinite justice (Rancière). This circulation not

only produces better-disciplined subjects of rights now more reliant than ever on particular and limited forms of governance (e.g., Arendt and Asad), but also produces an international divide between those rendered Good and Evil, the Just and the Corrupt, and the Saviors and the Damned. In doing so human rights has been critiqued as the political-moral foundation for a new form of Western imperialism (e.g., Žižek). While this may be the case, I hope to make clear in Chapters 1 and 2 that this so-called new form of Western imperialism is in fact better understood as the ontic manifestation of the metaphysical humanist projection of the subjectivity of the subject onto the multifarious worlds of the globe. As will become clear in Chapter 2, this projection that subjectivizes the globe while foreclosing possibilities of an otherwise is most clearly discerned in the notion of moral progress. See Hannah Arendt, *The Origins of Totalitarianism* (New York: Harcourt, Brace, Jovanovich, 1973); Talal Asad, "Redeeming the 'Human' through Human Rights," in *Formations of the Secular: Christianity, Islam, Modernity* (Stanford, Calif.: Stanford University Press, 2003), 127–58; Wendy Brown, "'The Most We Can Hope For . . .': Human Rights and the Politics of Fatalism," *South Atlantic Quarterly* 103, no. 2 (2004): 451–63; Jacques Rancière, "Who Is the Subject of the Rights of Man?" *South Atlantic Quarterly* 103, nos. 2–3 (2004): 308–9; Slavoj Žižek, "Against Human Rights," *New Left Review* 34 (July–August 2005): 115–31.

63. Needless to say, these critiques have been almost entirely ignored in the world of social and political movements. For despite these criticisms, the post–Cold War years, and particularly so since the late 1990s, have witnessed the increased "naturalization" of human rights. This "naturalization," in fact, can be gleaned in some of the most important anthropological studies of human rights in practice. Although many of these studies are quite critical of the ways human rights in practice often tend to support neoliberal and state governing apparatuses and limit political possibilities (e.g., Merry, Goldstein, Tate, and Goodale), such criticism is regularly set aside in favor of the possibility of a rightly enacted human rights regime that would be informed by anthropological knowledge. As one prominent anthropologist of human rights has put it, "The kind of anthropology of human rights that I and others have in mind is *both* critical and optimistic, both attuned to the problem of power within the current international human rights regime and sanguine about the potential role a reconfigured idea of human rights might play in projects for social change across a range of cultural, legal, and ethical terrains" (Goodale, 39). Or as another put it quite simply, "With all its flaws, [human rights] is the best we have" (Merry, 231). Indeed, such a perspective has become the policy of the American Anthropological Association with the 1999 adoption of the "Declaration on Anthropology and Human Rights,"

which concludes by stating that it is "incumbent on anthropologists to be involved in the debate on enlarging our understanding of human rights on the basis of anthropological knowledge and research." Thus, as Goodale (34) puts it, the AAA has become "a human rights advocacy NGO focused on vulnerable populations and emerging rights categories." See American Anthropological Association, "Declaration on Anthropology and Human Rights," 1999, http://humanrights.americananthro.org/1999-statement-on-human-rights/; Sally Engle Merry, *Human Rights and Gender Violence: Translating International Law into Local Justice* (Chicago: University of Chicago Press, 2006); Daniel M. Goldstein, "Human Rights as Culprit, Human Rights as Victim: Rights and Security in the State of Exception," in *The Practice of Human Rights: Tracking Law between the Global and the Local*, ed. Mark Goodale and Sally Engle Merry (Cambridge, U.K.: Cambridge University Press, 2007), 49–77; Winifred Tate, *Counting the Dead: The Culture and Politics of Human Rights Activism in Colombia* (Berkeley: University of California Press, 2007); Mark Goodale, *Surrendering to Utopia: An Anthropology of Human Rights* (Stanford, Calif.: Stanford University Press, 2009).

64. Lee Edelman describes reproductive futurism as "generat[ing] generational succession, temporality, and narrative sequence, not toward the end of enabling change, but, instead, of perpetuating sameness, of turning back time to assure repetition." See Edelman, *No Future: Queer Theory and the Death Drive* (Durham, N.C.: Duke University Press, 2004), 60; Caputo, *Radical Hermeneutics*.

65. Gadamer, *Truth and Method*, 300.

1. THE EFFECTIVE HISTORY OF RIGHTS

1. Gadamer, *Truth and Method*.

2. Ibid., 300–302.

3. Ibid., xxiv.

4. Wendy Brown puts it thus: "Human rights activism is a moral-political project and if it displaces, competes with, refuses or rejects other political projects, including those aimed at producing justice, then it is not merely a tactic but a particular form of political power carrying a particular image of justice, and it will behoove us to inspect, evaluate, and judge it as such." See Brown, "Most We Can Hope For . . . ," 453.

5. See for example Lynn Hunt, *Inventing Human Rights: A History* (New York: Norton, 2007); Micheline R. Ishay, *The History of Human Rights: From Ancient Times to the Globalization Era* (Berkeley: University of California Press, 2008).

6. See for example Samuel Moyn, *The Last Utopia: Human Rights in History* (Cambridge, Mass.: Belknap Press of Harvard University Press, 2010);

Stefan-Ludwig Hoffmann, ed., *Human Rights in the Twentieth Century* (Cambridge, U.K.: Cambridge University Press, 2011).

7. Cf. Reinhart Koselleck, *Futures Past: On the Semantics of Historical Time*, trans. Keith Tribe (New York: Columbia University Press, 1983); Stefan-Ludwig Hoffmann, "Koselleck, Arendt, and the Anthropology of Historical Experience," *History and Theory* 49, no. 2 (2010): 212–36.

8. Brian Massumi has recently described what he calls the operative logic of concepts in a similar manner. See Massumi, *Ontopower: War, Powers, and the State of Perception* (Durham, N.C.: Duke University Press, 2015).

9. Gadamer, *Truth and Method*, xxiv.

10. Villa, *Arendt and Heidegger*, 176; Barad, *Meeting the Universe Halfway*, 97.

11. Brian Goldstone, for example, argues that the concept of political sovereignty developed in confluence with the Christian notion of creation ex nihilo around the time of the Constantinian convergence of Roman imperial and Christian institutional power. Rome's absolute sovereignty is grounded in the "ur-expression of sovereign power," God's creation ex nihilo (105). See Goldstone, "Life after Sovereignty."

12. For an excellent discussion of these debates and their relation to heresy, dissent, and Church-imperial relations see Gordon Leff, *Heresy in the Later Middle Ages: The Relation of Heterodoxy to Dissent, c. 1250–c. 1450* (Manchester, U.K.: Manchester University Press, 1967).

13. Richard Tuck, *Natural Rights Theories: Their Origin and Development* (Cambridge, U.K.: Cambridge University Press, 1981), 20.

14. Consumption here is the key to the argument. If one only exercises simple use or *usus simplex facti*, and thus consumes and does not participate in trade or exchange of any kind (including usufruct), then and only then is one not exercising property rights.

15. Tuck, *Natural Rights Theories*, 17.

16. Saskia Sassen argues that because of its strong property rights late medieval burghers preferred Roman law over Church law or the various folk, customary, or local legal orders that arose after the collapse of the Roman Empire . She further claims that Christian doctrine "objected to private property," but this does not take account of the strong debates underway at the time within the Church over property rights and poverty, and the eventual defense of property rights as a God-given natural right. The outcome of these debates almost certainly had real connections to and consequences for similar moves for legally sanctifying property rights in secular law. See Sassen, *Territory, Authority, Rights: From Medieval to Global Assemblages* (Princeton, N.J.: Princeton University Press, 2006), 62–63.

17. Virpi Mäkinen, *Property Rights in the Late Medieval Discussion on Franciscan Poverty* (Leuven: Peeters, 2001), 95.

18. Tuck, *Natural Rights Theories*, 22.

19. Ibid.

20. Ibid.

21. Michel Villey is widely recognized as the most influential scholar arguing that William of Ockham was the first to posit a notion of subjective rights in the latter's argument against John XXII and based on his nominalist metaphysics. However, as both Tuck and Leff point out, William's famous response to John in his *Opus nonaginta dierum* is fought entirely on the terrain established by John in the *Quia vir reprobus*, and therefore elides the very foundation of John's argument that needed to be refuted in order to save the Franciscan position. In fact, Ockham accepts John's position that use entailed a right but argued that this was a natural right, not a right granted by human law, and therefore did not entail ownership. Thus, John XXII's defense of institutional power by means of subjective rights preceded that of William's argument that Villey emphasizes. For an important review of Villey's argument and a critique of his emphasis on William of Ockham see Brian Tierney, *The Idea of Natural Rights: Studies on Natural Rights, Natural Law, and Church Law, 1150–1625* (Grand Rapids, Mich.: Eerdmans, 2001).

22. When I write of the human rights industry I simply intend the fact that in the post–Cold War years an entire global industry has arisen around the proliferation of human rights and includes not only NGOs, social and political movements, international organizations, and governmental departments and ministries, but also university departments, graduate programs, degrees, and centers that produce the knowledge and the workforce to support this industry.

23. Tuck, *Natural Rights Theories*, 24.

24. William of Ockham, in fact, argued on just this point against John, claiming that the *dominium* given to Adam by God was not ownership over the world—this was only given after the fall—but rather should be understood as "governing and ruling with reason." See Leff, *Heresy in the Later Middle Ages*, 250–51.

25. Although there had been a shift in theoretical arguments within the universities that were increasingly emphasizing active rights, the *Quia vir reprobus* is, to the best of my knowledge, the first official and institutional articulation so strongly supporting active rights. See Tuck, *Natural Rights Theories*, 23.

26. Schürmann, *Heidegger on Being and Acting*, 112.

27. Ibid., 110–12.

28. Villa, *Arendt and Heidegger*, 177.

29. Tuck, *Natural Rights Theories*, 24.

30. Ibid., 52–54.

31. The title has also been translated as *On the Rights of War and Peace.*

32. David Brion Davis, *The Problem of Slavery in Western Culture* (Ithaca, N.Y.: Cornell University Press, 1966), 111–16.

33. Tuck, *Natural Rights Theories*, 77.

34. Qtd. in ibid., 78.

35. Qtd. in ibid., 79.

36. For an interesting discussion on the ambiguity of the term *servitus* in the work of Grotius and the implications of this ambiguity for questions of slavery, perpetual servitude, and sovereignty see Gustaaf van Nifterik, "Hugo Grotius on 'Slavery,'" in *Grotius and the Stoa* (Assen: Koninklijke Van Gorcum, 2004), 233–43.

37. It is interesting to note that Selden's essentially Grotian argument was developed in the context of diplomatic tensions between Britain and the Dutch over fishing rights in the North Sea and seagoing rights in the East Indies and elsewhere. These tensions took place within a larger international debate over rights to ocean waters between the main European colonial powers, as this right would significantly affect colonial trade, exploitation, and rule. Thus, Selden expanded on a weak notion of contract found in Grotius's *Mare Liberum* (*The Free Sea*) and *De iure belli ac pacis* and developed a strong notion of contract in his *Mare Clausum* (*The Closed Sea*) in order to refute Grotius's argument for open seas and to defend Britain's claim to fishing rights in the North Sea. See: Tuck *Natural Rights Theories*, 89; David Armitage, *The Ideological Origins of the British Empire* (Cambridge, U.K.: Cambridge University Press, 2000), 105–24.

38. Tuck, *Natural Rights Theories*, 143.

39. Ibid., 149–50.

40. If it is not entirely appropriate to refer to these as bourgeois revolutions, then they certainly can be labeled elite revolutions since members of the bourgeoisie and landed aristocracy primarily led them while utilizing a natural rights theory that supported the ideological foundations of mercantile capitalism. For example, property and free trade were central concepts in these natural rights theories, and their protection were considered a priority by the new governments formed: thus, James Madison's claim that the new U.S. government "ought to be so constituted as to protect the minority of the opulent against the majority." See for example Roger Normand and Sarah Zaidi, *Human Rights at the UN: The Political History of Universal Justice* (Bloomington: Indiana University Press, 2008), 13–14.

41. See for example James E. Gillespie, *The Influence of Oversea Expansion on England to 1700* (New York: Octagon Books, 1974), 262–73; Richard Tuck, *The Rights of War and Peace: Political Thought and the International Order from Grotius to Kant* (Oxford, U.K.: Oxford University Press, 1999); Anthony

Pagden, "Human Rights, Natural Rights, and Europe's Imperial Legacy," *Political Theory* 31, no. 2 (2003): 171–99; Moyn, *Last Utopia*, 21–23.

42. See for example Alice L. Conklin, "Colonialism and Human Rights, a Contradiction in Terms? The Case of France and West Africa, 1895–1914," *American Historical Review* 103, no. 2 (1998): 419–42; Uday Singh Mehta, *Liberalism and Empire: A Study in Nineteenth-Century British Liberal Thought* (Chicago: University of Chicago Press, 1999), 192.

43. Pagden, "Human Rights, Natural Rights, and Europe's Imperial Legacy"; Moyn, *Last Utopia*, 26.

44. Moyn, *Last Utopia*, 26; 30; Stefan-Ludwig Hoffmann, "Introduction: Genealogies of Human Rights," in *Human Rights in the Twentieth Century*, ed. Hoffmann, 9–10.

45. See for example Anil Seal, *The Emergence of Indian Nationalism: Competition and Collaboration in the Later Nineteenth Century* (Cambridge, U.K.: Cambridge University Press, 1968); Naomi Rosenthal et al., "Social Movements and Network Analysis: A Case Study of Nineteenth-Century Women's Reform in New York State," *American Journal of Sociology* 90, no. 5 (1985): 1022–54; Craig Calhoun, "'New Social Movements' of the Early Nineteenth Century," *Social Science History* 17, no. 3 (1993): 385–427; Leila J. Rupp, *Worlds of Women: The Making of an International Women's Movement* (Princeton, N.J.: Princeton University Press, 1997); Zaragosa Vargas, *Labor Rights Are Civil Rights: Mexican American Workers in Twentieth-Century America* (Princeton, N.J.: Princeton University Press, 2005); Normand and Zaidi, *Human Rights at the UN*, 15.

46. Moyn, *Last Utopia*, 30–31.

47. Mark Mazower, *Dark Continent: Europe's Twentieth Century* (New York: Vintage Books, 2000).

48. Ishay, *History of Human Rights*, 209.

49. Gaston V. Rimlinger, "Capitalism and Human Rights," *Daedalus* 112, no. 4 (1983): 51–79.

50. Douglas Galbi, "International Aspects of Social Reform in the Interwar Period," *Galbi Think!* June 12, 1993, http://www.galbithink.org/isr.pdf.

51. Jane Seymour, "Not Rights, but Reciprocal Responsibility: The Rhetoric of State Health Provision in Early-Twentieth-Century Britain," in *Assembling Health Rights in Global Context: Genealogies and Anthropologies*, ed. Alex Mold and David Reubi (London: Routledge, 2013), 23–41.

52. For a description of trends pointing toward the reform of the interwar political economic system in the Euro-American states and its relation to human rights see Ishay, *History of Human Rights*, 199–211.

53. Eric Hobsbawm, *The Age of Extremes: A History of the World, 1914–1991* (New York: Vintage, 1994), 138–41, 169–70, 274–75.

54. The role of the Soviet Union in this process does not change this, for ultimately the social rights it endorsed in the UDHR had already been endorsed by many leaders of the liberal-capitalist countries and most prominently by FDR prior to his death. It should be further noted that the Soviet Union abstained from voting for the UDHR. See Hoffmann, "Introduction," 17.

55. Moyn, *Last Utopia*, 59.

56. Johannes Morsink, *The Universal Declaration of Human Rights: Origins, Drafting, and Intent* (Philadelphia: University of Pennsylvania Press, 1999), 310–11.

57. Emphasis added.

58. Andrew Moravcsik, "The Origins of Human Rights Regimes: Democratic Delegation in Postwar Europe," *International Organization* 54, no. 2 (2000): 217–52.

59. Jeremi Suri, *Power and Protest: Global Revolution and the Rise of Détente* (Cambridge, Mass.: Harvard University Press, 2005).

60. Mark Mazower, "The Strange Triumph of Human Rights, 1933–1950," *Historical Journal* 47, no. 2 (2004): 379–98.

61. Moyn, *Last Utopia*.

62. Ibid., 98, 195, 212.

63. Ibid., 196–98.

64. Hoffmann, "Introduction," 23.

65. Alexei Yurchak, *Everything Was Forever, Until It Was No More: The Last Soviet Generation* (Princeton, N.J.: Princeton University Press, 2006).

66. See Celia Donert, "Charter 77 and the Roma: Human Rights and Dissent in Socialist Czechoslovakia," in *Human Rights in the Twentieth Century*, ed. Hoffmann, 191–211; Benjamin Nathans, "Soviet Rights-Talk in the Post-Stalin Era," in *Human Rights in the Twentieth Century*, ed., 166–90; Hoffmann, "Introduction," 23.

67. Tom Wolfe, "The 'Me' Decade and the Third Great Awakening," *New York*, August 23, 1976, http://nymag.com/news/features/45938/.

68. See for example Oleg Kharkhordin, *The Collective and the Individual in Russia: A Study of Practices* (Berkeley: University of California Press, 1999); Yurchak, *Everything Was Forever*.

69. Philip Alston, "The UN's Human Rights Record: From San Francisco to Vienna and Beyond," *Human Rights Quarterly* 16, no. 2 (1994): 375–90; Moyn, *Last Utopia*; Hoffmann, "Introduction," 2.

70. Nicolas Guilhot, *The Democracy Makers: Human Rights and the Politics of Global Order* (New York: Columbia University Press, 2005).

71. Justin Vaïsse, *Neoconservatism: The Biography of a Movement*, trans. Arthur Goldhammer (Cambridge, Mass.: Belknap Press of Harvard University Press, 2010).

72. Guilhot, *Democracy Makers*, 76.

73. David Harvey, *A Brief History of Neoliberalism* (Oxford, U.K.: Oxford University Press, 2005), 7.

74. Moyn, *Last Utopia*, 147.

75. There are, of course, many on the left who are very critical of human rights. Despite this, shall I say, radical fringe, overwhelmingly the left has supported and taken up the discourse of rights in one version or another. For some important critical responses to human rights see Wendy Brown, *States of Injury: Power and Freedom in Late Modernity* (Princeton, N.J.: Princeton University Press, 1995); Pheng Cheah, "Posit(ion)ing Human Rights in the Current Global Conjuncture," *Public Culture* 9, no. 2 (1997): 233–66; Alain Badiou, *Ethics: An Essay on the Understanding of Evil*, trans. Peter Hallward (London: Verso Books, 2001).

76. The connection between human rights and conservative forms of liberal capitalism was already well underway in the immediate postwar years in Europe, where the drafting and adoption of the European Convention on Human Rights was primarily led and influenced by right-wing European political elites. Leading this human rights movement were the British Conservatives, who saw human rights as a transnational space for the protection of classical liberal values and politics against both international communism and the noncommunist leftist parties, which were increasingly gaining power in national governments (e.g., the British Labour Party). Contrary to what had happened with the UDHR and various new postwar national constitutions, these conservative politicians and elites effectively maneuvered to have social rights left out of the European Convention. In doing so they revealed that the postwar human rights project in one form or another was a project for securing a particular form of nation-state-based liberal governance. See Marco Duranti, "Conservatism, Christian Democracy and the European Human Rights Project, 1945–1950" (Ph.D. diss., Yale University, 2009).

77. See for example Makoba J. Wagona, "Nongovernmental Organizations (NGOs) and Third World Development: An Alternative Approach to Development," *Journal of Third World Studies* 19, no. 1 (2002): 53–55; Roger Magazine, "An Innovative Combination of Neoliberalism and State Corporatism: The Case of a Locally Based NGO in Mexico City," *Annals of the American Academy of Political and Social Science* 590 (November 2003): 243–56; Sangeeta Kamat, "The Privatization of Public Interest: Theorizing NGO Discourse in a Neoliberal Era," *Review of International Political Economy* 11, no. 1 (2004): 155–76.

78. General Assembly Resolutions 48/134 and 48/121, respectively.

79. For example the UN's 1999 Declaration on the Right and Responsibility of Individuals, Groups and Organs of Society to Promote and Protect Universally Recognized Human Rights and Fundamental Freedoms.

80. Alston, "UN's Human Rights Record," 379, 388; Susan Marks, "Nightmare and Noble Dream: The 1993 World Conference on Human Rights," *Cambridge Law Journal* 53, no. 1 (1994): 61–62; Dianne Otto, "Nongovernmental Organizations in the United Nations System: The Emerging Role of International Civil Society," *Human Rights Quarterly* 18, no. 1 (1996): 107–41.

81. See for example Sabine Lang, "The NGO-ization of Feminism: Institutionalization and Institution Building within the German Women's Movement," in *Global Feminisms since 1945: Rewriting Histories*, ed. Bonnie G. Smith (London: Routledge, 2000), 290–304.

82. SustainAbility, "The 21st Century NGO: In the Market for Change," June 26, 2003, 18, http://sustainability.com/our-work/reports/the-21st-century-ngo/.

83. World Bank, *World Development Report, 1997 : The State in a Changing World* (New York: Oxford University Press, 1997); Wagona, "Nongovernmental Organizations (NGOs) and Third World Development"; Guilhot, *Democracy Makers*, 189.

84. For example, in 2002 it was reported that USAID gives at least 20 percent of its funding through NGOs. See Wagona, "Nongovernmental Organizations (NGOS) and Third World Development."

85. Ibid.; Magazine, "Innovative Combination of Neoliberalism and State Corporatism"; Kamat, "Privatization of Public Interest"; Margaret Sutton and Robert F. Arnove, eds., *Civil Society or Shadow State? State/NGO Relations in Education* (Greenwich, CT: Information Age, 2004); Guilhot, *Democracy Makers*, 182; Nicolas Guilhot, "Reforming the World: George Soros, Global Capitalism and the Philanthropic Management of the Social Sciences," *Critical Sociology* 33, no. 3 (2007): 447–77; Hoffmann, "Introduction," 21–22.

86. For a similar argument for the motivations of incipient democracies to support the new post–Second World War human rights regime see Moravcsik, "Origins of Human Rights Regimes."

87. See for example Asad, *Formations of the Secular*, 154; Merry, *Human Rights and Gender Violence*; Goodale and Merry, *Practice of Human Rights*; Jarrett Zigon, *HIV Is God's Blessing: Rehabilitating Morality in Neoliberal Russia* (Berkeley: University of California Press, 2011).

88. Judith Butler makes a similar argument concerning the historicity of names and words regarding hate speech. She writes, "The name has, thus, a *historicity*, what might be understood as the history which has become internal to a name, has come to constitute the contemporary meaning of a name: the sedimentation of its usages as they have become part of the very name, a sedimentation, a repetition that congeals, that gives the name its force" (36). For Butler such sedimentation is potentially broken up through continued

repetition. While this may apply to the hate speech about which she is here specifically referring, in this chapter I am making the exact opposite argument regarding political and moral concepts. Indeed, unlike hate speech, which must be repeated in order to be revealed as hurtful, abusive, or oppressive, political and moral concepts may simply be rejected as counterproductive. Because of this, genealogy is politically necessary in order to understand the proclivity carried by any particular concept. Since all concepts have a proclivity the question could always be asked: what is the particular proclivity of any particular concept? See Butler, *Excitable Speech: A Politics of the Performative* (London: Routledge, 1997), 36–38.

89. Cf. Massumi, *Ontopower*.

2. PROGRESS; OR, THE REPETITION OF DIFFERENTIAL SAMENESS

1. Jonathan Cohen and Daniel Wolfe, "Harm Reduction and Human Rights: Finding Common Cause," *AIDS* 22, no. S2 (2008): S93–S94.

2. Transatlantic Partners against AIDS, "HIV/AIDS, Law and Human Rights: A Handbook for Russian Legislators," 2005, 49.

3. Drug Policy Alliance, "Harm Reduction," n.d., http://www.drugpolicy.org/harm-reduction.

4. For example see Philippe Bourgois, "Disciplining Addictions: The Bio-Politics of Methadone and Heroin in the United States," *Culture, Medicine and Psychiatry* 24, no. 2 (2000): 165–95; Gordon Roe, "Harm Reduction as Paradigm: Is Better Than Bad Good Enough? The Origins of Harm Reduction," *Critical Public Health* 15, no. 3 (2005): 243–50; Katherine McLean, "The Biopolitics of Needle Exchange in the United States," *Critical Public Health* 21, no. 1 (2011): 71–79.

5. For example see Cohen and Wolfe, "Harm Reduction and Human Rights"; Drug Policy Alliance, "Harm Reduction"; Harm Reduction International, "What Is Harm Reduction?" n.d., https://www.hri.global/what-is-harm-reduction.

6. Both of these are found International Network of People Who Use Drugs, "Our Aims," n.d., http://inpud.net/en/our-aims.

7. Drug Policy Alliance, "Mission and Vision," n.d., http://www.drugpolicy.org/mission-and-vision.

8. See for example Occupy Wall Street, "Everyone Has the Right to Occupy Space, Safely," November 8, 2011, http://occupywallst.org/article/everyone-has-right-occupy-space-safely/.

9. Emphasis added in the following quotations in this paragraph.

10. Clarence J. Dias and David Gillies, *Human Rights, Democracy, and Development* (Montreal: International Centre for Human Rights and Democratic Development, 1993), 9.

11. Kofi A. Annan, "Foreword," in *The Universal Declaration of Human Rights: Fifty Years and Beyond*, ed. Yael Danieli, Elsa Stamatopoulou, and Clarence J. Dias (Amityville, N.Y.: Baywood, 1999), v.

12. Alex Wodak, "Health, HIV Infection, Human Rights, and Injection Drug Use," in *War on Drugs, HIV/AIDS, and Human Rights*, ed. Kasia Malinowska-Sempruch and Sarah Gallagher (New York: IDEA, 2004), 154.

13. Michael Ignatieff, *Human Rights as Politics and Idolatry*, ed. Amy Gutmann (Princeton, N.J.: Princeton University Press, 2001), 3–4.

14. Edelman, *No Future*, 60.

15. Mehta, *Liberalism and Empire*, 78–79.

16. Ibid., 77.

17. Ibid., 81–82; Conklin, "Colonialism and Human Rights."

18. Koselleck, *Futures Past*, 238.

19. Mehta, *Liberalism and Empire*, 89–97; Hoffmann, "Introduction," 3.

20. Hans Blumenberg, *The Legitimacy of the Modern Age* (Cambridge, Mass.: MIT Press, 1985), 30.

21. Ibid., 34.

22. Brown, *Politics out of History*, 6.

23. Moyn, *Last Utopia*.

24. Such rankings do of course occur but are usually done by particular nation-states for rather self-interested political purposes. Organizations such as Human Rights Watch that claim to be nonideological and objective in their assessment of human rights violations do not, for the most part, exclude any country or region from their watchful gaze.

25. As I showed in Chapter 1 this view can clearly be contested and deconstructed to reveal the political, economic, and ideological alliances the human rights industry has increasingly made since at least the 1970s. What I intend here is to convey the rhetoric and not the reality of human rights language and its manifestation in practice.

26. A certain family resemblance can be seen here between this vigilance against human rights abuses and the vigilance advocated by some Christianities against sin.

27. Jarrett Zigon, "Maintaining the 'Truth': Performativity, Human Rights, and the Limitations on Politics," *Theory and Event* 17, no. 3 (2014): https://muse.jhu.edu/article/553385.

28. Again this is the rhetoric of the human rights industry in general. See Chapter 1 for an entirely different story.

29. Transatlantic Partners against AIDS, "HIV/AIDS, Law and Human Rights," 49.

30. Kasia Malinowska-Sempruch, Jeff Hoover, and Anna Alexandrova, "Unintended Consequences: Drug Policies Fuel the HIV Epidemic in

Russia and Ukraine," in *War on Drugs, HIV/AIDS, and Human Rights*, ed. Malinowska-Sempruch and Gallagher, 203.

31. Ibid., 204.

32. This is of course false, as the heroin epidemic in Russia was already fully underway and perhaps reached its peak by 1999. Rather than the responsibility of foreign military adventures, the injecting drug use and HIV crises in Russia are primarily a result of the Russian state's inability to control its borders—including the widespread corruption of border guards—through which large amounts of the world's heroin supply flowed on its way to Europe and North America throughout the 1990s. See Louise Shelley, "The Drug Trade in Contemporary Russia," *China and Eurasia Forum Quarterly* 4, no. 1 (2006): 15–20.

33. Lev Levinson, "Russian Drug Policy: Stating the Problem and Revealing the Actual Picture," in *War on Drugs, HIV/AIDS, and Human Rights*, ed. Malinowska-Sempruch and Gallagher, 53.

34. Zigon, *HIV Is God's Blessing*.

35. Robert Heimer et al., "HIV and Drug Use in Eurasia," in *HIV/AIDS in Russia and Eurasia, Volume I*, ed. Judyth L. Twigg (New York: Palgrave Macmillan, 2006), 151.

36. Malinowska-Sempruch, Hoover, and Alexandrova, "Unintended Consequences," 196.

37. Mark G. Field, "The Health and Demographic Crisis in Post-Soviet Russia: A Two-Phase Development," in *Russia's Torn Safety Nets: Health and Social Welfare during the Transition*, ed. Mark G. Field and Judyth L. Twigg (New York: St. Martin's Press, 2000), 13.

38. Ibid., 18.

39. Malinowska-Sempruch, Hoover, and Alexandrova, "Unintended Consequences," 204–5.

40. Ibid., 205.

41. Ibid.

42. Transatlantic Partners against AIDS, "HIV/AIDS, Law and Human Rights," 12.

43. Ibid., 12–13.

44. See for example Luba Nebrenchina, *Drug Policy in Russia: Drug Users' Stories of Repression* (Moscow: ARF, 2009).

45. Brown, *Politics out of History*, chap. 2.

46. Ignatieff, *Human Rights as Politics and Idolatry*, 4.

47. Brown, *Politics out of History*, 36.

48. This could also be seen as the enactment of what Lauren Berlant calls cruel optimism—that is, "when something you desire is actually an obstacle to your flourishing. It might involve food, or a kind of love; it might be a

fantasy of the good life, or a political project. It might rest on something simpler, too, like a new habit that promises to induce in you an improved way of being. These kinds of optimistic relation are not inherently cruel. They become cruel only when the object that draws your attachment actively impedes the aim that brought you to it initially." The argument I have been making in this chapter suggests that human rights as the foundation of contemporary moralizing politics has become cruel. See Berlant, *Cruel Optimism* (Durham, N.C.: Duke University Press, 2011), 1.

49. Edelman, *No Future*. See also Renata Salecl, *The Spoils of Freedom: Psychoanalysis and Feminism after the Fall of Socialism* (London: Routledge, 1994).

3. WORLDS AND SITUATIONS

1. Cf. Merry, *Human Rights and Gender Violence*; Goodale, *Surrendering to Utopia*.

2. Cf. Critchley, *Infinitely Demanding*. See also Rancière, *Dissensus*.

3. Schürmann, *Heidegger on Being and Acting*.

4. Lauren Berlant has also written of situations but in a way that more closely resembles what I call "breakdown" than how I use the concept situation here. See Berlant, *Cruel Optimism*, 5–6; Jarrett Zigon, "Moral Breakdown and the Ethical Demand: A Theoretical Framework for an Anthropology of Moralities," *Anthropological Theory* 7, no. 2 (2007): 131–50; Zigon, *HIV Is God's Blessing*.

5. Lear, *Radical Hope*, 118.

6. Cf. Anna Lowenhaupt Tsing, *Friction: An Ethnography of Global Connections* (Princeton, N.J.: Princeton University Press, 2005), 267; Lear, *Radical Hope*.

7. Cf. Povinelli, *Economies of Abandonment*.

8. "World," *Online Etymology Dictionary*, n.d., http://www.etymonline.com/index.php?term=world.

9. João de Pina-Cabral, "World: An Anthropological Examination (Part 1)," *HAU: Journal of Ethnographic Theory* 4, no. 1 (2014): 49–73.

10. See for example Martin Heidegger, "The Thing," in *Poetry, Language, Thought*, trans. Albert Hofstadter (New York: Harper & Row, 1975), 163–86.

11. Cf. Nancy and Barrau, *What's These Worlds Coming To?* Preamble.

12. Anna Lowenhaupt Tsing, *The Mushroom at the End of the World: On the Possibility of Life in Capitalist Ruins* (Princeton, N.J.: Princeton University Press, 2015), 21–25.

13. For a similar argument see Ella Myers, *Worldly Ethics: Democratic Politics and Care for the World* (Durham, N.C.: Duke University Press, 2013), 101–3.

14. Anna Lowenhaupt Tsing, "Worlding the Matsutake Diaspora: or, Can Actor-Network Theory Experiment with Holism?" in *Experiments in Holism*, ed. Ton Otto and Nils Bubandt (Oxford, U.K.: Blackwell, 2011), 57, 63.

15. Tsing, *Mushroom at the End of the World*, 21–23.

16. See Arendt, *Human Condition*, 192.

17. See for example Tracy B. Strong, *Politics without Vision: Thinking without a Banister in the Twentieth Century* (Chicago: University of Chicago Press, 2012), 89, 313–15.

18. Arendt, *Human Condition*. See also Villa, *Arendt and Heidegger*, 92–94.

19. Myers, *Worldly Ethics*.

20. Leslie Paul Thiele, *Timely Meditations: Martin Heidegger and Postmodern Politics* (Princeton, N.J.: Princeton University Press, 1995).

21. Myers, *Worldly Ethics*, 100.

22. Ibid.

23. Pina-Cabral, "World: An Anthropological Examination (Part 1)," 66. See also João de Pina-Cabral, "World: An Anthropological Examination (Part 2)," *HAU: Journal of Ethnographic Theory* 4, no. 3 (2014): 149–84.

24. Tim Ingold, "One World Anthropology" (talk presented at The Human Condition: Reinventing Philosophical Anthropology Conference, Aarhus University, 2015).

25. Eduardo Kohn, *How Forests Think: Toward an Anthropology beyond the Human* (Berkeley: University of California Press, 2013).

26. Morton, *Hyperobjects*.

27. Andrew J. Mitchell, "The Fourfold," in *Martin Heidegger: Key Concepts*, ed. Bret W. Davis (Durham, U.K.: Acumen, 2010), 215.

28. Cf. Martin Heidegger, "Building Dwelling Thinking," in *Poetry, Language, Thought*, 152–53; Kathleen Stewart, "Afterword: Worlding Refrains," in *The Affect Theory Reader*, ed. Melissa Gregg and Gregory J. Seigworth (Durham, N.C.: Duke University Press, 2010), 339–53.

29. Jeff Malpas, *Heidegger and the Thinking of Place: Explorations in the Topology of Being* (Cambridge, Mass.: MIT Press, 2012), 38.

30. Tim Ingold similarly describes what he calls environment. Ingold subscribes to a single-world ontology, so it is unclear how specifically environments fit into, as it were, this one world. Regardless, it would seem that Ingold would similarly describe world—even if a single world—for as he puts it, "The world we both inhabit [he and a seagull] is one that undergoes continual formation as our respective lives, and those of countless other creatures, gradually unfold" (505). See Ingold, "Epilogue: Towards a Politics of Dwelling," *Conservation and Society* 3, no. 2 (2005): 501–8.

31. Jean-Luc Nancy, *Being Singular Plural* (Stanford, Calif.: Stanford University Press, 2000), 11.

32. Critchley, *Infinitely Demanding*, 113.

33. Laclau and Mouffe, *Hegemony and Socialist Strategy*.

34. Schürmann, *Heidegger on Being and Acting*, 142.

35. Muñoz similarly writes of potentiality as "present but not actually

existing in the present tense" (9), and its centrality to a politics similar to the politics of worldbuilding I am writing about here. See José Esteban Muñoz, *Cruising Utopia: The Then and There of Queer Futurity* (Durham, N.C.: Duke University Press, 2009), 9.

36. Giorgio Agamben, *Potentialities: Collected Essays in Philosophy*, trans. Daniel Heller-Roazen (Stanford, Calif.: Stanford University Press, 1999), 179.

37. Povinelli, *Economies of Abandonment.*

38. Allison writes about what she calls zones of possibility in very similar ways. See Allison, *Precarious Japan*, Chap. 6.

39. Muñoz, *Cruising Utopia*, 1.

40. On nonlinear temporalities and acting see Jarrett Zigon, "Hope Dies Last: Two Aspects of Hope in Contemporary Moscow," *Anthropological Theory* 9, no. 3 (2009): 253–71; and Zigon, "Temporalization and Ethical Action," *Journal of Religious Ethics* 42, no. 3 (2014): 442–59.

41. Cf. Maurice Merleau-Ponty, *The Visible and the Invisible*, trans. Alphonso Lingis (Evanston, Ill.: Northwestern University Press, 1997).

42. Malpas, *Heidegger and the Thinking of Place*, 40.

43. Heidegger, "Thing," 179.

44. Cf. Jean-Luc Nancy, *The Creation of the World or Globalization*, trans. François Raffoul and David Pettigrew (Albany: State University of New York Press, 2007).

45. Elizabeth A. Povinelli, "Routes/Worlds," *E-Flux Journal* 27 (September 2011): 7.

46. Similarly, Nancy writes that the "unity of a world is nothing other than its diversity, and its diversity is, in turn, a diversity of worlds." I would substitute "diversity of situations" for his "diversity of worlds." See Nancy, *Creation of the World or Globalization*, 109.

47. By now it should already be clear that I conceive of situations in a way that contrasts with the Situationists' notion of a constructed situation. Guy Debord defined the central task of the Situationists as the construction of situations. For example, he writes, "Our central idea is the construction of situations, that is to say, the concrete construction of momentary ambiences of life and their transformation into a superior passional quality." See Debord, "Report on the Construction of Situations and on the International Situationist Tendency's Conditions of Organization and Action," *Bureau of Public Secrets*, 1957, http://www.bopsecrets.org/SI/report.htm.

48. On radical worlds and incommensurability see Elizabeth A. Povinelli, "Radical Worlds: The Anthropology of Incommensurability and Inconceivability," *Annual Review of Anthropology* 30, no. 1 (2001): 319–34.

49. Badiou, *Ethics*.

50. In the last few decades several philosophers and theorists have offered various ontologies for thinking the singular multiple. These have included, for example, the assemblages of Deleuze and Guattari, the set logic of situations and worlds put forth by Badiou, the collectives of Latour, and the being singular plural of Nancy. Each of these, I would argue, whether articulated or not, have been either directly or indirectly inspired by Heidegger's notion of world as gathering and fourfold. Although each of these thinkers have to a greater or lesser extent influenced my thinking on the singular multiple, Heidegger remains my primary source of inspiration. See Gilles Deleuze and Félix Guattari, *A Thousand Plateaus: Capitalism and Schizophrenia*, trans. Brian Massumi (Minneapolis: University of Minnesota Press, 1987); Alain Badiou, *Being and Event*, trans. Oliver Feltham (London: Continuum, 2005); Alain Badiou, *Logic of Worlds: Being and Event, 2*, trans. Alberto Toscano (London: Bloomsbury, 2013); Bruno Latour, *Reassembling the Social: An Introduction to Actor-Network-Theory* (Oxford, U.K.: Oxford University Press, 2005); Nancy, *Being Singular Plural*. For Heidegger on multiplicity and the gathering of worlds see Heidegger, *Being and Time*; and "Building Dwelling Thinking."

51. Anthropologists are likely most familiar with the concept of assemblage through the work of Ong and Collier. However, my use of assemblage is based on a Heideggerian reading of Manuel DeLanda's interpretation of Deleuze and Guattari, and I have written elsewhere on what I call moral and ethical assemblages. See Aihwa Ong and Stephen J. Collier, *Global Assemblages: Technology, Politics, and Ethics as Anthropological Problems* (Malden, Mass.: Blackwell, 2005); Manuel DeLanda, *A New Philosophy of Society: Assemblage Theory and Social Complexity* (London: Continuum, 2006); Jarrett Zigon, "Moral and Ethical Assemblages: A Response to Fassin and Stoczkowski," *Anthropological Theory* 10, nos. 1–2 (2010): 3–15; Zigon, *HIV Is God's Blessing*; and Jarrett Zigon, "A Moral and Ethical Assemblage in Russian Orthodox Drug Rehabilitation," *Ethos* 39, no. 1 (2011): 30–50.

52. William L. Marcy, *The Politics of Cocaine: How U.S. Foreign Policy Has Created a Thriving Drug Industry in Central and South America* (Chicago: Lawrence Hill Books, 2010), 10.

53. Ibid.; Winifred Tate, "Congressional 'Drug Warriors' and U.S. Policy towards Colombia," *Critique of Anthropology* 33, no. 2 (2013): 214–33.

54. Marcy, *Politics of Cocaine*, 135.

55. Qtd. in ibid., 137.

56. Michael Kenney, "From Pablo to Osama: Counter-Terrorism Lessons from the War on Drugs," *Survival* 45, no. 3 (2003): 187–206; Vanda Felbab-Brown, "Counterinsurgency, Counternarcotics, and Illicit Economies in Afghanistan: Lessons for State-Building," in *Convergence: Illicit Networks and National Security in the Age of Globalization*, ed. Jacqueline Brewer, Michael

Miklaucic, and James G. Stavridis (Washington, D.C.: National Defense University Press, 2013), 189–209.

57. Thomas M. Sanderson, "Transnational Terror and Organized Crime: Blurring the Lines," *SAIS Review of International Affairs* 24, no. 1 (2004): 52.

58. Ibid., 55–58; Felbab-Brown, "Counterinsurgency, Counternarcotics, and Illicit Economies in Afghanistan."

59. Radley Balko, *Rise of the Warrior Cop: The Militarization of America's Police Forces* (New York: PublicAffairs, 2013).

60. For this and other information see New York Civil Liberties Union, "Stop-and-Frisk Data," n.d., http://www.nyclu.org/content/stop-and-frisk-data; and New York Civil Liberties Union, "Analysis Finds Racial Disparities, Ineffectiveness in NYPD Stop-and-Frisk Program; Links Tactic to Soaring Marijuana Arrest Rate," May 22, 2013, http://www.nyclu.org/news/analysis-finds-racial-disparities-ineffectiveness-nypd-stop-and-frisk-program-links-tactic-soar.

61. Bryan Stevenson, "Drug Policy, Criminal Justice and Mass Imprisonment" (working paper prepared for the First Meeting of the Global Commission on Drug Policies, Geneva, January 24–25, 2011), 3.

62. Cf., for example, Gupta and Ferguson, "Beyond 'Culture,'" 18; Critchley, *Infinitely Demanding*; Povinelli, *Economies of Abandonment*, 109–10.

63. A significant difference between the politics of worldbuilding I am attempting to delineate and the political worldly ethics of Ella Myers can be seen precisely on this point of an issue. Myers claims that the object of her politics is not the world in general but instead what she calls worldly things. This is how she describes them: "A *worldly thing* [is] shorthand for what is actually a constellation rather than a unitary object. It is useful shorthand for thinking about democratic politics, however, because *worldly thing* helps denote that a particular issue has been successfully politicized" (101). Here Myers articulates that the object of her worldly politics is in fact what I would call a situation, that is, a non-totalizable assemblage or what she calls a constellation, but as "shorthand" she will elide this complexity in order to issueify it. In her attempt to simplify with this shorthand, I suggest, Myers is simply repeating the issue-focused individualized singularity of the politics of the a priori. See Myers, *Worldly Ethics*.

64. See for example Badiou, *Being and Event*, 24.

65. Badiou, *Logic of Worlds*, 598.

66. Ibid., 156.

67. Ibid., 37–38.

68. Ibid., 101.

69. Ibid.

70. Ibid., 113, 118–19.

71. Ibid., 66.

72. This book, then, could be read as a response to Michael Fischer's recent call for a politics that better thinks the human as intertwined in worlds with nonhumans without falling for the trappings of a sustained antihumanism. I would not, however, name this a "new humanistic politics" as does Fischer, but prefer to call it a politics of worldbuilding. See Michael M. J. Fischer, "The Lightness of Existence and the Origami of 'French' Anthropology: Latour, Descola, Viveiros de Castro, Meillassoux, and Their So-Called Ontological Turn," *HAU: Journal of Ethnographic Theory* 4, no. 1 (2014): 349.

73. Laclau and Mouffe, *Hegemony and Socialist Strategy*, xviii, 58, 65.

74. Ibid., 86.

75. Ibid., 167.

76. See John Dewey, *The Public and Its Problems* (New York: Henry Holt, 1927).

77. Levi R. Bryant, "Symptomal Knots and Evental Ruptures: Žižek, Badiou, and Discerning the Indiscernible," *International Journal of Žižek Studies* 1, no. 2 (2007): http://zizekstudies.org/index.php/IJZS/article/view/33/30.

78. Kathleen Stewart, *Ordinary Affects* (Durham, N.C.: Duke University Press, 2007); Berlant, *Cruel Optimism*; Allison, *Precarious Japan*.

79. C. Jason Throop, "Moral Moods," *Ethos* 42, no. 1 (2014): 65–83.

80. For the necessity of thinking the political without event, see Oliver Human, "Potential Novelty: Towards an Understanding of Novelty without an Event," *Theory, Culture & Society*, 32, no. 4 (2015): 45–63.

81. Connolly, *Fragility of Things*, 7–9.

82. Ibid., 41, 137.

83. Ibid., 134–36.

84. Caputo, *Radical Hermeneutics*.

85. Cf. Human, "Potential Novelty."

86. Morton, *Hyperobjects*, 4.

87. Ibid., 7.

88. Ibid., 1.

89. See for example Graham Harman, *Tool-Being: Heidegger and the Metaphysics of Objects* (Chicago: Open Court, 2002).

4. AN ETHICS OF DWELLING

1. Critchley, *Infinitely Demanding*, 6–9.

2. Ibid., 8.

3. Ibid., 9. In fact, Critchley gets dangerously close to articulating what I call the politics of the a priori when he prioritizes the necessity of subject formation as the first step of politics, a political subject that would then demand

rights. It is here that I most differ from Critchley despite our essential agreement on politics responding to a demand that arises from a situation in a world (see, e.g., p. 91).

4. I have written elsewhere of the relation between breakdown and ethics at both the personal and societal levels. See for example Zigon, "Moral Breakdown and the Ethical Demand"; Zigon, "Within a Range of Possibilities: Morality and Ethics in Social Life," *Ethnos* 74, no. 2 (2009): 251–76; Zigon, *HIV Is God's Blessing*. For other, and sometimes similar, notions of breakdown see Lear, *Radical Hope*; Berlant, *Cruel Optimism*; Allison, *Precarious Japan*.

5. See for example James Laidlaw, "For an Anthropology of Ethics and Freedom," *Journal of the Royal Anthropological Institute* 8, no. 2 (2002): 311–32; Joel Robbins, *Becoming Sinners: Christianity and Moral Torment in a Papua New Guinea Society* (Berkeley: University of California Press, 2004); Robbins, "Between Reproduction and Freedom: Morality, Value, and Radical Cultural Change," *Ethnos* 72, no. 3 (2007): 293–314; Zigon, "Moral Breakdown and the Ethical Demand"; Zigon, *HIV Is God's Blessing*; C. Jason Throop, *Suffering and Sentiment: Exploring the Vicissitudes of Experience and Pain in Yap* (Berkeley: University of California Press, 2010); James D. Faubion, *An Anthropology of Ethics* (Cambridge, U.K.: Cambridge University Press, 2011).

6. Jarrett Zigon, "Narratives," in *A Companion to Moral Anthropology*, ed. Didier Fassin (Malden, Mass.: Wiley-Blackwell, 2012), 204–20; Jarrett Zigon, "On Love: Remaking Moral Subjectivity in Postrehabilitation Russia," *American Ethnologist* 40, no. 1 (2013): 201–15; Zigon, "Attunement and Fidelity: Two Ontological Conditions for Morally Being-in-the-World," *Ethos* 42, no. 1 (2014): 16–30.

7. See for example Didier Fassin, "Beyond Good and Evil? Questioning the Anthropological Discomfort with Morals," *Anthropological Theory* 8, no. 4 (2008): 333–44; Joel Robbins, "On the Pleasures and Dangers of Culpability," *Critique of Anthropology* 30, no. 1 (2010): 122–28.

8. Throughout this chapter I use the shorthand morality/ethics or ethics/morality when discussing anthropological studies and approaches, since as of yet there is no agreement by anthropologists as to what either concept means or which is more useful—and thus they are often used interchangeably, or one is simply chosen rather than the other.

9. Michael Lambek, "Toward an Ethics of the Act," in *Ordinary Ethics: Anthropology, Language, and Action*, ed. Lambek (New York: Fordham University Press, 2010), 39.

10. Veena Das, "Ordinary Ethics," in *Companion to Moral Anthropology*, ed. Fassin, 134.

11. See for example Robbins, *Becoming Sinners*; Zigon, "Moral Breakdown and the Ethical Demand"; Throop, *Suffering and Sentiment*.

12. Veena Das is correct to criticize my misrepresentation of ordinary language philosophy as concerned with "linguistic problems," which I wrote in a previous version of this chapter published elsewhere. I certainly did not intend by this unfortunate phrase problems "on the model of linguistics" as Das writes. Rather, what I meant, and I hope I have conveyed clearly here, is that philosophical problems emerge from the "bewitchment" we often undergo because of the abstraction of language from its context of use—that is, the form of life within which language has meaning. Thus, for example, Wittgenstein famously writes in the *Philosophical Investigations*, "For philosophical problems arise when language *goes on holiday*" (PI 38); and "Philosophy is a battle against the bewitchment of our intelligence by means of language" (PI 109). See Veena Das, "What Does Ordinary Ethics Look Like?" in *Four Lectures on Ethics: Anthropological Perspectives*, ed. Michael Lambek, Veena Das, Didier Fassin, and Webb Keane (Chicago: HAU Books, 2015), 58; Jarrett Zigon, "An Ethics of Dwelling and a Politics of World-Building: A Critical Response to Ordinary Ethics," *JRAI* 20, no. 1 (2014): 746–64; Ludwig Wittgenstein, *Philosophical Investigations*, trans. G. E. M. Anscombe. (Englewood Cliffs, N.J.: Prentice Hall, 1958).

13. Michael Lambek, "Introduction," in *Ordinary Ethics*, ed. Lambek, 2.

14. Ibid.

15. See for example Zigon, "Moral Breakdown and the Ethical Demand"; Zigon, *HIV Is God's Blessing*.

16. Lambek, "Introduction," 28.

17. Lambek, "Toward an Ethics of the Act," 39.

18. Michael Lempert, "No Ordinary Ethics," *Anthropological Theory* 13, no. 4 (2013): 370–93.

19. Lambek, "Introduction," 28.

20. See for example Laidlaw, "For an Anthropology of Ethics and Freedom"; Robbins, "Between Reproduction and Freedom"; Zigon, "Within a Range of Possibilities"; Cheryl Mattingly, "Two Virtue Ethics and the Anthropology of Morality," *Anthropological Theory* 12, no. 2 (2012): 161–84.

21. Lambek in *Ordinary Ethics*, ed. Lambek, 39, 61, 7, 9, 10, 11.

22. Lambek, "Introduction," 11–12.

23. Das, "Ordinary Ethics," 136.

24. Lambek, "Toward an Ethics of the Act," 40.

25. Talal Asad, *Genealogies of Religion: Discipline and Reasons of Power in Christianity and Islam* (Baltimore: Johns Hopkins University Press, 1993), 47.

26. Lambek, "Introduction," 2.

27. Veena Das, *Life and Words: Violence and the Descent into the Ordinary* (Berkeley: University of California Press, 2007), 7–8.

28. Zigon, "Human Rights as Moral Progress?"; Brown, *Politics out of History*.

29. For this and more information see for example http://www.drugpolicy.org/ and https://www.opensocietyfoundations.org/.

30. Brown, *Politics out of History*.

31. Lambek, "Introduction," 1.

32. Anne Allison has similarly written of what she calls a politics of sociality that has emerged in Japan in response to the unbearableness some precariat experience. See for example Allison, *Precarious Japan*, 58–59.

33. For an excellent and concise history of the concept of dignity see Michael Rosen, *Dignity: Its History and Meaning* (Cambridge, Mass.: Harvard University Press, 2012).

34. For similar articulations of politics that aim at dwelling in a world and the openness such dwelling entails, see Thiele, *Timely Meditations*; Strong, *Politics without Vision*.

35. C. Jason Throop has written on the relation between ethnographic practice/analysis and the phenomenological epoché. See Throop, "On Inaccessibility and Vulnerability: Some Horizons of Compatibility between Phenomenology and Psychoanalysis," *Ethos* 40, no. 1 (2012): 75–96.

36. For this and other information see "Stop-and-Frisk Data," *New York Civil Liberties Union*, n.d., http://www.nyclu.org/content/stop-and-frisk-data; and "Analysis Finds Racial Disparities, Ineffectiveness in NYPD Stop-and-Frisk Program; Links Tactic to Soaring Marijuana Arrest Rate," *New York Civil Liberties Union*, May 22, 2013, http://www.nyclu.org/news/analysis-finds-racial-disparities-ineffectiveness-nypd-stop-and-frisk-program-links-tactic-soar.

37. See Zigon, "Moral Breakdown and the Ethical Demand"; Zigon, "On Love."

38. Cf. Ingold, "Epilogue," 507.

39. Heidegger, "Building Dwelling Thinking."

40. Heidegger, ". . . Poetically Man Dwells . . . ," in *Poetry, Language, Thought*, 211–29.

41. Cf. Ingold, "Epilogue"; Graham Harman, "The Politics of Truth, Power, and Dwelling," *Attempt Magazine* 1 (2015): 32–40.

42. See for example Thiele, *Timely Meditations*, 72–73; Strong, *Politics without Vision*, 306, 313–15.

43. Lear, *Radical Hope*, 51.

44. Thiele, *Timely Meditations*, 156–57.

45. Tim Ingold, *The Perception of the Environment: Essays on Livelihood, Dwelling and Skill* (London: Routledge, 2011), 173.

46. Heidegger, "Building Dwelling Thinking," 161; Povinelli, *Economies of Abandonment*.

47. Nancy, *Creation of the World or Globalization*, 54.

48. Michael Jackson, *Existential Anthropology: Events, Exigencies and Effects* (Oxford, U.K.: Berghahn Books, 2005).

49. For a similar characterization of the discipline see for example James F. Weiner, *Tree Leaf Talk: A Heideggerian Anthropology* (Oxford, U.K.: Berg, 2003); T. M. S. Evens, "Some Ontological Implications of Situational Analysis," *Social Analysis* 49, no. 3 (2005): 46–60; Ingold, *Perception of the Environment*; Martin Holbraad, *Truth in Motion: The Recursive Anthropology of Cuban Divination* (Chicago: University of Chicago Press, 2012).

50. Zigon, "Attunement and Fidelity."

51. Ingold, *Perception of the Environment*, 186–87.

52. Susan Boyd, Donald MacPherson, and Bud Osborn, *Raise Shit! Social Action Saving Lives* (Winnipeg: Fernwood, 2009), 66.

53. Ibid., 36.

54. "Downtown Eastside by the Numbers," *Eastside Stories: Diary of a Vancouver Beat Cop*, May 20, 2012, http://www.beatcopdiary.vpd.ca/2012/05/20/downtown-eastside-by-the-numbers/.

55. Ben Christopher, "How Vancouver's War on Drugs Began," *The Tyee*, March 21, 2012, https://thetyee.ca/News/2012/03/21/Vancouver-Drug-Policy/.

56. Because he is known around the globe for his activism in Vancouver, I am using Bud Osborn's real name.

5. WORLDBUILDING AND ATTUNEMENT

1. For a similar argument see Myers, *Worldly Ethics*, 91, 101–3.

2. Villa, *Arendt and Heidegger*, 173.

3. Arendt, *Human Condition*, 318.

4. See for example Michel Foucault, *The History of Sexuality, Vol. 1: The Will to Knowledge*, trans. Robert Hurley (London: Penguin, 1978). See also Andrew Barry, Thomas Osborne, and Nikolas Rose, eds., *Foucault and Political Reason: Liberalism, Neo-liberalism, and Rationalities of Government* (Chicago: University of Chicago Press, 1996).

5. Giorgio Agamben, *Homo Sacer: Sovereign Power and Bare Life*, trans. Daniel Heller-Roazen (Stanford, Calif.: Stanford University Press, 1998).

6. See for example Barry, Osborne, and Rose, *Foucault and Political Reason*; Paul Rabinow, *Anthropos Today: Reflections on Modern Equipment* (Princeton, N.J.: Princeton University Press, 2003); Miriam Ticktin, *Casualties of Care: Immigration and the Politics of Humanitarianism in France* (Berkeley: University of California Press, 2011); Didier Fassin, *Humanitarian Reason: A Moral History of the Present* (Berkeley: University of California Press, 2011); Zigon, *HIV Is God's Blessing*; Carlo Caduff, "The Semiotics of Security: Infectious Disease Research and the Biopolitics of Informational Bodies in

the United States," *Cultural Anthropology* 27, no. 2 (2012): 333–57; Allison, *Precarious Japan*.

7. Nikolas Rose, *The Politics of Life Itself: Biomedicine, Power, and Subjectivity in the Twenty-First Century* (Princeton, N.J.: Princeton University Press, 2007).

8. See for example Barry, Osborne, and Rose, *Foucault and Political Reason*; Asad, *Formations of the Secular*; Zigon, *HIV Is God's Blessing*.

9. Raffoul, *Origins of Responsibility*, 40.

10. Aristotle, "Nicomachean Ethics," in *The Basic Works of Aristotle*, ed. Richard McKeon (New York: Random House, 1941), bk. III.

11. See Immanuel Kant, *Critique of Pure Reason*, trans. Werner S. Pluhar (Indianapolis: Hackett, 1996), sec. Third Conflict of Transcendental Ideas.

12. See Immanuel Kant, *Fundamental Principles of the Metaphysics of Morals*, trans. Thomas K. Abbott (New York: Macmillan, 1949); Immanuel Kant, *Critique of Practical Reason*, trans. T. K. Abbott (Amherst, N.Y.: Prometheus Books, 1996).

13. Raffoul, *Origins of Responsibility*, chap. Introduction.

14. Rancière, *Dissensus*, 94.

15. Harm Reduction International, "What Is Harm Reduction?" n.d., https://www.hri.global/what-is-harm-reduction.

16. See for example Bourgois, "Disciplining Addictions"; Roe, "Harm Reduction as Paradigm"; McLean, "Biopolitics of Needle Exchange in the United States."

17. Zigon, *HIV Is God's Blessing*.

18. Barad, *Meeting the Universe Halfway*, 107.

19. I thank Nicky van Oostrum, who did her master's thesis as part of my larger project on anti–drug war politics, for her excellent research on this job training and other issues of responsibilization in Honolulu harm reduction programs. See Nicky van Oostrum, "Rights, Responsibility, and the HIV/AIDS Pandemic: Global Impact on Moral and Political Subjectivity on the Island O'ahu in Hawai'i" (M.A. diss., University of Amsterdam, 2012).

20. Rancière, *Dissensus*, 94.

21. See for example Bennett, *Vibrant Matter*, 7; Kohn, *How Forests Think*.

22. Barad, *Meeting the Universe Halfway*, 396.

23. Ibid., 185.

24. Rancière, *Dissensus*.

25. Brown, *Politics out of History*.

26. Barad, *Meeting the Universe Halfway*, 182.

27. Lambek, "Toward an Ethics of the Act."

28. Barad, *Meeting the Universe Halfway*, 182.

29. Ibid.

30. Bennett, *Vibrant Matter*, 122.

31. Barad, *Meeting the Universe Halfway*, 391.

32. Raffoul, *Origins of Responsibility*, 32–33, 165.

33. Emmanuel Levinas, *Totality and Infinity: An Essay on Exteriority*, trans. Alphonso Lingis (Pittsburgh, Pa.: Duquesne University Press, 2011), 291.

34. Maurice Blanchot, *The Infinite Conversation*, trans. Susan Hanson (Minneapolis: University of Minnesota Press, 1993), 73; Critchley, *Ethics-Politics-Subjectivity*, 264.

35. For a similar critique see Bonnie Washick and Elizabeth Wingrove, "Politics That Matter: Thinking about Power and Justice with the New Materialists," *Contemporary Political Theory* 14, no. 1 (2015): 63–89.

36. Qtd. in Barad, *Meeting the Universe Halfway*, 391. See Emmanuel Levinas, *Otherwise Than Being, or Beyond Essence*, trans. Alphonso Lingis (Pittsburgh, Pa.: Duquesne University Press, 2011), 139.

37. Levinas, *Otherwise Than Being*, 114.

38. This is part of Barad's definition of the metaphysics of individualism. See Barad, *Meeting the Universe Halfway*, 107.

39. Cf. Raffoul, *Origins of Responsibility*.

40. See Boyd, MacPherson, and Osborn, *Raise Shit!* 36, 81.

41. Ibid., 66.

42. Zigon, "Attunement and Fidelity."

43. Kathleen Stewart has written similarly about what she calls atmospheric attunement. See Stewart, "Atmospheric Attunements," *Rubric* 1 (2010): 1–14.

44. Zigon, "Attunement and Fidelity." See also Zigon, "Moral Breakdown and the Ethical Demand"; Zigon, *HIV Is God's Blessing*; Zigon, "On Love."

45. James Laidlaw, *The Subject of Virtue: An Anthropology of Ethics and Freedom* (Cambridge, U.K.: Cambridge University Press, 2014), 124–29.

46. See for example Zigon, "Moral Breakdown and the Ethical Demand"; Zigon, "Within a Range of Possibilities"; Zigon, *HIV Is God's Blessing*; Zigon, "On Love"; Zigon, "Attunement and Fidelity."

47. Laidlaw, *Subject of Virtue*, 117.

48. Ibid., 149.

49. "[Thought] is what allows one to step back from this way of acting or reacting, to present it to oneself as an object of thought and to question it as to its meaning, its conditions, and its goals. Thought is freedom in relation to what one does, the motion by which one detaches oneself from it, establishes it as an object, and reflects on it as a problem." See Michel Foucault, *Ethics, Subjectivity, and Truth: Essential Works of Foucault, 1954–1980*, vol. 1, ed. Paul Rabinow (New York: New Press, 1997), 117. See also Zigon, "Moral Breakdown and the Ethical Demand," 137; Laidlaw, *Subject of Virtue*, 102.

50. Zigon, "On Love"; Jarrett Zigon and C. Jason Throop, "Moral Experience: Introduction," *Ethos* 42, no. 1 (2014): 1–15; Zigon, "Attunement and Fidelity."

51. Throop, "Moral Moods."

52. Laidlaw, *Subject of Virtue*, 119.

53. Zigon, "Moral Breakdown and the Ethical Demand," 138.

54. Robbins, *Becoming Sinners*.

55. Faubion, *Anthropology of Ethics*.

56. Cheryl Mattingly, *Moral Laboratories: Family Peril and the Struggle for a Good Life* (Berkeley: University of California Press, 2014).

57. See for example Webb Keane, *Ethical Life: Its Natural and Social Histories* (Princeton, N.J.: Princeton University Press, 2015), 133.

58. Lambek, "Introduction."

59. Laidlaw, *Subject of Virtue*, 128.

60. I thank Jason Throop for suggesting this way of expressing existential comfort.

61. Laidlaw, *Subject of Virtue*, 128.

62. Ibid., 126.

63. See Zigon, "Attunement and Fidelity."

64. Allison, *Precarious Japan*, 84, 128.

65. Ibid., 175.

66. Ibid., 174.

67. It should be noted that in many places such service centers do provide referrals to other services provided at other centers that are similarly linear. Thus, in contrast to a world of emerging possibilities, this referral system connects isolated points and involves a good deal of layered difficulties of bureaucracy.

68. For some phenomenological analyses of space, place, and its design as openness, see Malpas, *Heidegger and the Thinking of Place*; Lena Hopsch, Marco Cesario, and Rachel McCann, "Traveling, Inhabiting, and Experiencing: A Phenomenology for Public Transit," *Environmental and Architectural Phenomenology* 25, no. 1 (2014): 9–14; Jeff Malpas, "Rethinking Dwelling: Heidegger and the Question of Place," *Environmental and Architectural Phenomenology* 25, no. 1 (2014): 15–23.

69. For various reasons some of these, such as the vending machine, computers, and coffee, did not remain in the bank very long after my initial time in the Downtown Eastside.

70. Raffoul, *Origins of Responsibility*, 303; Jacques Derrida and Elisabeth Roudinesco, *De Quoi Demain . . . : Dialogue* (Paris: Fayard/Galilée, 2001), 90–91.

EPILOGUE: CRITICAL HERMENEUTICS

1. A more ethnographically focused book on the political and ethical activity of the anti–drug war movement is forthcoming. In that book I will attempt a critical hermeneutics as an anthropology of potentiality in order to show ethnographically how the not-yet is practiced.

2. Cf. John Caputo on Heidegger's analysis of repetition and futurity (p. 91), and Caputo's notion of radical hermeneutics in general. Caputo, *Radical Hermeneutics.*

3. Gadamer, *Truth and Method*, xxxvii–xxxviii.

4. See for example Caputo, *Radical Hermeneutics.*

5. Cf. Thomas Schwarz Wentzer, "The Meaning of Being," in *The Routledge Companion to Phenomenology*, ed. Sebastian Luft and Søren Overgaard (New York: Routledge, 2014), 307–17.

6. On hermeneutic understanding as standing in the midst of, or "expos[ing] oneself to," "the groundlessness of things," see Caputo, *Radical Hermeneutics*, 205.

7. Schürmann, *Heidegger on Being and Acting*, 61.

8. For a very interesting assessment of the influence of Heidegger on Foucault see Alan Milchman and Alan Rosenberg, eds., *Foucault and Heidegger: Critical Encounters* (Minneapolis: University of Minnesota Press, 2003); for the quotations in the text, see page 3 of the introductory chapter in this book, titled "Toward a Foucault/Heidegger *Auseinandersetzung*."

9. Laidlaw, *Subject of Virtue*, 103.

10. Caputo, *Radical Hermeneutics*; Schürmann, *Heidegger on Being and Acting.*

11. Schürmann, *Heidegger on Being and Acting*, 289.

12. Ibid., 78.

13. Caputo, *Radical Hermeneutics*, 212.

INDEX